"I spend much time helping organizations capture requirements and even more time helping them recover from not capturing requirements. Many of them have gone through some motions regarding requirements as if they were sleepworking. It's time to wake up and do it right—and this book is going to be their alarm clock."

—Jerry Weinberg, author of numerous books on productivity enhancement

"In today's complex, fast-paced software development environment, collaboration—the intense peer-to-peer conversations that result in products, decisions, and knowledge sharing—is absolutely essential to success. But all too often, attempts to collaborate degenerate into agonizing meetings or ineffectual bull sessions. Ellen's wonderful book will help you bridge the gap—turning the agony of meetings into the ecstasy of effective collaboration."

—Jim Highsmith, a pioneer in adaptive software development methods

"Requirements by Collaboration *presents a wealth of practical tools and techniques for facilitating requirements development workshops. [It] is suitable—no, essential reading—for requirements workshop facilitators. It will help both technical people and customer representatives participate in these critical contributions to software success."*

—Karl Wiegers, Principal Consultant, Process Impact, author of *Software Requirements*

"The need for this particular book, at this particular time, is crystal clear. We have entered a new age where software development must be viewed as a form of business problem solving. That means direct user participation in developing 'requirements,' or more accurately, in jointly working the business problem. That, in turn, means facilitated sessions. In this book, Ellen Gottesdiener provides a wealth of practical ideas for ensuring that you have exactly the right stuff for this all-important area of professional art."

—Ronald G. Ross, Principal, Business Rule Solutions, LLC, Executive Editor,
  www.BRCommunity.com

"Gottesdiener's years of software development experience coupled with her straight-forward writing style make her book a perfect choice for either a senior developer or a mid-level project manager. In addition to her technical experience, her knowledge of group dynamics balance the book by educating the reader on how to manage conflict and personality differences within a requirements team—something that is missing from most requirements textbooks. . . .[It] is a required 'handbook' that will be referred to again and again."

—Kay Christian, ebusiness Consultant, Conifer, Colorado

"Requirements by Collaboration *is a 'must read' for any system stakeholder. End users and system analysts will learn the significant value they can add to the systems development process. Management will learn the tremendous return they may receive from making a modest time/people investment in facilitated sessions. Facilitators will discover ways to glean an amazing amount of high-quality information in a relatively brief time."*

—Russ Schwartz, Computer System Quality Consultant, Global Biotechnology Firm

"In addition to showing how requirements are identified, evaluated, and confirmed, Ellen provides important guidance based on her own real-world experience for creating and managing the workshop environment in which requirements are generated. This book is an engaging and invaluable resource for project teams and sponsors, both business and IT, who are committed to achieving results in the most productive manner possible."

—Hal Thilmony, Senior Manager, Business Process Improvement (Finance), Cisco
  Systems, Inc.

"Project managers should read this book for assistance with planning the requirements process. Experienced facilitators will enrich their knowledge. New facilitators can use this book to get them up to speed and become more effective in less time."

—Rob Stroober, Competence Development Manager and Project Manager, Deloitte &
  Touche Consultdata, The Netherlands

"While many books discuss the details of software requirement artifacts (e.g., use cases etc.), Ellen's new book zeros in on effective workshop techniques and tools used to gather the content of these artifacts. As a pioneer in requirements workshops, she shares her real-life experiences in a comprehensive and easy-to-read book with many helpful examples and diagrams."

—Bill Bird, Aera Energy LLC

"Requirements by Collaboration is absolutely full of guidance on the most effective ways to use workshops in requirements capture. This book will help workshop owners and facilitators to determine and gain agreement on a sound set of requirements, which will form a solid foundation for the development work that is to follow."

—Jennifer Stapleton, Software Process Consultant and author of DSDM: The Method
  in Practice

"This book provides an array of techniques within a clear, structured process, along with excellent examples of how and when to use them. It's an excellent, practical, and really useful handbook written by a very experienced author!"

—Jean-Anne Kirk, Director DSDM Consortium and IAF Professional Development

"Ellen has written a detailed, comprehensive, and practical handbook for facilitating groups in gathering requirements. The processes she outlines give the facilitator tools to bring together very different perspectives from stakeholders elegantly and with practical, useable results."

—Jo Nelson, Principal, ICA Associates, Inc., Chair, IAF (2001–2)

Requirements by Collaboration

REQUIREMENTS BY COLLABORATION

Workshops for Defining Needs

ELLEN GOTTESDIENER

✦ Addison-Wesley

Boston ▪ San Francisco ▪ New York ▪ Toronto ▪ Montreal
London ▪ Munich ▪ Paris ▪ Madrid
Capetown ▪ Sydney ▪ Tokyo ▪ Singapore ▪ Mexico City

The publisher offers discounts on this book when ordered in quantity for special sales. For more information, please contact:

Pearson Education Corporate Sales Division
201 W. 103rd Street
Indianapolis, IN 46290
(800) 428-5331
corpsales@pearsoned.com

Visit AW on the Web: www.aw.com/cseng/

Library of Congress Control Number: 2002101262

ISBN 0-201-78606-0
Text printed in the United States on recycled paper at RR Donnelley Crawfordsville in Crawfordsville, Indiana.
7th Printing, February 2010

To Shirley and Mendy Gottesdiener

CONTENTS

LIST OF FIGURES   XVII

LIST OF TABLES   XIX

PREFACE   XXI

The Organization of This Book   xxiii

Acknowledgments   xxiv

PART ONE   OVERVIEW OF REQUIREMENTS WORKSHOPS   1

CHAPTER 1   GETTING STARTED WITH REQUIREMENTS WORKSHOPS   3

Essential Requirements   4

Difficulties with Requirements   5

Requirements Levels   6

Surfacing User Requirements   7

User Requirements Models   7

Requirements Workshops   9

Workshops and Collaboration   10

Workshops and Facilitation   11

How Workshops Differ from Typical Meetings   11
  Workshop Products   14

Types of Requirements Workshops   14
  Other Uses for Workshops   14

Workshops and Iterative Development   16

Making the Business Case for a Requirements Workshop   17

When Not to Use Requirements Workshops   17

Summing Up   18

For More Information   19

CHAPTER 2   WORKSHOP DELIVERABLES: MINING COAL,
             EXTRACTING DIAMONDS   21

The Evolution of Requirements   22
Business Requirements   24
User Requirements   25
Software Requirements   27
Model Views, Focuses, and Levels of Detail   27
    Model Views   28
    Model Focus   30
    Level of Detail   32
    Building the Models   35
    As-Is Models   36
    Multiple Models   36
Model Briefings   37
    Actor Map   37
    Actor Table   37
    Business Policies   38
    Business Rules   38
    Context Diagram   39
    Decision Table or Decision Tree   39
    Domain Model   39
    Event Table   40
    Glossary   40
    Process Map   41
    Prototype   41
    Relationship Map   41
    Scenarios   42
    Stakeholder Classes   42
    Statechart Diagrams   43
    Use Cases   43
    Use Case Map   44
    Use Case Package   44
    User Interface Navigation Diagram   44
For More Information   45

CHAPTER 3   INGREDIENTS OF A SUCCESSFUL REQUIREMENTS
             WORKSHOP   47

A Shared Purpose   47
The Right People   48
Shared Space   50
Wise Groups   51

Pre-Work   52

Focus Questions   53

Serious Play   54

Trust   55

Process Variety   56

Doneness Tests   57

Collaborative Closure   59

Flexible Structure   60

Using Both Sides of the Brain   61

Frequent Debriefs   63

PART TWO   REQUIREMENTS WORKSHOP FRAMEWORK   65

CHAPTER 4   PURPOSE: SHARING A COMMON GOAL   67

Writing Your Workshop Purpose Statement   68
  Don't Assume Anything   68
  Seek the Stories   70
  Link Workshop Purpose with Project Vision   70
Defining Project Scope   72
Identifying the Workshop Sponsor   74
Defining the Workshop Planning Team   75
Sample Purpose Statements   76
  Purpose for Horizontal Top-Down Requirements Workshop   76
  Horizontal Middle-Out Requirements Workshop   77
  Horizontal Bottom-Up Requirements Workshop   77
  Vertical Strategy Requirements Workshop   77
  Zigzag Strategy Requirements Workshop   78
Tips   78
Questions to Ask Stakeholders   79
  Questions Related to Project Purpose   79
  Questions Related to Workshop Purpose   80
For More Information   80

CHAPTER 5   PARTICIPANTS: ROLES PEOPLE PLAY   83

Workshop Roles   84
The Workshop Sponsor   86
The Project Sponsor   86
  Having Sponsors in the Workshop   88
  Sponsor Kick-and-Close   88

Content Participants   89
    Surrogate Users   92
    Ensuring Attendance   94
The Recorder   95
The Facilitator   96
    Facilitator as Planner and Designer   97
    Facilitator as Process Leader   98
    Facilitator Observation and Intervention Skills   100
    Other Facilitator Considerations   101
    Should You Hire an Outside Facilitator?   101
Observers   103
On-Call Subject Matter Experts   105
Tips   106
Questions to Ask Stakeholders About Participant Roles   106
For More Information   106

CHAPTER 6   PRINCIPLES: GROUND RULES FOR THE WORKSHOP   109

Forming, Storming, Norming, and Performing 110
Basic Ground Rules   111
Special Ground Rules   113
    Values-Based Ground Rules   114
    Culturally Aware Ground Rules   115
Introducing and Testing Ground Rules   116
Hidden Agendas   117
Decision-Making Ground Rules   119
    Product and Process Decisions   120
    Collaborative Decision Making   121
Decision Rules   122
    Reaching Closure   126
    A Real-World Example   128
Tips   129
Questions to Ask Stakeholders About Ground Rules   129
For More Information   130

CHAPTER 7   PRODUCTS: ENDING WITH THE BEGINNING   133

Output Products   134
    Making Deliverables Visually Rich   135
    Select Models Aligned with the Business Problem   136
    Use Multiple Models   138
    Mix Text and Diagrammatic Models   139

Mix Focuses and Views   140
Define the Level of Detail   141
Iteratively Deliver Requirements   142
Prioritize the Deliverables   143
Partition Requirements Across Workshops   145
Define Doneness Tests   145
Metaphors   149
Doneness Testing and Decision Making   149

Intangible Output Products   150
Input Products   152
The Workshop Agenda   152
Draft Models   152
System and User Documentation   154
Pre-Work   154
Templates   155
Workshop Aids   157

The Workshop Repository   160
Tips   160
Questions to Ask Stakeholders About Products   162
For More Information   162

CHAPTER 8   PLACE: BEING THERE   165

Workshop Logistics   166
Room Setup   168
Creating Sticky Walls   168
Preparing the Workshop Room   169
Different Time and Place Options   170
Videoconferencing   171
Collaborative Technology   172
Collaborative Technology Variants   174
Collaborative Technology: A Caveat   175
Tips   175
Place Checklists   176
For More Information   176

CHAPTER 9   PROCESS: PLAN THE WORK, WORK THE PLAN   179

Opening the Workshop   180
The Opener   181
Designing Activities   182
Sequencing Activities   183
Framing Activities   185

Mini-Tutorials 185
Elements of a Workshop Activity 186
Sample Workshop Activity 188
Estimating Activity Time 191
Using Focus Questions 191
Imagine This . . . 193
QA As You Go 194

Collaborative Modes 199

Collaboration Patterns 200

Wall of Wonder 200
Divide, Conquer, Correct, Collect 201
Multi-Model 203
Expand Then Contract 203
The Sieve 205
Combining Collaboration Patterns 208

Collaborative Techniques 209

Techniques for Guiding the Flow 210

The Parking Lot 210

Group Dynamics 211

Conflict 212

The Value of Conflict 212
Group Dysfunction 213
How to Deal with Difficult Participants 214

Fun and Games 215

Closing the Workshop 217

The Show-and-Tell 218
Addressing Parking Lot Items 219
Final Debrief 219

Tips 219

Tools for the Workshop Process 220

For More Information 220

PART THREE REQUIREMENTS WORKSHOP DESIGN
            STRATEGIES 223

CHAPTER 10 WORKSHOP NAVIGATION STRATEGIES 225

The Horizontal Strategy 225

Picking Your Horizontal Strategy 226
The Top-Down Approach 228

The Middle-Out Approach 230
   The Bottom-Up Approach 233
The Vertical Strategy 233
   Pick a Starting Model 233
   Pick a Primary Focus 235
   Start at the Scope Level or the High Level 235
   Move Over 236
   The Vertical Strategy with Multiple Workshops 236
The Zigzag Strategy 238
Comparing the Strategies 240

CHAPTER 11   WORKSHOP CASE STUDIES   241

SalesTrak 241
   What Worked Well 244
   Pitfalls and Learning Points 245
RegTrak 245
   What Worked Well 247
   Pitfalls and Learning Points 250
HaveFunds 250
   What Worked Well 253
   Pitfalls and Learning Points 254
BestClaims 255
   What Worked Well 256
   Pitfalls and Learning Points 258

CHAPTER 12   MOVING FORWARD   261

Making the Case to Management 262
   The Business Value of Requirements Workshops 263
   Critical Success Factors 264
   Surfacing Problems 264
How to Evaluate Workshops 265
   What to Report 266
   Deliverable Data to Capture 267
   Cost Benefit Data to Capture 267
   Happy Sheets 268
   The Post-Workshop Survey 268
   Improvement Data 268
   Regular Workshop Debriefs 269

Integrating Workshops into the Requirements Phase 269
Becoming a Skilled Requirements Workshop Facilitator 271
    The IAF 272
    How Much Must the Facilitator Know? 273
    What Do Business Users Need to Know? 274
Ground Rules for the Facilitator 274
Epilogue 277
For More Information 277

APPENDIX   COLLABORATION PATTERNS   279
GLOSSARY   287
BIBLIOGRAPHY   303
INDEX   315

LIST OF FIGURES

Figure 1-1   Overlapping Requirements Levels   6
Figure 1-2   Types of Requirements Workshops   15
Figure 2-1   Requirements Levels (Based on Wiegers, 1999)   23
Figure 2-2   Model View, Focus, and Level of Detail   28
Figure 2-3   Overlap among Requirements Views   29
Figure 2-4   The Six Great Focus Questions   31
Figure 2-5   Model Focus and Level of Detail   34
Figure II-1   The Requirements Workshop Process   66
Figure 6-1   The Group Development Process   110
Figure 6-2   Common Decision Rules   124
Figure 6-3   Degree of Agreement Scale   126
Figure 7-1   Workshop Inputs and Outputs   134
Figure 7-2   Threading Multiple Models Through a Workshop   139
Figure 7-3   Iteratively Delivering Requirements in a Workshop   142
Figure 7-4   Partitioning Requirements Across Workshops   146
Figure 7-5   Workshop Iterations Integrating Pre-Work, Post-Work, and QA   161
Figure 8-1   Time and Place Meeting Options   170
Figure 9-1   Structure of a Requirements Workshop   180
Figure 9-2   Structuring an Activity   183
Figure 9-3   How Models Thread Together   184
Figure 9-4   Elements of a Workshop Activity   187
Figure 9-5   Sample Steps for an Activity   189
Figure 9-6   Results of a Self-Reflecting Activity   198
Figure 9-7   Wall of Wonder Steps   200
Figure 10-1   Horizontal Top-Down Strategy   229
Figure 10-2   A Horizontal Middle-Out Strategy in Action   231

Figure 10-3   A Vertical Strategy   234

Figure 10-5   Zigzag Strategy, with Focus on Business Rules   239

Figure 10-4   Zigzag Strategy, Starting with Events   239

Figure 11-1   SalesTrak Workshop Activity Flow   243

Figure 11-2   RegTrak Workshop Activity Flow   248

Figure 11-3   HaveFunds Workshop Activity Flow   252

Figure 11-4   BestClaims Workshop Activity Flow   257

Figure 12-1   Integrating Requirements and Reviews into the Requirements Process   270

LIST OF TABLES

Table 2-1   Requirements Models by View   30

Table 2-2   Focus Questions Versus Requirements Models   32

Table 2-3   Requirements Models by Focus   33

Table 2-4   Requirements Models by Level of Detail   35

Table 4-1   Sample Project Vision and Workshop Purpose Statements   72

Table 5-1   Workshop Roles   85

Table 7-1   Visual Deliverables   135

Table 7-2   Heuristics for Selecting Requirements Models   137

Table 7-3   Sample Matrix for Doneness Testing   148

Table 7-4   Poster Symbols   158

Table 8-1   Physical Location Considerations   167

Table 8-2   Onsite versus Offsite Location Considerations   168

Table 8-3   Collaborative Technology Pluses and Minuses   173

Table 9-1   Sample Activity Template   190

Table 9-2   Guidelines for Estimating Activity Time Requirements   192

Table 10-1   Picking Your Horizontal Strategy   226

Table 10-2   Comparing Navigation Strategies   240

Table 12-1   Team and Project Problems That Impact Workshop Success   265

PREFACE

"What is softest in the world drives what is hardest in the world."
—Lao-Tzu

To be successful, software projects need solid requirements and collaborating teams. Problems with requirements are one of the primary causes of software project failure. To make matters worse, the rush to use technologies to collaborate over time and space, or to try to substitute fast development, has resulted in lots of bad software. Many people on both sides of the software divide—developers and users—have complaints about their interrelationships.

Requirements by Collaboration explains how to plan and hold workshops to meet two essential needs: efficiently defining user requirements while building positive, productive working relationships. Similar structured workshops are called joint requirements, accelerated design, group design, or Joint Application Design or Development (JAD) sessions. These workshops are about getting the requirements accurately, quickly, and collaboratively, through shared vision and clear communications. By collaborating in this way, you establish relationships, achieve mutual understanding, and build trust.

Successful workshops don't just happen. Facilitating a requirements workshop is *simple*, but it's not *easy*. These workshops require forethought, planning, and design on the part of the workshop facilitator as well as its stakeholders.

This book focuses on the essential tools you need for planning and leading requirements workshops. It integrates user requirements modeling, including use cases, business rules, and collaborative techniques. It teaches you the basic principles of designing and facilitating requirements workshops and gives you an overview of the deliverables of these workshops. It also shows you workshop design strategies. This book is a complement to other books on requirements gathering as well as those that deal with software engineering, requirements, modeling, and facilitation. To guide your study of these related topics, most chapters include references and information about further reading.

The aim of this book is to be practical, not theoretical. It's based on my real-world experiences from the numerous projects I've facilitated for clients as well as a series of courses I've written and delivered to clients in a variety of industries. The goals of this book are to provide a focused perspective on user requirements elicitation and to promote techniques that enhance the ongoing relationship between software and business people.

A unique aspect of this book is its discussion of *collaboration patterns*: reusable collections of group behavior applied to software projects. Collaboration patterns extend the idea of "process patterns" (work methods) by exploiting the power of software and customer groups working in tandem to achieve project goals.

You can think of collaboration as a continuous feedback loop that enhances both the quality and the speed of communication, and thereby of the products created in workshops. For this reason, the techniques described in this book use collaboration patterns coupled with clearly defined user requirements documentation and diagrams.

Anyone who participates in initiating, eliciting, analyzing, verifying, validating, or approving requirements for software will find this book useful. The focus is on perspectives, ranging from those of project sponsors to analysts, with the goal of providing a common understanding of user requirements from concept through specification. Readers of this book include people who will facilitate requirements workshops; project, product, and business managers overseeing the requirements process; and participants in requirements workshops. Project roles include analyst, project manager, product manager, developer, architect, quality assurance analyst, tester, and requirements engineer.

Like life itself, workshops are often surprising. You plan, and plan you must. But then unexpected things happen when people get together. A workshop rarely follows its original plan because when people get together, things get messy and sloppy; mistakes are made, discussions go off-track, the unexpected occurs. Yet this is when great ideas spring forth. With steady guidance from the facilitator, the group can achieve wonders.

THE ORGANIZATION OF THIS BOOK

The body of this book contains 12 chapters within three parts.

Part One, Overview of Requirements Workshops, contains three chapters.

- Chapter 1, Getting Started with Requirements Workshops, describes the problems associated with eliciting requirements and the basic concepts of the requirements workshop.
- Chapter 2, Workshop Deliverables: Mining Coal, Extracting Diamonds, provides a high-level overview of the various models that are the primary deliverables of a requirements workshop. Each of these models expresses a particular point of view, provides perspective on a certain focus, and achieves a varying level of detail. The chapter also explains how the workshop facilitator selects the most appropriate models for the workshop.
- Chapter 3, Ingredients of a Successful Requirements Workshop, describes the elements you need to achieve success with a requirements workshop.

Part Two, Requirements Workshop Framework, contains six chapters.

- Chapter 4, Purpose: Sharing a Common Goal, describes how to specify *why* a given workshop is being held. A concise statement of purpose is the starting point for defining the other elements of a workshop: *who*, *how*, *what*, *where,* and *when*. Shared purpose is also an essential element for participants to become an effective working group.
- Chapter 5, Participants: Roles People Play, describes the various roles played by workshop attendees. It also explains what to do if surrogate or substitute users will attend your workshop and why the facilitator should be neutral and should have knowledge about requirements models. The chapter discusses the importance of participation by business subject matter experts, sponsors, and software stakeholders.
- Chapter 6, Principles: Ground Rules for the Workshop, describes basic ground rules, special ground rules, ways to uncover hidden agendas, and decision-making ground rules.
- Chapter 7, Products: Ending with the Beginning, discusses workshop products in detail. It describes how to determine the right level of precision, perform "doneness tests," and divide a product across multiple sessions (or multiple products across a single session). It also shows how to promote efficiency by using pre-work and self-assigned post-work.

- Chapter 8, Place: Being There, describes "same time, same place" focus, recording modes (including posters and collaborative software tools), and location logistics.

- Chapter 9, Process: Plan the Work, Work the Plan, describes the design and flow of workshop activities and shows you how to create a comprehensive agenda to serve as your roadmap. The chapter discusses how to open and close the workshop and defines collaborative modes, focus questions, collaboration patterns, sponsor "show and tell," group dynamics, and location logistics.

Part Three, Requirements Workshop Design Strategies, contains three chapters.

- Chapter 10, Workshop Navigation Strategies, describes three roadmaps for structuring requirements workshops: horizontal, vertical, and zigzag.

- Chapter 11, Workshop Case Studies, illustrates the book's principles and strategies with several case studies drawn from requirements workshops that I've facilitated.

- Chapter 12, Moving Forward, explains how to make workshops a best practice, including using data to improve workshops, selling workshops to management, integrating workshops into your requirements process, ensuring that subject matter experts and the workshop facilitator have the needed knowledge and skills, and identifying helpful ground rules.

The book also includes a Glossary, which contains definitions for all terms introduced in the body of the text. The Bibliography lists books and articles that contain relevant material. Finally, the Appendix describes a set of collaboration patterns, referenced in the main body, that I have found helpful in facilitating requirements workshops.

My Web site (http://www.ebgconsulting.com) contains a variety of assets that are useful for planning, facilitating, quality checking, and reviewing requirements workshops. These assets include questions; templates, worksheets, and forms; checklists; resources such as workshop techniques; and links to online resources.

ACKNOWLEDGMENTS

I am deeply appreciative of many friends, colleagues, and loved ones who made this book possible. Their support, encouragement, and feedback made all the difference. For more than a year and a half, many of them weaved in and out at various stages of the writing process, helping me in myriad ways.

I am grateful to all my colleagues in the areas of requirements, project and process, software development methods, and professional facilitation. They provided me with opportunities to share experiences and knowledge from which I was able to learn, synthesize, adapt, and refine. I am grateful to the many clients whom I had the honor to work with over the years. By engaging me, they provided me with live learning labs in which I could evolve many of the techniques and ideas presented in this book.

Thanks very much to my reviewers: Scott Ambler, Lynda Lieberman Baker, Karla Becker, James Bielak, Bill Bird, Erran Carmel, Kay Christian, Bernie DeKoven, Esther Derby, Gary Evans, Simon Herbert, Jim Highsmith, Capers Jones, Darryl Kulak, Brian Lawrence, Keri McBride, Bob Moir, Jo Nelson, Fred Niziol, Gary Purser, Joe Quick, Paul Reed, Ellen Robinson, Ron Ross, Russ Schwartz, Roger Schwarz, Richard Spector, Tom Spitzer, Jennifer Stapleton, Rob Stroober, Hal Thilmony, Steve Tockey, Kirk Wilson, and Lindsay Wilson. Thanks to Kendall Scott for his work on the glossary and smoothing out some of my tables into text. Special thanks to Michael Erickson for his wonderful cartoons, and to Bill Bird for his humor, enthusiasm, and hard work on the figures.

I appreciate the special encouragement I received from numerous people, including Ingrid Bens, Larry Constantine, Janet Danforth, Patricia Ferdinandi, Naomi Karten, Norm Kerth, and Meilir Page-Jones. Thanks to Donna Wills, for her trust and friendship many years ago; she was my first mentor in the business world, and from her I learned many valuable things.

I offer my deep gratitude to Jerry Weinberg and Karl Wiegers, my very special writing mentors and friends, who encouraged, cajoled, critiqued, and helped me keep the faith throughout this whole process.

Thanks to my buddies Andy Bradtke, Alix Litwak, Curt Chuvalas, Debbie Romjue-Bailey, Marla Tasch, Theresa Markowitz, Wendy Melemed, Mindy Stein, and Laurie Robinson for their ongoing support, listening ear, and encouragement throughout this effort.

I am grateful to my wonderful acquisitions editor, Peter Gordon, and to the helpful team at Addison-Wesley, including Jacqui Doucette, Dana Weightman, Susannah Buzard, Kate Saliba, Melanie Buck, and many more behind the scenes supporting this effort. Thanks to Kim Arney Mulcahy for her wonderful work on the pages. A very special debt of gratitude to my fabulous and fantastic copy editor, Betsy Hardinger, who is not only a wonderful copy editor but also has been writing mentor to me.

I close with thanks to my sons Ben and Noah, who tolerated many hours of Mom working. Most especially, gratitude to Jeffrey Radding, the love of my life, who was patient and completely confident that I would reach this place.

PART ONE

OVERVIEW OF REQUIREMENTS WORKSHOPS

Chapters 1, 2, and 3 explain how requirements workshops can be helpful and describe the deliverables of the workshops as well as ingredients for workshop success.

1

GETTING STARTED WITH REQUIREMENTS WORKSHOPS

"The hardest single part of building a software system is deciding precisely what to build."
—Fred Brooks

"We're sorry, but your transaction cannot be completed."

Ed stared at the blinking pop-up screen. The next line was even more puzzling:

"Reason—invalid action."

Ed was trying to use his bank's online system to transfer money from his savings account into checking. He had inadvertently overdrawn his checking account and was being charged for bounced checks. To transfer the funds, he figured it would be easier to use the online system instead of going to the ATM in the shopping center 20 minutes away. After all, Ed was a programmer and a big fan of new technology.

But now he was stumped. "Maybe I hit a wrong key or something," he thought.

He tried again. Same result. A third try gave the same cryptic response.

Frustrated, Ed called the bank and keyed through the automated response line. After waiting on hold for 9 minutes, he finally reached a human being and described the problem.

"You can't do that," the customer service representative told him bluntly.

"What do you mean?" Ed yelled. "I'm overdrawn and need to make a transfer right away! I've made online transfers before!"

The voice explained that Ed couldn't transfer money into an account with a negative balance.

Ed was incredulous. "You mean if I brought a check into the bank, the teller wouldn't be able to transfer the money?"

"Oh no, they could do that. You just can't do it online."

"Can I do it at the automated teller machine?"

"Oh sure, the ATM will do that."

So Ed drove 20 minutes to the ATM—the same amount of time he'd spent trying to get his need met online.

Ed was the victim of a requirements catch-22. When his bank's online system was being designed, no one considered this scenario. As a result, the requirements for the system were inconsistent or missing. To the online system—but not to a teller or an ATM—an account with a zero balance was invalid.

ESSENTIAL REQUIREMENTS

Alas, most of us can relate to Ed's predicament: being on the receiving end of discourteous or unsatisfactory software. Avoiding this situation is one of the most vexing problems in software development. Failing to get requirements right, or to get all the right requirements, almost always leads to big problems, including the enormous cost of reworking mistakes discovered later in the software development life cycle. Worse, you risk losing customers or market share when you deliver software with defects, such as the missing or conflicting requirements that Ed experienced. If your software misses market needs, you put your entire business at risk. (For industry data on the costs of requirements, see "The Business Value of Requirements Workshops" in Chapter 12.)

Many requirements problems originate with people and not technology itself. After all, the term *requirements* is broadly used to mean the needs of or conditions to be satisfied on behalf of two different groups of constituents: users and suppliers.

The user base includes customers and users. *Customers* are the people who sponsor a development project with money and resources. For commercial and business systems software, the customers are the people or organizations who commission a software project. For shrink-wrap software, the customers are the end users of the software or perhaps buyers who don't use the software. *Users*, also known as *direct users* or *end users*, interact directly with the software. *Suppliers* design and create the software. This group includes people in the software organization who perform roles such as developers, architects, analysts, software engineers, testers, and project managers.

DIFFICULTIES WITH REQUIREMENTS

Requirements definition is complicated when multiple, conflicting needs arise from a diverse group of users and customers. Software organizations typically aren't armed with tools and techniques for negotiating and prioritizing requirements issues. As a result, software releases get planned from a software-only perspective, and customers are frustrated when their requirements don't receive priority. On the other hand, software development teams can be faced with impossible delivery cycles when customer demands dictate releases without the software organization's input. Also, some requirements take precedence over others for architectural reasons, something that business people generally don't have the experience or knowledge to understand.

Another obstacle can be the lack of involvement and participation of the right people. Business people need the software, but often they don't invest the time to define their needs. Software people keep coming back to business people for clarification, but they may receive different requests from different users. Software project managers often complain—rightly so—that they can't get the customers to provide the right *domain experts*, or *subject matter experts* (SMEs), to specify the user requirements. Delivery dates are often mandated without prioritized requirements, or the software team makes its own choices on which requirements to deliver.

Software professionals, too, contribute to the difficulties inherent in requirements gathering. Listening closely to the voice of the customer isn't easy if you're focused on software internals. Software people are often eager to try out the newest technologies, tools, and methods to solve their clients' development woes. This attitude often leads to a focus on *building the product right* rather than *building the right product*. Too often, software people go overboard with complex models and documentation. Or they rush to code, building the wrong software or writing code laden with defects.

Another consequence of poorly defined requirements is harder to measure but just as treacherous. *Scope creep* is often cited as the highest risk for any software development project (Jones, 1996). Unrestrained by carefully developed requirements and a mutual agreement between customers and product developers, the scope of the project expands as the work proceeds. Changing requirements because of changing market and business conditions is largely unavoidable; the problem is the avoidable scope creep that happens when you haven't clarified and prioritized requirements.

REQUIREMENTS LEVELS

Software requirements derive from *user requirements,* which in turn derive from *business requirements*. There are overlaps among these requirements levels, as shown in Figure 1-1.

Requirements can be documented in different ways:

- Business requirements can be recorded in a project charter, initiation document, or vision document.
- User requirements can be documented in a user requirements document, or a use case document if use cases are the primary technique being used to express the system's functionality.

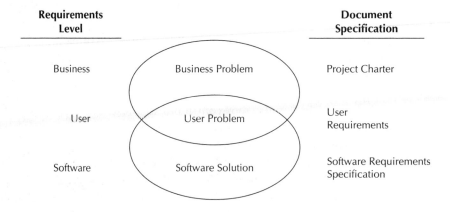

Requirements Level		Document Specification
Business	Business Problem	Project Charter
User	User Problem	User Requirements
Software	Software Solution	Software Requirements Specification

FIGURE 1-1 OVERLAPPING REQUIREMENTS LEVELS SPECIFICATION

- Requirements documentation can also take the form of a software requirements specification. Some organizations use a generic "requirements document" that includes both user and software requirements.

- User requirements span business and software requirements, thus bridging the needs of the business to those of the software.

SURFACING USER REQUIREMENTS

We often talk about how tough it is to capture user requirements. The term *capture* implies that we must catch and imprison requirements. In reality, though, the software organization must acquire and keep user requirements in trust. The ultimate knowledge of user requirements, and the decision making with regard to their quality, rests with the business people who sponsor a software project. At the same time, though, business people need to understand and prepare for the impact that software will have on operations.

User requirements have always been difficult to *surface* (uncover) and clarify. Many industry experts assert that defining user requirements is the most difficult task of software development. One of the biggest sources of difficulty is gaps in communication between software and business people—gaps that result in less than stellar customer-supplier relationships. Each side uses its own acronyms and jargon. Unless people on both sides have experienced each other's roles, they have trouble truly appreciating each other's legitimate concerns. This problem exists for both external software development organizations and software groups supporting internal business organizations. Models, discussed in the next section, help bridge these communication gaps.

USER REQUIREMENTS MODELS

User requirements are the needs that users have. To express user requirements, you can create text-based functional hierarchies; for many business systems, user requirements models augment these functional hierarchies. In some cases, detailed user requirements models can substitute for text hierarchies.

A *requirements model* is a high-level blueprint for a software product. It takes the form of a diagram, list, or table, often supplemented with text, that depicts a user's needs from a particular point of view. Examples of user requirements models include event lists, use cases, data models, class models, business rules, actor maps, prototypes, and user interface navigation diagrams. Chapter 2 defines and discusses these models.

Business Change

Software changes people's lives in large ways and small. Consider the software you deal with, whether it's your word processor or your favorite Internet bookstore site. Recall the first time you used it. What surprised you? What annoyed you? How long did it take for you to be comfortable? Did you ever feel delight? If your software was "upgraded," were you forced to see and act in new ways?

When you define user requirements, you gain a real understanding of how people's lives will change. Perhaps workers will have a new sequence of tasks to perform, new forms to use, and different screens—perhaps even different people—to interact with. All these things translate into change.

Anticipating and facilitating change should begin during user requirements discovery. Business customers, for example, need to make sure that they can deliver business assets such as operational guidelines, standard operating procedures, training materials, and help information.

Requirements workshops can play a role in making your software project more successful, allowing the affected people to participate in identifying and designing the changes. For this reason, you should ensure that these users participate in the workshops. If this isn't possible, engage user surrogates who truly appreciate the needs of their constituents, and incorporate brief requirements reviews with users to ensure that their needs have been appropriately represented.

I sometimes recommend that training or performance improvement experts observe workshops, or at least see the deliverables and workshop documentation, because they need to understand and facilitate the job change. In addition, I encourage participants to add to the "parking lot" (see Chapter 9) any item that falls into the category of business change planning. Later, in your workshop wrap-up, you'll make sure that someone will pass that important information to the people who need to know it.

Whatever its form, the primary purpose of a requirements model is to *communicate*. Defining requirements is a discovery process for users and customers. User requirements evolve from the process of users "trying out" their requirements through models.

Requirements models speak to users as well as software people. As users create and modify the models, their understanding of their requirements changes and evolves—in other words, the requirements become clearer.

Defining requirements with models works independently of software development methodology or technology. If you're using a formal, disciplined development methodology, you're likely to need more models that contain greater detail.

With fewer formal and prescribed methodologies, you'll create only a few models, and the models aren't likely to be very precise. In either case, models are needed. This is true whether you're using traditional technologies and languages or "bleeding-edge" tools.

Requirements Workshops

Now we're ready for a formal definition of the subject of this book. A *requirements workshop* is a structured meeting in which a carefully selected group of stakeholders and content experts work together to define, create, refine, and reach closure on *deliverables* (such as models and documents) that represent user requirements. The benefit of the workshop process is that it nurtures team communication, decision making, and mutual understanding. Workshops are also an effective way to bring together customers, users, and software suppliers to improve the quality of software products without sacrificing time to delivery. These sessions tend to commit users to the requirements definition process and promote their sense of *ownership* of the deliverables and, ultimately, of the system.

Requirements workshops can bridge communication gaps among project stakeholders. Co-creating models in a requirements workshop expedites mutual learning and understanding. By asking focused questions in the workshop, the workshop *facilitator* (see the later section "Workshops and Facilitation") helps participants define requirements at different levels of specificity.

You might start with a scope workshop (see "Types of Requirements Workshops") to outline the terrain, defining what the software will deliver and getting agreement on a starting set of functionality. If there's agreement on scope, you might begin with user interactions and evolve your detailed user requirements models from that point. In any case, workshops provide a forum in which customers and users can make informed decisions about delivery trade-offs and priorities.

A successful workshop requires the participation of key project stakeholders. Each workshop is treated as a mini-project that's woven into the fabric of a software or business project. Like any project, each workshop requires planning, role clarification, and infrastructure. It has a beginning, a middle, and an end. Deliverables are defined beforehand, but they'll change as the group learns.

Requirements workshops are based on the premise that a small group of knowledgeable, motivated people is more effective than one or two development "heroes." They're also based on the premise that, as Jerry Weinberg said, "One of us is not as smart as all of us." You tap the collective wisdom of the group to get your user requirements. This requires collaboration and facilitation.

WORKSHOPS AND COLLABORATION

Collaboration occurs when all members of a group or team share a common purpose, there's mutual trust, and everyone uses agreed-upon approaches for the work. The members operate like a jazz ensemble: multiple voices interwoven, playing together and individually, generously and inventively, sharing a single theme.

Collaboration doesn't just happen; teams don't just form and jell automatically. Rather, collaboration must be engineered into a team's work. Requirements workshop participants should include a healthy mix of business and software people who share a common goal and have stakes in the same project. A key element of successful collaborative workshops is that the participants agree ahead of time to the workshop purpose, principles for participation, and products. They also determine a decision-making process ahead of time; this permits the group to reach closure on their deliverables and the actions they will take after the workshop.

COLLABORATION IS LIKE JAZZ.

WORKSHOPS AND FACILITATION

> *"Facilitation is the art of leading people through processes toward agreed-upon objectives in a manner that encourages participation, ownership, and productivity from all involved."*
>
> —David Sibbet, *Effective Facilitation*, 1994,
> The Grove Consultants International, San Francisco, CA.

A requirements workshop is a *facilitated* group meeting. The facilitated group process of each workshop must be custom-designed for the specific group needing to deliver requirements for a specific project. The interactions in the session let the participants discover, elaborate, clarify, and close the project's requirements.

Roget's Thesaurus lists the following synonyms for the noun *facilitate*: *easing, smoothing,* and *expediting*; as a verb, *to facilitate* yields *ease, grease the wheels, smooth,* and *pave the way*. Does that describe the meetings you attend in your work? Probably not. If you're typical, at least half your meetings are unproductive and a waste of your time. A facilitated workshop is different from these meetings in several key ways that you'll explore in the next section.

Meeting Madness

The cost of ineffective meetings is staggering. The average person attends seven to ten meetings a week, half of which are unproductive, and the average meeting involves nine people (two managers, four co-workers, two subordinates, and one outsider) who have as little as two hours' prior notice. As you'll see, this does *not* fit my definition of a workshop. What's more, the average meeting has no written agenda, and its purported purpose is completed only half the time.

Meeting participants complain that they waste time discussing irrelevant issues. Many people feel pressured to espouse opinions with which they privately disagree, or they feel they have little or no influence on the discussion. They don't consider the results creative; most of them, in fact, think that underlying issues outside the scope of the official agenda are the *real* subjects under discussion.

HOW WORKSHOPS DIFFER FROM TYPICAL MEETINGS

The requirements workshops described in this book are a modern-day variant of Joint Application Design (JAD), also known as Joint Application Development. On the surface, facilitated workshops are like meetings in that both involve people meeting together at the same time, and both (presumably) follow a logical flow. But there are significant differences.

Some of the differences have to do with responsibilities:

- Meetings are led by a manager or leader, who generally has done minimal preparation; requirements workshops are led by a neutral facilitator who has prepared intensively.
- Meetings require little or no *pre-work* by the attendees; requirements workshops generally require a fair amount of pre-work, including the creation of products that serve as candidates for workshop inputs.
- The authority to make decisions in meetings rests with the meeting leader, and that authority may not even be a topic of discussion; in a requirements workshop, each decision has an associated decision rule. There's a decision process, and authority can rest with one or more people (but not the facilitator).

Other differences involve the approach:

- Meetings are about information exchange; requirements workshops are about information discovery and creation.
- In a meeting, people often interact very little; interactions among people in requirements workshops are intense and varied, and the participants perform activities as individuals, members of subgroups, and members of the group as a whole.
- Meetings allow little or no time for playful activities; requirements workshops encourage "serious play" to promote innovation and foster teamwork.

Still other differences between meetings and facilitated workshops are connected to the documentation produced by participants:

- Meetings rarely involve producing deliverables; requirements workshops involve participants creating and verifying deliverables such as requirements models.
- Meetings rarely require inputs in the form of work products; requirements workshops almost always require that participants create things such as draft models.
- Meetings use visual media sparingly, if at all; requirements workshops make heavy use of visual media such as posters, sticky notes, cards, and diagrams.

The Roots of Joint Application Design

The JAD workshop technique originated at IBM in the late 1970s. (JAD is a trademark of IBM.) Officially, the *D* stands for *design*, but many people use it to stand for *development* to indicate that the technique applies across the entire software development life cycle. The original purpose of JAD was to help groups to overcome obstacles in achieving high-quality requirements and design deliverables and to promote active customer involvement.

The core models produced in traditional JAD workshops are logical data models, process models (in the form of functional decomposition and data flow diagrams), character-based user interface screen designs, and report layouts. In the mid-1980s, when rapid application development (RAD) became popular, JAD became a favored way to define user requirements quickly. As object-oriented development and the Internet became widely used, JAD reemerged as a way to accelerate delivery of requirements.

Perhaps the most important distinctions between workshops and meetings are the presence of specific process roles—facilitator and recorder—in workshops and the fact that workshops deliver specific, predefined products.

A neutral *facilitator* assists the group by leading the workshop planning process and then guiding the group through the workshop. A person serving in another process role, the *recorder* (or *scribe*), might also assist by capturing the group's work in real time.

Neither the facilitator nor the recorder operates as a content expert, nor does either collaborate in product creation. As a result, they're free to focus on the process. As the group becomes more familiar with the workshop process, the facilitator's role in controlling the process can be relaxed.

The facilitator's job is to balance the needs of content, process, and people.

- Balancing *content* involves ensuring that the necessary user requirements are delivered at the right level of detail and with the necessary degree of quality.
- *Process* balancing requires the facilitator to design a sequence of activities that follows a logical progression within the specified time constraints, to promote participation, and to keep participants energized and engaged.

▪ Balancing *people* needs is also a key responsibility of the facilitator. This involves helping participants to build their relationships, exploiting the strengths of different styles of thinking, learning, and interacting, and helping participants become a high-performing group.

WORKSHOP PRODUCTS

A key difference between workshops and meetings is that workshops deliver specific, predefined products. These include tangible products, such as requirements models. Workshops also deliver important intangible products, such as mutual learning, increased understanding, decisions, motivation, and teamwork.

All these products are specifically planned ahead of time, and workshop planners need time to define what to deliver, what level of detail the materials should contain, and how the intangibles will be achieved. A useful guideline is that you'll need at least one day of planning time to facilitate one day of workshop. This investment is substantial, but the benefits can be vast.

During your workshop, participants use one model to test another, and in so doing they uncover missing and erroneous requirements. Because each requirements model connects in some way to at least one other, you can also use one model to elicit another. In this way, participants more easily see connections. They quickly learn to iterate across multiple models in the workshop, and that leads to the delivery of more complete requirements.

OTHER USES FOR WORKSHOPS

Elements of requirements workshops, such as process planning, product delivery, and process roles, can be applied in other settings. For example, you can use facilitated workshops to launch a project by delivering elements documented in the project charter or vision document. In fact, you might usefully create the scope-level requirements I discuss in this book during the chartering process. Other good uses of workshops include project planning, strategic planning, process improvement, and problem solving.

TYPES OF REQUIREMENTS WORKSHOPS

Throughout this book, I explain how you can use workshops to elicit, specify, review, quality-check, and reach closure on user requirements deliverables.

Figure 1-2 shows a sequence of three types of requirements workshops. (Note that the deliverables are examples; Chapter 2 contains full lists of the deliverables for each type of workshop.)

Although each project is unique, this diagram gives you a basis for defining the deliverables of any of the workshop types. For example, you might use multiple half-day workshops to deliver high-level requirements.

These workshops are preceded by an agreed-upon charter document or vision document and possibly a charter workshop. Typically, in a charter workshop, you deliver goals, objectives, a communication plan, roles and responsibilities, and perhaps the same deliverables as for scope workshops (discussed next). After you read Chapters 4 through 9, which together provide a framework for

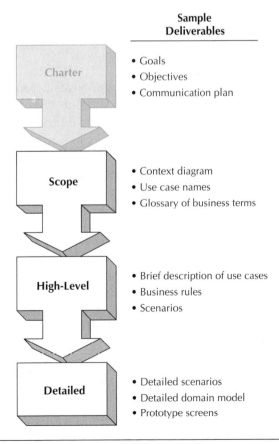

Sample Deliverables

Charter
- Goals
- Objectives
- Communication plan

Scope
- Context diagram
- Use case names
- Glossary of business terms

High-Level
- Brief description of use cases
- Business rules
- Scenarios

Detailed
- Detailed scenarios
- Detailed domain model
- Prototype screens

FIGURE 1-2 TYPES OF REQUIREMENTS WORKSHOPS

designing scope, high-level, and detailed user requirements workshops, you should have a good idea of how charter workshops can work for you.

In the ensuing workshops, you refine the user requirements, moving from a high level of abstraction to more detailed requirements. In a *scope workshop*, you take a bird's-eye view to determine which user requirements should be included. The deliverables from the scope workshop clarify the items to be elaborated in your *high-level workshop*, and its deliverables are in turn refined in detail in the *detailed workshop*. If the scope of your project is fairly well contained, you can combine workshop levels. In practice, workshop categories often overlap.

As you move through the workshops, you also prioritize your requirements. In one of my workshops, for example, we integrated prioritization with high-level modeling and then detailed modeling. I asked participants to write brief use case descriptions and then to prioritize the entire set of use cases. From there, the participants created detailed use cases, scenarios, and business rules. In our final workshop activity, the participants revisited these priorities and adjusted the earlier list based on their deeper understanding.

Requirements workshops are often repeated, with each workshop delivering a set of requirements in a certain state or degree of completeness. You decide which products you need and tailor the outcomes appropriately. If time is of the essence, you might decide to deliver less precise user requirements, realizing that the trade-off will be more defects and rework during development. For projects in which quality is king, you'll want to deliver a more comprehensive set of requirements.

WORKSHOPS AND ITERATIVE DEVELOPMENT

Many software projects with fast delivery cycles have adopted an *iterative* development life cycle. This involves delivering cohesive chunks of the product incrementally over the course of numerous *releases*. In each release, you use a development life cycle that loosely follows the stages of defining, designing, developing, testing, and implementing.

With this technique, you can initially focus your workshops on high-priority areas and get started with software development, deferring lower-priority requirements for later exploration. This approach reduces the risks associated with trying to get all the requirements right at the very beginning of the requirements stage.

Iterative life cycles make use of *prototypes* to elicit or verify requirements. This method gives customers and users early visibility of the software, and that tends to promote their ongoing involvement. Iterative prototyping complements, or can be integrated into, requirements workshops. Workshops are woven into early iterations either to define the requirements in terms of a prototype or to create a *low-fidelity* prototype: a representation of screens or screen flows created on a whiteboard or poster or with posts (sticky notes) on a wall. These types of prototypes tend to reduce the risks associated with software prototypes.

MAKING THE BUSINESS CASE FOR A REQUIREMENTS WORKSHOP

Some organizations shy away from workshops, reluctant to invest the time it takes to plan and execute them. Others claim that gathering people together in the same place at the same time is cost-prohibitive. But requirements workshops can provide a substantial return on investment, as outlined in the section "The Business Value of Requirements Workshops" in Chapter 12.

Requirements workshops provide business value by reducing the time it takes to gather requirements, by increasing team productivity, and by reducing risks associated with software projects.

Requirements workshops also contribute to customer and user satisfaction because they allow customers and users to participate directly in defining their needs. In one project I facilitated, we defined requirements using models, such as user interface prototypes, built during workshops; as a result, not one high- or medium-priority defect originated with requirements. The long-term prognosis for a project that uses requirements workshops is better because the workshops help build a healthy project community early in the project's life. In addition to delivering requirements, workshops enhance team interactions, trust, and collaboration. They show by example the value of maintaining active customer involvement in the software development process.

WHEN NOT TO USE REQUIREMENTS WORKSHOPS

Requirements workshops are most beneficial when the project conditions are appropriate. If your project is small and low-risk, I don't recommend using workshops. However, if your requirements are complex and you value the side effects of collaboration—trust, mutual understanding, and participation—then require-ments workshops may be for you.

Requirements workshops are most appropriate for business software or commer-cial software when you can get the participation of knowledgeable customers, users, or surrogates. Requirements for real-time systems are less visible to cus-tomers, so requirements workshops are probably not suitable.

Size matters, so be careful not to overload the workshops with too many people. The number of participants should not exceed 16 unless you use 2 facilitators. Most workshops have between 7 and 12 participants. Each additional person can add more time to the workshop or reduce the number of deliverables. Strive for the minimum number of participants who can represent the collective needs of customers, users, testers, designers, and analysts.

If you can't identify a workshop sponsor (see Chapter 5), you won't have the necessary commitment to ensure that the right players participate and to prepare for a successful session. For some organizations, it isn't feasible to gather users or their surrogates at the same time and place. In that case, you might consider using collaborative software tools that allow people to gather in a different time–different place virtual environment (see "Different Time and Place Options" in Chapter 8). Be aware that you'll need a skilled facilitator who can lead the process and also use the tool.

Planning requirements workshops takes time. If management won't allow time for planning and pre-work, your workshop results are likely to be mediocre.

Finally, don't use workshops unless you have a facilitator who is neutral to the outcome, experienced with group processes, and knowledgeable about the deliv-erables to be created in the session. These skills can be developed within your organization and shared across projects.

In lieu of workshops, you can use techniques such as observation, interviews, surveys, prototypes, competitive analysis, and product complaint data. Of course, these techniques can be powerful in combination with workshops, if workshops seem to be a fit for you.

SUMMING UP

There's no standard formula for requirements workshops. Each project, business situation, and group of people will combine to make each workshop unique.

Preparing for the requirements workshop requires collaboration. It permits you to tap into the collective wisdom of all the project stakeholders. You can use the fundamentals provided in this book as a guide for planning, designing, and running your own requirements workshops.

Further Readings

FOR MORE INFORMATION

Doyle and Strauss (1976) is a must-read for facilitators and meeting leaders. The key ideas in this book inspired Chuck Morris's creation of JAD.

Gause and Weinberg (1989) is a fun and straightforward look at the ambiguities of requirements and also their human side. The authors devote a number of pithy chapters to workshop-like events and discuss making meetings work for everybody, idea-generating meetings, right-brained methods, and facilitating in the face of conflict.

Highsmith (2000) presents a compelling case for using a collaborative and adaptive approach to software development. He devotes a chapter to great teams and their ability to collaborate. The book also includes a discussion on the value of using JAD workshops as an important means of collaboration.

Jones (2000) offers assessment, benchmark, and empirical data from thousands of projects, of all types and from all countries, presented by perhaps the world's most prolific researcher on software projects. Because software is the most labor-intensive and error-prone product of the twentieth century, the one purpose of Jones's quest for data is to minimize software project failure. His data continues to support JAD and requirements workshops as a best practice to significantly reduce scope creep and as a means to gather stable requirements with less downstream rework.

Keil and Carmel (1995) presents research showing that successful software development projects have more "links": channels and techniques in which customers and developers exchange information.

McConnell (1996) is a classic book on software development best practices. It devotes a chapter to JAD, promotes the value of customer-inclusive practices, and summarizes industry data about the high cost of requirements defects.

Wood and Silver (1995), an updated version of the authors' classic 1989 JAD book, describes the phases of classic JAD, related participatory approaches, tools and techniques, and group dynamics. This is an easy-to-read and friendly book useful to any JAD facilitator.

Zahniser (1993) presents an approach to requirements workshops using cross-functional teams, storyboards, concurrent modeling, and multiple orthogonal models.

2

WORKSHOP DELIVERABLES: MINING COAL, EXTRACTING DIAMONDS

"Example is the best precept."
—Aesop

When you examine a precious gem such as a diamond, you see different things depending on how light hits it, the angle of your view, and your distance from it. When you rotate the gem, you see new things. Each time you look, you might discover new wonders, each one different from the others yet equally valid. Even a slight twist of the gem gives you a richer appreciation of it.

You should treat your user requirements in a similar manner, seeking to examine them in a way that enriches your understanding. A good way to do that is by using multiple requirements models.

Requirements models offer a variety of ways to represent user requirements; these models serve as the primary deliverables of your workshop. Each requirements model expresses a particular point of view, provides perspective on a certain focus, and achieves a specific level of detail. As a facilitator, you must understand which models are available and how they interrelate. Your requirements will be more complete and correct if you build more than one of these models in each of your workshops.

It's critical that you select the most appropriate models to solve the business problem at hand and then design your workshops to deliver those models. Typically, the participants create part of one model, which in turn reveals elements of another. Having multiple models speeds the user requirements discovery process while also increasing the correctness of the requirements. Taken together, these models weave a story of your user requirements.

This chapter is designed to provide initial answers to the following questions:

- What is the context for user requirements?
- In what ways can I understand requirements models?
- What are the possible models that participants can deliver in workshops?
- What is the context in which these models fit into a software project?
- What is the purpose of each model?
- What questions does each model answer?
- What view of the world does each model take?
- What is the primary focus of each model?
- What are some questions I might ask to explain what the model is communicating?

The first few sections of the chapter describe the terminology associated with re-quirements models, including requirements level, model level, model view, and model focus. The last section provides overviews of each of the 19 models. Each model is summarized according to its purpose, focus, format, level of detail, key elements, and relationship to other models.

You don't need to define or adopt all these models; for a given requirements workshop, you need only define a subset. The key is to become adept at picking the right model for the right problem. You'll also save time by having some of the participants create parts of the target model before the workshop. This pre-work not only allows the group to jump-start the modeling work but also prepares them mentally for the thinking they'll need to do during the workshop.

THE EVOLUTION OF REQUIREMENTS

Requirements define the operational capabilities of a system or a process that must exist to satisfy a legitimate business need. The generic term *requirements* covers both *functional* requirements, which specify the functionality that users expect, and *nonfunctional* requirements, which include user quality attributes such as performance; system requirements such as security and maintainability; and system constraints such as database and language.

Taken together, these types of requirements are based on *business* requirements: the reasons for undertaking a project. No requirements should exist without a good business reason that make them valid. Each requirement should be testable and verified throughout the development process.

Figure 2-1 shows the various requirements levels and illustrates how they evolve.

You can use a variety of models to depict requirements at each level. Within each level, some models can be created with more or less detail.

When you plan your workshop, you may find that you need to define higher-level business requirements before diving into more detail. On one project I worked on, the business sponsor believed that he needed a new system. Rather than jump into user requirements, though, the workshop participants need to understand the broader business context.

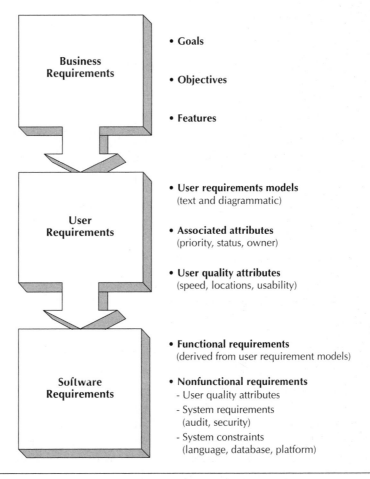

Business Requirements
- Goals
- Objectives
- Features

User Requirements
- User requirements models
  (text and diagrammatic)
- Associated attributes
  (priority, status, owner)
- User quality attributes
  (speed, locations, usability)

Software Requirements
- Functional requirements
  (derived from user requirement models)
- Nonfunctional requirements
  - User quality attributes
  - System requirements
    (audit, security)
  - System constraints
    (language, database, platform)

FIGURE 2-1 REQUIREMENTS LEVELS (BASED ON WIEGERS, 1999)

We conducted a two-day workshop in which the participants created a relationship map (described later in this chapter). The workshops, and the resulting model, helped the business stakeholders to understand their higher-level business requirements before deciding whether and how software should be used. This work also gave the software team a deeper understanding of the business, and that allowed them to be more effective partners. Subsequently, the business stakeholders saw several opportunities to simplify their policies and processes, and they implemented changes. They also pinpointed where and how to target the use of technology and launched an automation project.

In other cases, everyone may have a good understanding of the business context, and your project is ready to dive into detailed user requirements. Your job is to select the best models, define how much detail each model should provide, establish "doneness tests" (see Chapter 7) for them, and design a workshop structure that permits participants to create models quickly.

Wherever possible, you'll supplement the user requirements with nonfunctional requirements information to shorten the time required to define software requirements. For example, in one workshop in which the group defined use cases, participants associated each use case with usage information, including locations where the use case would be needed, the approximate number of actors initiating the use case, the minimum and maximum response time needed, and the frequency of use.

The following subsections describe the requirements levels.

BUSINESS REQUIREMENTS

Business requirements are the higher-level needs that, when addressed, will permit the organization to do things such as increase revenue, reduce costs, improve service, and meet regulatory requirements.

Business requirements are usually defined in a project *charter document* that answers the question, Why do this project? (Some organizations call the document a *vision document, initiation document,* or *business case.*) The business requirements in this document are typically written in broad strokes. For example, your charter might include a list of software features or functions such as "provide users with an easy-to-use and up-to-date inventory search capability." These functions, in turn, should be associated with one or more business goals, such as "retain existing customers."

Your charter is a tool for marshaling people, money, and other organizational resources. Many organizations require sponsor sign-off of a formal charter document before any project is launched. The charter document should describe the project infrastructure in terms of the six questions to be answered:

- Why: business vision, goals, and objectives
- What: organizational, financial, temporal, and functional scope
- Who: staffing, roles, and responsibilities
- How: project controls; success metrics; assumptions and critical success factors; team and user education, coaching, and training; risks and risk mitigation strategies
- Where: locations of staff and potential users and customers
- When: high-level work plan and release strategy

USER REQUIREMENTS

User requirements bridge the requirements of the business and the requirements of the software. It's this bridge that's most often difficult to cross because the languages, models, knowledge, and work styles of the players on either side are different. This is where I focus this book: using workshops to facilitate understanding while concurrently creating the models to represent the needs of business stakeholders.

Gause and Weinberg (1989) broadly define a *user* as anyone who affects or is affected by the product. This definition includes people and things (devices, databases, external systems) that interact directly with the system being modeled as well as other people and things that receive system by-products (decisions, secondary reports, questions). To elicit user requirements more completely in workshops, you may need to include stakeholders other than direct users.

You can specify user requirements in a separate user requirements document. This document typically includes the definitions of stakeholder classes, functional scope, detailed user requirements, quality attributes such as speed, usability, and capability (if possible), and general attributes such as priority, version, and status. Or your organization might choose to integrate user requirements into your software specification document. Some organizations include user requirements in their charter document.

BUSINESS CHANGE A seldom mentioned aspect of software development is that it provokes change in the behavior of business users. Direct users must

Is *User* a Dirty Word?

The term *users* implies people who interact directly with the software. When I was an assembler and COBOL programmer in the early 1980s, *user* was a dirty word. Hoping to reduce user dissatisfaction with the software organization, the company I worked for launched a new policy: Don't call the people who have requirements "users"; instead, call them "customers."

Alas, improving the sordid state of software–business relationships doesn't happen merely because of changing a word. Ever since software has been around, perception on both sides has been lousy.

On the software development side, users are the people who cannot or will not tell you what they want—and they keep changing their minds anyway. As Ed Yourdon has pointed out, the software industry is the only one that calls its customers "users" (the illegal drug trade excepted). On the business side, software people can't seem to understand the users' real-life business pressures. Developers also take too long to do anything, and they insist on using obtuse language. Software people want to be precise in an imprecise world, and they don't deliver the right stuff on time.

Relationships among people with different perspectives and needs are formed one person at a time. Although well-run requirements workshops aren't a panacea, you'll find that they'll go a long way toward establishing better understanding and communications among software and business people.

interact with software in new ways. The business workflow often changes, along with procedures, policies, and interactions among people. As you uncover user requirements, your users will be faced with decisions about how and where to change their work.

To understand how the business will change, various stakeholders can ask these questions:

- Who is doing what work?
- What is the flow of work?
- Who makes what decisions?
- What will the system do for me? What won't it do for me?
- Which jobs will change?
- What handoffs will there be?
- Which forms and documents do I use?

- What operating procedures do I follow?
- What policies and rules are different? Who needs to know about these changes?

I recommend that business stakeholders create a *business change document* at the time they're capturing user requirements. This document should include current and changed business processes, impacted organizations and roles, changes to documentation (such as manuals), guidelines, standard operating procedures, plans for user training and education, a communication plan, and a change management plan.

Software Requirements

Software operates within certain constraints, which are the functional and nonfunctional requirements that make up software requirements. The *doing* parts of software are the functions that derive directly from your user requirements. Typically, these functions are expressed as text decompositions of a list of user requirements. In classic software engineering, functional requirements are decomposed into lower-level functions, forming a functional hierarchy.

The *being* parts of software are the nonfunctional needs that must be satisfied, including the users' desired quality attributes, technical requirements related to auditing and security, quality attributes such as capacity and reliability, and constraints such as platform and database. These nonfunctional requirements are often critical distinguishing aspects of a software product. After all, you certainly wouldn't use a Web site that's slow or unreliable. For this reason, it's important to discover nonfunctional requirements, which you can often elicit simultaneously with functional requirements.

Note that if you have well-defined user requirements that employ some of the models described in this chapter, you may not need to convert those models into classic text-based functional requirements.

Model Views, Focuses, and Levels of Detail

You model primarily to facilitate communication. Models can be depicted with words, drawings, or both. The process of modeling allows you to elicit, discover, and specify views of the problem domain or other area of study. To select the most appropriate requirements models to use in your workshop, you must understand their basic purposes and what they can communicate. Figure 2-2 presents

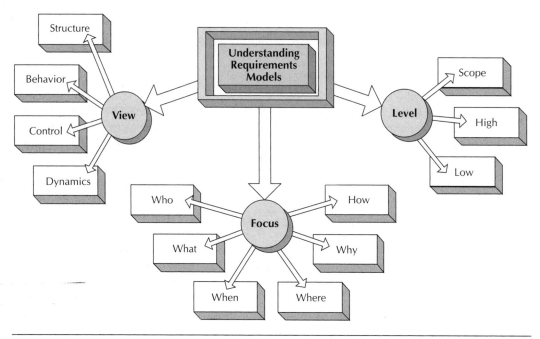

FIGURE 2-2 MODEL VIEW, FOCUS, AND LEVEL OF DETAIL

the concepts I'll use to help you gain that understanding: model view, focus, and level of detail.

MODEL VIEWS

User requirement models can be categorized by four views.

1. Models that primarily express *behavior* are oriented toward processes, tasks, or sequences. Examples include use cases, use case maps, and process maps.

2. A model with a *structural* view describes parts and their relationship, as in data models and class models.

3. *Dynamic* models describe how things change over time; examples include event tables and statechart diagrams.

4. Views that are *control*-oriented describe decisions and policies that provide guidance to the other views. Business policies, business rules, and decision tables or trees represent control requirements.

Figure 2-3 shows the overlaps among these views.

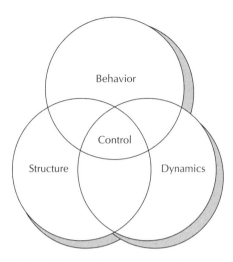

FIGURE 2-3 OVERLAP AMONG REQUIREMENTS VIEWS

Although each view implies aspects of the other views, each one speaks to a single primary view. For example, a data model is a structural view of requirements, but the connections among data entities in the model imply behavioral rules. Similarly, a use case model is primarily behavioral, but it has some dynamic and structural aspects. Table 2-1 groups the 19 basic requirements models by view.

One of your first tasks is to help the team pick the right model for the right problem. This requires that you grasp enough of the problem to know which model view is your best starting point. Many project teams choose behavioral models, such as use cases, as their core user requirements view; however, behavior models may not be appropriate for all business systems.

Some problem domains are more structural in nature, such as those in which the primary task of the software will be to store information and respond to queries. Others are dynamic: Time affects the state of business information, and the software must store information and act on it based on state. Still others depend on enforcing or analyzing sets of complex and interconnected rules.

One project team asked me to facilitate a workshop in which they assumed that they'd create use cases. After asking some questions about the business problem they were trying to solve, who would use the system, and how it would be used, I understood their problems to be more structural. In particular, the users and plant managers needed to query and analyze financial information. To define the

TABLE 2-1 REQUIREMENTS MODELS BY VIEW

View	Requirements Model
Behavioral	Actor map
	Actor table
	Context diagram
	Process map
	Prototype
	Relationship map
	Scenarios
	Stakeholder classes
	Use cases
	Use case map
	Use case package
	User interface navigation diagram
Structural	Domain model
	Glossary
Dynamic	Event table
	Statechart diagrams
Control	Business policies
	Business rules
	Decision table, decision tree

first-cut user requirements, we conducted our workshop using questions, a data model, and policies rather than use cases.

MODEL FOCUS

Many of us know about the six great focus questions: *who, what, when, where, why,* and *how.* Rudyard Kipling's poem "The Elephant's Child" refers to these questions as the "six honest serving men." John Zachman (1987) uses them as the "columns" of his systems architecture. Journalists use them as guidance for writing a story. I use these questions as a shortcut to describe the requirements models according to focus, as illustrated in Figure 2-4.

You won't answer all these questions, nor will you deliver all the models. Instead, you'll decide which are the most important models for your problem domain. You'll design a workshop flow by asking questions in a manner that

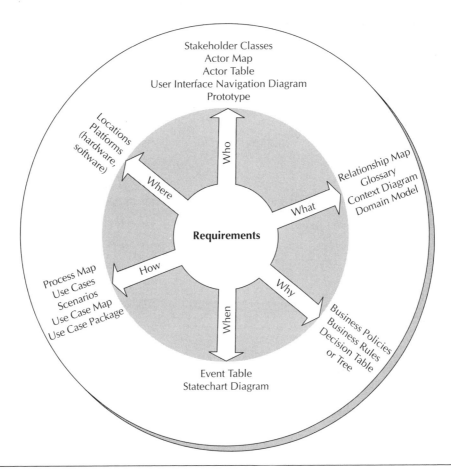

FIGURE 2-4 THE SIX GREAT FOCUS QUESTIONS

allows participants to follow a natural progression of understanding their requirements, as shown in Table 2-2.

These aren't the only questions to ask. Each model has elements that you will expand on so that you can ask specific questions that will yield the other model elements you need. These questions are woven into your collaboration patterns (see Chapter 9); these patterns provide a framework for group or subgroup activities that generate requirements models. For example, with a use case model, you can ask questions such as, How will the work be done? What goals must the actors accomplish using the system? How do events get handled?

Table 2-3 groups the 19 basic requirements models by focus.

TABLE 2-2 FOCUS QUESTIONS VERSUS REQUIREMENTS MODELS

Focus	Question Model (Text and/or Diagrams)
Why do this project?	Goals, objectives, vision
What do we mean?	Glossary
Who's affected by the project? Who affects it?	Stakeholder classes
What's going to happen?	Relationship map Context diagram
When will it happen? What will result?	Event table
What processes will go on?	Process map Use cases (at high level)
Who does it?	Actor table Actor map
What policies do we have?	Business policies
How will it be done?	Use case packages Use cases (at detailed level)
What are examples of what will happen?	Scenarios
What data is needed? When will that data change?	Domain model Statechart diagrams
What must be true?	Business rules Decision table, decision tree
In what sequence will things be done?	Use case map
What will the system look like?	User interface navigation diagram Prototypes

LEVEL OF DETAIL

Each model can be described along a continuum of how much or how little detail it contains. These levels include the following:

- *Scope level*, in which you understand the context of the requirements
- *High level*, in which you describe requirements using broad strokes
- *Detailed level*, which contains many elements and steps

TABLE 2-3 REQUIREMENTS MODELS BY FOCUS

Focus	Requirements Model
Who	Actor map
	Actor table
	Prototype
	Stakeholder classes
	User interface navigation diagram
What	Context diagram
	Domain model
	Glossary
	Relationship map
When	Event table
	Statechart diagrams
Why	Business policies
	Business rules
	Decision table, decision tree
How	Process map
	Scenarios
	Use cases
	Use case map
	Use case packages

Figure 2-5 shows requirements models by focus (the six key questions) and these three levels of detail.

Some models can be captured at varying levels of precision; you'll need to decide how far to go in your workshop with a given model. For example, high-level use cases include use case names, brief descriptions, and use case headers, whereas detailed use cases include those elements plus step-by-step sequences that describe the interactions between the actors and the systems; they also describe exceptions that can occur.

You can use various strategies in your requirements workshop to get the level of detail you want. For example, you can obtain agreement before the workshop on a list of use cases, which will give you a jump-start on your high-level use cases. In one workshop I facilitated, the software team had drafted use cases at a detailed level, but these didn't satisfy the business stakeholders. Still, the use cases provided a starting point for defining detailed use cases along with companion

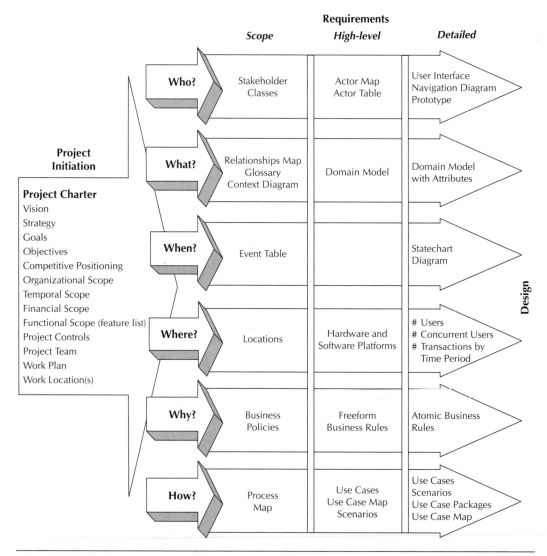

FIGURE 2-5 MODEL FOCUS AND LEVEL OF DETAIL

models: scenarios, business rules, a prototype (in the form of static screen shots), and a domain model.

In practice, requirement models don't fit neatly into a single level; they can cross levels. For example, Figure 2-5 shows the actor table and actor map together as one high-level model, but you might actually draft them during a project charter workshop because they flow naturally from defining the impacted organizations.

TABLE 2-4 REQUIREMENTS MODELS BY LEVEL OF DETAIL

Level(s)	Model
Scope	Business policies
	Context diagram
	Event table
	Process map
	Relationship map
	Stakeholder classes
Scope (and other levels)	Glossary
High	Actor map
	Actor table
High and detailed	Domain model
	Scenarios
	Use cases
	Use case map
Detailed	Business rules
	Decision table, decision tree
	Prototype
	Statechart diagrams
	Use case packages
	User interface navigation diagram

Similarly, you might provide a list of expected software functions in the form of use cases in your charter.

Table 2-4 groups the 19 basic requirements models by level of detail.

BUILDING THE MODELS

You might not elicit your requirements models in top-down order. In fact, often you'll iterate among the levels. Your participants might need to begin by walking through prototype screens and use case steps, particularly if you're replacing an existing system. Some projects may have well-defined scope, and the team may be ready to jump into high-level requirements. Each project is unique, and you'll need to consider factors such as team size, location, degree of customer and user involvement, past history with software development, existing documentation and software, and team modeling experience in deciding the best way to elicit user requirements in workshops. This topic is discussed more fully in Chapter 10.

As-Is Models

When you decide which models to use, consider whether you need to create any *as-is* models to represent the current business or user environment. For example, participants might create a process map and an actor map depicting their current workflow. You can do this during the workshop as a way for everyone to understand which operations need to remain the same and which ones need to be eliminated.

This technique is similar to business process reengineering (BPR), which generally requires time to evaluate as-is workflow models in order to discover problems such as delays, inadequate or incorrect information, and unnecessary policies. Rather than do this during your requirements workshop, you can arrange for participants to draft as-is models before the workshop; then when you're modeling future user requirements, you can use the models as a reference point or to get the juices flowing.

A pitfall of as-is modeling involves taking too much time and intellectual energy getting the models "just right." You can spend a lot of time modeling the current user environment at the expense of envisioning the future, *to-be* environment. This trap, along with other political and management issues raised by a focus on current work processes, is one reason that BPR tends to be downplayed in software projects.

If you decide to use as-is models, pick only one or two models, and don't model them too precisely. Be clear on why you need them. In one of my workshops, the planning team created an as-is process map in order to identify roles to involve in the workshop. We also used this map during our doneness testing (see "QA As You Go" in Chapter 9) to ensure that the requirements, in the form of use cases, weren't missing any important steps.

Multiple Models

A requirements model describes one aspect of the problem at hand; no single model can describe all aspects of the problem nor all the requirements. To gain a complete understanding of the requirements, you need multiple models. As you begin to define one model, elements of another emerge. For example, as you specify use cases, you'll begin to capture data elements (which you should capture in a domain model), define business rules, and define more glossary items. This combination of models or a subset thereof yields higher quality user requirements than relying on one model such as a data flow diagram.

To facilitate the creation of more complete user requirements, I recommend using the Multi-Model collaboration pattern in requirements workshops. See the Appendix for a briefing about this pattern. Chapter 9 includes examples of this pattern in use.

"Concern for man and his fate must always form the chief interest of all technical endeavors. Never forget this in the midst of your diagrams and equations."

—Albert Einstein

MODEL BRIEFINGS

The following subsections present "briefings" about the 19 basic requirements models. These short descriptions are not meant to fully exploit the communication power of the model; their purpose is only to summarize each model. (Refer to Tables 2-1 through 2-4 to see the relevant view, question, focus, and level of detail for each model.)

ACTOR MAP

An *actor map* (also known as an *actor hierarchy*) defines the relationships among the actors in the actor table (see the next section) in terms of how their roles are shared and disparate. The map shows both human and nonhuman actors arranged into hierarchies.

An actor map is particularly useful when you're answering questions such as, Who needs to interact with the system in similar ways? and Which roles are unique? As with the actor table, each actor in the actor map is likely to initiate at least one use case. The actor map can also help you make decisions about new and changed job roles.

ACTOR TABLE

An *actor table* (also known as a *direct users list* or an *actor catalog*) defines the roles played by people and things that will interact directly with the system. The contents of an actor table typically include names, brief descriptions, physical locations, and necessary job aids.

An actor table is particularly useful when you're answering questions such as, What are the responsibilities of the people who will interact with the system? and How can we reuse specific information about these users for other requirements or for downstream projects? Each actor in the table is likely to initiate at least one use case. The actor table can also help you surface issues involving where (at which physical locations) to roll out the system and in which order.

BUSINESS POLICIES

Business policies (also known as *guidelines, high-level business rules, standards,* or simply *policies*) define the principles and regulations that influence the behavior and structure of the business being modeled. These policies provide the basis for decomposing business rules (see the next section). It's useful to collect policies in a table that groups them and also shows the source, the *owner* (the entity that has the authority to create and enforce the policy), and the change status of each policy.

Business policies are particularly useful when you're answering questions such as, What are the policies we must enforce? and Why do we need this policy? Each policy will contain multiple business terms defined in the glossary, and, as implied earlier, policies will map to multiple lower-level business rules. Business policies can also help you elicit issues about which policies will be enforced in software versus those enforced as part of human workflows.

BUSINESS RULES

Business rules (also known as *free-form business rules, atomic business rules, constraints,* or *invariants*) are specific guidelines, regulations, and standards that must be adhered to. Attributes of business rules include the owner, the source, the source category (for example, human or document), jurisdiction, and relative complexity.

Business rules are particularly useful when you're answering questions such as, What policies must we enforce? and Why do we need this particular policy? Business rules are represented on a number of other models, such as statechart diagrams (in the form of guard conditions), data models (connected with attributes and relationships), and use cases (each of which generally requires several business rules).

Business rules are really the heart of your functional requirements; they represent the reasoning you do, and the decisions you make, when you're deciding on these requirements.

CONTEXT DIAGRAM

A *context diagram* (also known as a *scope model, level-zero data flow diagram, context-level use case,* or *system context use case*) shows the system as a whole in its environment. On this diagram,

- The system is a bubble in the center; the system is seen as a *black box* that manipulates input and produces output in a way that's not visible to or controllable by viewers
- Interfaces and actors appear as boxes or stick figures
- Inflows and outflows are arrows labeled with nouns

A context diagram is particularly useful when you're answering questions such as, What does the system get? and When do things happen, and what are the results of those things happening? The inflows equate to business events, the outflows to event responses, and the actors to actors in a use case model. The context diagram can also help you address the "big picture" scope of your system.

DECISION TABLE OR DECISION TREE

A *decision table* (also known as a *logic table*) or a *decision tree* (also known as a *decision diagram*) describes the conditions associated with particular actions or decisions, along with the constraints on the associated behavior. A decision table shows rules as rows and conditions as columns, with an X in each cell for each action that should be taken by the person performing the behavior. A decision tree shows decision points as diamonds (as on a flowchart) and actions as boxes.

Decision tables or trees are particularly useful when you're answering questions such as, What conditions influence various decisions? and What is the order in which the system will check those conditions? Each of the conditions on the table is a component of an atomic business rule; the data elements associated with these conditions should be represented in the data model or class model. Decision tables are also useful when you're dealing with complex business rules or when the order in which conditions are checked is important in the context of the problem domain.

DOMAIN MODEL

A *domain model* (also known as a *conceptual data model* or *conceptual class model*) defines groups of information that must be stored in the system and the relationships among these groups. The model contains at least a list of business objects, data entities, or classes, and it can also contain a diagram that shows objects, entities, or classes and the relationships among them. The detailed domain model should also contain attributes for each item.

A domain model is particularly useful when you're answering questions such as, What information does each action need? and What will the structure look like when I've enforced the business rules? Each object, entity, or class should be defined in the glossary; attributes are likely to be represented in prototypes and use cases. A domain model can also help you to ensure that your data is clean or help you to determine requirements for cleaning data as necessary.

EVENT TABLE

An *event table* (also known as an *event list*) defines the triggers of events to which the system responds. Some of these responses involve visible outputs; others change only internal information; still others do both. You list events and responses in various formats, such as *subject+verb+object* or *"time to"+verb+object*. It's also useful to add columns to an event table to address things such as frequency.

An event table is particularly useful when you're answering questions such as, When will things happen, and what will result? and When does the system need to do something? Each term in an event table is likely to be associated with an element of your data model or class model. An event table can also provide a greater level of precision than a context diagram, which doesn't allow you to show temporal events.

GLOSSARY

A *glossary* (also known as a *business glossary, concepts catalog,* or *project glossary*) defines the meanings of all business terms relevant to the system being built. These terms serve as the foundation for all requirements models and business rules; the goal of the glossary is to provide a common vocabulary on which all of the stakeholders can agree.

A glossary is particularly useful when you're answering questions such as, What are the meanings of the business terms we use? and What are the business concepts we use? Each term in the glossary is likely to be associated with elements of many other models, such as data or class models and use cases. The glossary can also help you reach mutual understanding—among people from different functional groups or product life cycles—of the big picture of the system.

PROCESS MAP

A *process map* (also known as a *swimlane diagram, workflow map,* or *cross-functional process map*) shows the organization context in terms of the flows of inputs and outputs across functions or roles for a specific work process. On this diagram,

- Horizontal lanes represent the functions or roles
- Boxes represent the steps in the process
- Diamonds represent decisions
- Arrows show the flow of work

A process map is particularly useful when you're answering questions such as, How is the work done? and What decisions are made along the way, and who makes these decisions? The inputs and outputs generally match up with domains or data attributes in a class model or data model; subsets of process steps may map to use cases. A process map can also help clarify the current flow of work in a complex, cross-functional process, as well as provide insight about how the process might work better if you were to redesign it.

PROTOTYPE

A *prototype* (also known as *user interface prototype* or *window user interface*) is anything that captures the look and feel of the user interface to be built for the new system and allows users to play with it. A prototype can take the form of a fully working, albeit bare-bones, "system," or something more low-tech, such as screen shots and low-fidelity sketches (for example, Visio diagrams).

A prototype is particularly useful when you're answering questions such as, What are the human actors' views of the system? and What information do the users provide, and where do they provide it? You should use prototypes to test your scenarios, and the data represented in the prototypes should be represented in your domain model. A prototype can also be useful, early in requirements gathering and analysis, as a bottom-up way to define use cases, the domain model, and business rules.

RELATIONSHIP MAP

A *relationship map* (also known as an *organizational context diagram*) shows the organization context in terms of the relationships that exist among suppliers and external customers. In particular, the diagram shows the functions that out-siders and your organization perform and the inputs and outputs from these functions. Rectangles represent each entity; arrows between the rectangles rep-resent function inputs and outputs that go across entities. You can also have function arrows within a rectangle.

A relationship map is particularly useful when you're answering questions such as, Who or what parts of our organization are involved? and What do external cus-tomers and suppliers provide? You can generally use the inputs and outputs of a re-lationship map to represent high-level information on your context diagram. A relationship map can also help you look for opportunities to design changes to busi-ness processes in the form of overloaded functions (those that have too many in-puts, too many outputs, or both).

SCENARIOS

Scenarios (also known as *use case scenarios, business scenarios, business-level scenarios, high-level scenarios,* or *concrete use cases*) describe typical uses of the system as narratives or stories. Each narrative can be a few sentences or a few paragraphs.

Scenarios are particularly useful when you're answering questions such as, What are examples of things actors might encounter? and How will examples play out? Each scenario should have the ability to be "played out" in the context of a path through a use case (see "Use Cases" later in this chapter), and the scenario should use terms from the glossary and the data model or class model. Scenarios can also help you test your use cases and discover new ones; unhappy scenarios can also reveal new business rules.

STAKEHOLDER CLASSES

Stakeholder classes (also known as *user classes*) define the people who care about—and the people who *should* care about—the system being developed. You compile these classes, for people such as customers and suppliers, in a list or a table. It's useful to extend your classification of stakeholders with an *inclusion strategy* that ranks how the requirements of each stakeholder will be treated and how each stakeholder will be involved.

Stakeholder classes are particularly useful when you're answering questions such as, Who will the system affect? and Who will affect the system? The stake-holders that you classify as direct users will map to your actors in a use case model. The stakeholder classes can also help you to ensure that you know about, and involve, the right people in the right ways.

STATECHART DIAGRAMS

Statechart diagrams (also known as *state diagrams, state models, domain statechart diagrams,* or *entity life history diagrams*) define how time affects your domain model, in terms of the possible states that elements of that model can assume and the transitions between those states. A Unified Modeling Language (UML) statechart diagram includes the following kinds of symbols:

- A solid circle that represents the initial or starting state
- A bull's-eye that represents the final or ending state
- Rectangles with rounded corners that represent full states
- Solid lines with feathered arrows that represent transitions

Statechart diagrams are particularly useful when you're answering questions such as, What happens to a domain over time? and What behavior is the system responsible for handling in response to state changes? Each transition should be associated with at least one business event or temporal event; you can also assign guard conditions to transitions, each of which is a business rule of some sort. Statechart diagrams can also reveal new states that are associated with use cases, business rules, and data specifications.

USE CASES

Use cases (also known, in this context, as *essential use cases* or *abstract use cases*) describe the major functions that the system will perform for external actors, and also the goals that the system achieves for those actors along the way. Use cases can contain a number of different pieces of information, but at minimum, they have names and basic courses of action (the *mainstream* paths); exception conditions and variant paths are included in detailed use cases.

Use cases are particularly useful when you're answering questions such as, How will we meet our project goals? and What tasks make up each action that an actor triggers? Use cases generally use the names of members of the domain model; use case triggers are business events or temporal events. Use cases are initiated by one or more actors. Use cases can also help you refine your event table, actor map, and business rules because it's easy to add references to those as you explore use cases.

USE CASE MAP

A *use case map* (also known as a *use case navigation diagram, use case dependency diagram, use case flow diagram,* or *use case activity diagram*) illustrates the predecessor and successor relationships among use cases. This diagram can take various forms—for example, it can be a UML activity diagram that shows use cases where activities would normally be—but a use case is represented as the standard UML ellipse labeled with the use case name, and dependencies are dashed lines with feathered arrows.

A use case map is particularly useful when you're answering questions such as, What does a typical work sequence look like? and How do the project's various actions relate to one another? A use case map can also help you develop your strategy for revealing and testing use cases, business rules, and scenarios you might have missed.

USE CASE PACKAGE

Use case packages (also known as *use case groups*) are cohesive groups of use cases that can form things such as a logical architecture, a test group, or a release of the system. You use a UML package diagram to show a use case package and also show dependencies among use case packages.

Use case packages are particularly useful when you're answering questions such as, Which actions form logical groupings? and What are the dependencies among use cases? You should allocate each of your use cases to one package. Use case packages can also be useful in helping your customers to prioritize their requirements and helping the project manager to plan the division of work among the members of the development team.

USER INTERFACE NAVIGATION DIAGRAM

A *user interface navigation diagram* (also known as *dialog map, user interface storyboard,* or *screen transition diagram*) shows the layout of the user interface (screens, windows, dialog boxes, HTML pages) and the possible navigation paths among the interface elements. The features of this diagram include

- Boxes, which represent the major elements
- Arrows, which show the allowable transitions among the elements
- Text, which names the user actions or GUI events triggering transitions

User interface navigation diagrams are particularly useful when you're answering questions such as, How will things look and feel when a human actor interacts with the system? and How does actor behavior affect the views? Each use case will have an associated navigation diagram; each transition represents an actor or system action described in that use case.

User navigation diagrams can also be useful before serious prototyping efforts begin, because these diagrams reduce the risk that the customers will think that the prototypes are the system.

Further Readings

FOR MORE INFORMATION

Beyer and Holtzblatt (1998) presents an approach to requirements and design that involves "in context" interviewing (watching and questioning users in their actual workspaces) followed by modeling workshops.

Cockburn (2000) is a well-written, practical guide to use cases that includes advice on scoping use cases as well as writing them.

Constantine and Lockwood (1999) describes a user-centered approach to requirements and design that employs user and task models, low-fidelity prototypes, and modeling workshops.

Damelio (1996) is a concise and highly focused guide to process maps, relationship maps, and swimlane diagrams.

Date (2000) is an introduction to business rules from a relational database perspective.

Davis (1993) is a pre-UML textbook that presents a comprehensive set of the models and methods associated with requirements analysis.

Fowler (1999) describes the essentials of the UML in a concise, easy-to-read guide. The author cuts to the core of each of the UML models.

Kulak and Guiney (2000), a readable and useful treatment of use cases, presents an iterative approach to use cases along with numerous examples.

McGraw and Harbison (1997) describes the authors' scenario-based engineering process, which centers on user scenarios elicited via workshops, interviews, and field observations.

McMenamin and Palmer (1994) describes the classic and timeless event-driven models and also explains the key idea of separating "essential" views of the system from implementation views.

Robertson and Robertson (1999) presents a process for high-quality requirements that uses their Volere requirements specification template. The book also presents numerous models, including use cases, data flow diagrams, and data models, and it describes useful concepts such as fit criteria, requirements trawling, and a work breakdown structure for their requirements process.

Ross (1998) describes the basic reasons that business rules are at the core of user requirements.

Rummler and Brache (1995), written by pioneers who invented relationship mapping and process mapping, presents the associated models as part of the authors' process improvement methodology.

Simsion (2001) is a well-written and comprehensive guide to data modeling.

Wiegers (1999) is a comprehensive, practical, and readable guide to requirements modeling and management. The author provides overviews of several requirements models, describes the importance of the "voice of the customer," and offers detailed information about requirements tracing and management.

3

Ingredients of a Successful Requirements Workshop

"Cookery is not chemistry. It is an art. It requires instinct and taste rather than exact measurements.
—Marcel Boulestin

 This chapter explores the essential ingredients for building a great requirements workshop. As with facilitation, each ingredient is simple—but not easy. Because humans think in a nonlinear manner, the unpredictable will occur in workshops. The ingredients discussed in this chapter actually exploit the possibilities of unpredictability and enable the group to manage the requirements process elegantly, honestly, and effectively for all stakeholders. This chapter is an overview of each of these ingredients. Later chapters illustrate them in detail.

A Shared Purpose

Unproductive requirements meetings are like any other unproductive meeting: They're boring and longer than they should be. Topics move in circles. Conclusions and decisions are elusive. Not everyone participates (whereas some participate too much). The content moves up and down with regard to the level of detail.

Requirements workshops offer a better way to gather requirements quickly and decisively because the purpose of these workshops is crystal-clear. Before the gathering, the stakeholders in the requirements process perform considerable work to ensure a successful workshop. Among the outcomes of that pre-work is a clear, concise statement of purpose—the *shared purpose*—that all the participants understand and share a stake in. To begin with the end in mind, a requirements workshop begins with a statement about the workshop's purpose.

If you don't establish a shared purpose, you run the following risks:

- Undefined project goals, objectives, or vision
- Unrealistic expectations for the workshop
- A misguided focus on the requirements deliverables before the current state of the project and the requirements are understood
- Failure to gather information from a cross section of project and requirements stakeholders

To make the best use of your shared purpose, you should implement these keys to success:

- Before your requirements workshops, hold a project charter or "visioning" workshop if the purpose isn't as clear as it should be.
- If the scope of the requirements is unclear, conduct a scope workshop.
- Plan for your workshops as the project is being commissioned.
- Ratify the workshop's statement of purpose with project stakeholders beforehand.
- Remind the participants about the workshop's purpose throughout each session.

Note also the following interactions and trade-offs associated with a shared purpose:

- Performing information gathering while you're trying to define the purpose helps you to identify the right people for the workshop (see the next section).
- There's a time trade-off between conducting a workshop sooner and doing it later after you've defined the shared purpose.

THE RIGHT PEOPLE

You accelerate your project by having the right people together at the same time and in the same place to clarify your requirements. The *right people* means customers, users, and software suppliers. Each of these groups has gaps in its knowledge and experience that another can fill:

- Customers are sometimes disconnected from the work context of direct users.
- Users sometimes don't know the "big picture" that provides a context for funding a project.
- Users as well as customers may not have a grasp of the technical trade-offs they face when defining some of their requirements.
- Suppliers may not understand customers' pressures and the day-to-day task needs of the users.

One of the outcomes of your workshops is to ease communications among these sometimes incongruent groups. A well-planned and well-run workshop is a forum for listening, sharing, and learning for each group.

Having the right people requires sponsorship. The very acts of identifying these people before the workshop, gathering them during the workshop, and dealing with them appropriately after the workshop communicate volumes to the project team about the importance of getting it right, fast.

The following risks are associated with trying to find the right people:

- Having to fall back on surrogate (substitute) users instead of the actual direct users
- Concerns about freeing up key people to attend the workshop
- Concerns about travel expenses
- Not having decision makers in the workshop
- Failing to involve people who have downstream stakes in the workshop products

To make the best use of the right people, you should implement these keys to success:

- Obtain both business and software sponsor commitment.
- Conduct reviews of workshop deliverables with the larger user community.
- Make a business case for having the right people at the workshop.
- Ensure that workshop participants are included in reviewing and reaching closure on any post-workshop deliverables.
- Provide incentives for participants, such as toys and fun in the workshop, release from some normal work responsibilities, and recognition from management and peers after the workshop.

Note also the following interactions and trade-offs associated with identifying the right people:

- Defining the shared purpose (see the preceding section) helps in defining the right people.
- There's a trade-off between delivering requirements of lesser quality with the help of surrogate users and delivering higher-quality requirements over a longer period of time with direct users.

SHARED SPACE

The workshop sponsor makes it possible for people to be present, to prepare, and to participate in *shared space*. Funding for that time and workshop space is necessary.

Experienced software project managers of geographically distributed project teams have learned that even though technology can facilitate communications, the team must periodically gather in person to reconnect. After all, we are human, and people communicate in many ways other than words and pictures. We communicate with voice inflection, facial expressions, and the myriad nonverbal behaviors that are possible to read or hear only when we gather at the same time and place.

Shared space is not just a room; it includes places and tools that allow content to be shared by the participants. This includes whiteboards, posters, "sticky" walls or notes, colored markers, a laptop computer with a drawing tool and a word processing program, a printer, a laptop projector, a whiteboard recorder, digital camera, or any combination of these tools.

The following risks are associated with the use of shared space:

- A lack of available space
- Insufficient wall space

To make the best use of shared space, you should implement these keys to success:

- Schedule your workshop for an offsite location.
- Schedule your workshop several weeks in advance.

Note also the following interactions and trade-offs associated with shared space:

- Setting up shared space establishes an environment for serious play (see "Serious Play" later in this chapter) and the ability to exploit the "wise groups" ingredient (see the next section).

WISE GROUPS

A requirements workshop is based on Aristotle's premise that "the whole is more than the sum of its parts. The part is more than a fraction of the whole." By your judgment, some of the participants are smart, experienced, and knowledgeable, whereas others may have less knowledge on certain content or less experience in software projects, or they may be newer to the project. Nevertheless, this collection of people is much wiser than any one person in the room. In other words, *groups are wise*.

The group's strength lies in its diversity. Because software projects are rarely solo efforts—they require the collective efforts of numerous individuals—the work must be done by a community of people gathered for a shared purpose.

Highly regarded leaders recognize this. Consider those leaders you admire and seek to be near. They act more like facilitators than directors. They listen more than they talk. They trust more than they test. They challenge and cajole rather than threaten and scare. So, too, must you trust in this wisdom and engineer a group process that taps into the group's collective wisdom and energy.

The following risks are associated with relying on the wisdom of a group:

- Not having the right mix of knowledge and experience
- Vocal or organizationally powerful group members dominating the group
- Hidden agendas surfacing during the workshop
- *Groupthink*, the situation in which people feel compelled to conform to the group

To give yourself the best chance to exploit group wisdom, you should implement these keys to success:

- Use an experienced facilitator.
- Ensure that the group has the right mix of people.

- Before the workshop, define ground rules and criteria for decision making.
- Agree on ground rules at the start of the workshop.
- Use a variety of interaction modes (individual, small group, and whole group; parallel and reciprocal) to promote participation and creativity.

Note also the following interactions and trade-offs associated with this ingredient:

- Wise groups require the right people; group wisdom is promoted by the use of collaborative closure.
- There's a trade-off between gathering requirements in a linear manner, over a longer period of time, and gathering them in a shorter period of time during intense, highly focused workshops.
- Groups can't be truly wise without the presence of an atmosphere of honesty and willingness to confront difficult project trade-offs.

Pre-Work

A workshop is a process; it has inputs, outputs, and transformations. You always use *pre-work* for input, no matter how untested, unclear, or controversial. The inputs are draft requirements of some sort and at some level of detail, along with your agenda, tools, and templates or forms. In this way, you're starting before the workshop actually happens. After all, a workshop is an event in the project process and not an end in itself. It should therefore flow along with other project activities and weave seamlessly into the flow of deliverables.

The following risks are associated with the ingredient of pre-work:

- Inadequate time to prepare
- Inaccessibility of key players
- No materials to use as a basis

To effectively use pre-work, you should implement these keys to success:

- Develop pre-work assignments for participants.
- Acquire or develop guidelines and templates for the modeling technique you're using.
- Build draft models to use as workshop inputs, even if they're known to be erroneous or incomplete.

Note also the following interactions and trade-offs associated with pre-work:

- Starting with something requires participation by the right people and a knowledgeable planning team.
- There's a trade-off between, on the one hand, scheduling the workshop earlier and producing less and, on the other hand, delaying the workshop to allow time to prepare and then delivering more in less time.

FOCUS QUESTIONS

Each task you ask people to do in a workshop begins with a clear focus question. The questions you ask are more important than any other communication you make in a requirements workshop, and that's why *focus questions* are the answer. Requirements models emerge when participants begin to collaboratively explore the answers to the questions.

Your questions center on generating and evaluating *products* (the requirements themselves) and *process* (assessing and enhancing the group's work). You must choose the right questions to ask at the right time.

You'll sometimes ask questions about choices: "Which of these user goals are most important?" "What criteria are important in selecting the requirements for this release?" You'll need the answers to these questions in order to capture non-functional requirements and to help the group make decisions about priorities.

Sometimes you'll ask questions about process: "Is this a good way to discover the data requirements?" "Does the sequence of activities we're doing make sense?"

Questions direct the flow of the group's work. Your questions allow participants to generate, redirect, evaluate, assess, reflect, expand, filter, and elaborate content. Most importantly, you want to create an environment in which participants themselves have the freedom and honesty to ask questions of one another.

The following risks are associated with the use of focus questions:

- Having inadequate time to prepare
- Asking the wrong questions
- Not having a portion of a model to use as a basis for focus questions

- Not knowing how models connect with each other
- Leading the group to predetermined answers

To ensure effective use of focus questions, you should implement these keys to success:

- Have draft models as inputs.
- Learn about the various kinds of models that you can build in requirements workshops.
- Prepare focus questions before the workshop and plan which questions to use when.
- To help jump-start the group, provide sample answers to focus questions.

Note also the following interactions and trade-offs associated with focus questions:

- Focus questions combine well with the pre-work ingredient.
- You rely on the right people to hear and respond to the questions.

SERIOUS PLAY

All high-performing groups engage in *serious play*. This oxymoron has two meanings. First, it means playing with models as a means of innovation, invention, and collaboration (Schrage, 2000). This involves interacting with user requirements models during a workshop to shape requirements, which is the heart of the workshop activity. Serious play also means having fun in meetings as a means of enhancing the group's productivity, energy, and relationships.

The group often holds celebrations, and the participants tease and cajole one another, all the while producing results. Without a doubt, the most productive and memorable workshops include elements of fun. Humor serves to relieve tension, introduce joy, and courteously reveal difficult truths.

You can facilitate fun for a group by using playful activities and tools such as colored pens, sticky notes, and toys. Use whatever is fun and reinforces the principle that everyone contributes to finding incomplete or incorrect requirements and, most importantly, helps the group achieve its goals.

The following risks are associated with serious play:

- Too much play can be perceived as frivolous and time-wasting.

To ensure effective use of serious play, you should implement these keys to success:

- Use play tactically—for quick energizers (see Chapter 6), during breaks, or as a means to help the group create deliverables.
- Engage management in play to demonstrate that it's acceptable.
- Use an opening activity that introduces playfulness.
- To allow time for people to get comfortable, make play optional.
- Debrief each activity that uses play to see whether people enjoyed it, thereby reinforcing the use of play.

Note also the following interactions and trade-offs associated with serious play:

- It works best with shared space.
- It's useful in combination with the pre-work ingredient.
- There's a trade-off between the appearance of frivolity and the effect of making people more comfortable and creative.

TRUST

A group with *trust* acts interdependently—relying on its members' mutual strengths and putting faith in individuals' skills and knowledge, helping them feel secure that they can do their best. They're able to recover from problems quickly and without personal offense. In workshops, this can have powerful effects. Trust saves time, and that enables quicker delivery of products of higher quality. Better yet, these behaviors tend to get transferred to the project as a whole, and teams begin to jell.

The irony is that it takes time to build trust, but once it's established, it saves time. Many of us are impatient or unwilling to make the time in our workshops to build trust. This effort must commence at the outset. You begin to build trust before the workshop, and then you choose activities early in the workshop that reinforce a sense of safety and mutual trust.

The following risks are associated with trust:

- Interference from company and project politics
- Personality conflicts

To ensure that trust is indeed a substitute for time, you should implement these keys to success:

- Uncover hidden agendas before the workshop.
- Conduct a workshop orientation meeting.
- Conduct a workshop opener that allows people to become comfortable and learn about one another.
- Define ground rules to help promote participation and an open exchange of information.
- Clarify how decisions will be made.
- Use *dyads* (two-person subgroups) or *triads* (three-person subgroups) for activities early in the workshop.
- Openly acknowledge any conflict and its source.
- Allow time for trust to be built.

Note also the following interactions and trade-offs associated with trust:

- The ingredient of wise groups and the collaborative closure technique (see "Collaborative Closure" later in this chapter) combine well with this ingredient.
- There's a trade-off between taking the time to build trust and the ability of the group to produce and reach closure on deliverables more quickly.

PROCESS VARIETY

When I facilitate a workshop, I use a number of techniques to maintain energy, creativity, and motivation. For example, sometimes I form small subgroups to work in parallel on portions of a single deliverable, such as a list of business rules for a use case or perhaps a use case itself. Smaller groups provide more opportunities for participation. This is an example of how you can use *process variety* during a workshop.

The best approach is to rotate among individual, subgroup, and whole-group work. This method provides participants with a change of pace and makes the workshop more interesting. Individual time—time for solo activities such as jotting down a list of use cases, filling out a prioritization matrix, walking around the room silently reviewing work on the wall, or creating sticky notes containing data elements—allows people to have time to think and integrate the information they're working on.

Working in subgroups builds trust, enhances learning, and allows multiple content areas to be worked on concurrently. Using whole-group, or *plenary*, activities returns the group to its "wholeness," builds common purpose, allows group norms to develop, and permits closure.

The following risks are associated with process variety:

- Facilitator inexperience with parallel subgroup work
- Not mixing small-group work throughout the workshop
- Overloading the workshop with too many deliverables
- Participant confusion

To be effective using process variety, you should implement these keys to success:

- Plan each activity in detail, step-by-step.
- Keep participants involved in each step of the process.
- Introduce each workshop activity by explaining the process to be used.
- Regroup in a plenary session to review subgroup deliverables.

Note also the following interactions and trade-offs associated with process variety:

- The ingredients wise groups and collaborative closure combine well with process variety.
- Doneness tests (see the next section) work well with an iterative workshop process in which you deliver sets of requirements across a series of workshops in a short time (see "Iteratively Deliver Requirements" in Chapter 7).
- There's a trade-off between possible confusion and the quality and speed that an iterative process promotes.

DONENESS TESTS

Suppose you're baking brownies or cookies from a mix. Do you rely on the instructions on the back of the box to know when your cookies or brownies are done? If you're like me, when you bake with your children, you teach them to test for doneness by using a toothpick or similar tool. So it is with your workshop products. You must have a way to know when the products of your workshop—use cases, events, business rules, and so on—are done. You need *doneness tests*.

DONENESS TESTS ARE USEFUL.

For this reason, you establish a set of criteria before the workshop to judge whether each deliverable is complete, clear, and correct enough to be acceptable. You decide how precise each deliverable must be, and you devise questions to ask about it to test its doneness. You might, for example, use a combination of a quality assurance (QA) checklist and a decision rule for each product.

Doneness tests have the added benefit, for the project as a whole, of forcing the team to decide the acceptable threshold for model completeness before they can move on to design and coding.

The following risks are associated with doneness tests:

- Lack of knowledge about the deliverables
- An unclear decision-making process

To be effective with doneness tests, you should implement these keys to success:

- Understand each deliverable's possible level of detail and criteria for quality.
- Use QA checklists and walkthroughs in the workshop.
- Cross-check portions of a model that relate to portions of another model.
- Allow participants to test one another's deliverables for quality.

Note also the following interactions and trade-offs associated with doneness tests:

- Doneness tests work well in combination with process variety.
- There's a trade-off between having a looser process and lower-quality models and spending more time in the workshop to produce models of higher quality.

COLLABORATIVE CLOSURE

One of the greatest challenges of workshops is reaching *collaborative closure*— making decisions that are congruent with the goals of the group and that are satisfactory to the individuals who influence or implement the decisions. To reach collaborative closure, stakeholders participate in the decision-making process in a way that meets the needs of individuals and the group, includes the diverse views of all stakeholders, and enhances the group's ability to continue to work effectively together.

If you make important decisions in a noncollaborative manner, you risk making poor requirements decisions that are difficult to sustain. And without a decision rule, people are vague about when, and even whether, a decision has been made. They delay taking action on the requirements, and that wastes valuable time and money. Effective workshops, on the other hand, result in timely, high-quality decisions. The participants learn from divergent perspectives, listen to each other's interests, make reasonable choices, and come to closure. Good decision-making groups seek inclusive decisions that merge the best of all available options.

Perhaps just as important, if the decision turns out not to be the best one, these teams can recognize it and recover. They've learned how to balance the content of the decision with the process of arriving at it.

The following risks are associated with collaborative closure:

- Inability or unwillingness to identify a person in charge of making the decision rule
- Unwillingness to select a collaborative decision rule
- Group "churning" around decisions
- Not having the right people to participate in decision making
- An unclear decision-making process

To reach collaborative closure, you should implement these keys to success:

- Before the workshop, define ground rules for decision making.
- Choose a participatory decision rule.
- Regularly ask the group whether it's ready to check for agreement.
- Display deliverables that need closure in the workshop room.
- Have stakeholders return for a show-and-tell presentation so that participants can share their results.

Note also the following interactions and trade-offs associated with collaborative closure:

- Doneness tests combine well with collaborative closure.
- There's a trade-off between leaving topics open due to business uncertainties and avoiding project delays when you reach closure.

FLEXIBLE STRUCTURE

Requirements workshops change shape and structure as they proceed, but they aren't on-the-fly sessions. They require a lot of forethought and planning on the part of all of the stakeholders. This planning allows the group and facilitator to move nimbly, change direction, adjust, and yet stay the course—a process I call *flexible structure*.

You start your workshop with a planned sequence of activities. Then things change. The group members gather and act . . . like people. As a result, the flow of the session must be adjusted. The level of detail for your models gets adjusted. Some requirements get jettisoned, and others get elevated. Learning happens, prior ideas get thrown out, and new ones merge. Hidden issues emerge and require time to discuss (or time to decide whether they should be discussed). People disagree, agree to disagree, and agree they weren't really disagreeing.

You can never anticipate everything that might happen when a group with a common goal starts to collaborate. Yet the very act of planning permits change. All your workshop planning is based on the need to provide a focused environment in which collaboration can occur. Despite the myths around creativity, it's only possible in a structured yet flexible environment.

The following risks are associated with a flexible structure:

- Insufficient planning time
- Designing a workshop process before knowing what deliverables are needed
- Lack of facilitator experience with workshop design
- Inability of the facilitator to change the process on-the-fly

To work effectively with a flexible structure, you should implement these keys to success:

- Use a planning team.
- Reuse workshop agendas.
- Hold periodic *huddles*: fast, stand-up consultation meetings with the planning team during the workshop.

Note also the following interactions and trade-offs associated with flexible structure:

- The frequent debriefs ingredient (see "Frequent Debriefs" later in this chapter) is a good fit with flexible structure.

USING BOTH SIDES OF THE BRAIN

Our brains are two-sided; each side works differently and supplements the other. The right side is more adept at dealing with things that are visual and random, whereas the left side is stronger at linear and analytical tasks. This means that we can exploit the capabilities of each side of the brain by using text (for the left brain) and diagrams (for the right brain). In addition, using visual models contributes to speed, whereas using text-based documentation contributes to accuracy. You need words for that. Thus, it's important to *use both sides of the brain*.

Be aware that each participant comes with a preference for his own learning style. Thus, the workshop will be more productive when you can incorporate multiple learning styles. Use both visual and textual documentation, continually weaving the two styles into your collaborative workshops. Defining requirements involves learning and discovery. Using various kinds of visual and text models helps you tap into different styles of learning: auditory, visual, and kinesthetic (physically doing things, such as drawing a picture of a user's workflow). The models are emergent, iteratively taking form and shape from within the context of the modeling elements.

WE WORK BEST WHEN WE USE BOTH SIDES OF OUR BRAIN.

The following risks are associated with using both sides of the brain:

- Unwillingness by the facilitator or the participants to use a variety of models
- Lack of precision in, or guidelines for, diagrammatic models
- Overcrowding of diagrammatic models with too much information

To use both sides of the brain effectively, you should implement these keys to success:

- Use both text and visual ways to represent user requirements.
- Break requirements models into component parts, and build them in chunks.
- Ask participants to cross-check one another's models or portions of models.
- Use techniques, such as cards, posts, and posters, whereby participants can draw, write, and physically manipulate tools in the workshop room.
- Integrate energizers to unleash creative thinking, promote serious play, and increase trust.

Note also the following interactions and trade-offs associated with using both sides of the brain:

- Both serious play and process variety help participants use both sides of their brains.
- There's a trade-off between generating more models and a higher volume of information to track, and the higher quality of requirements that tends to result from doing both text and diagrams.

FREQUENT DEBRIEFS

"Evolution is chaos, with feedback," said physicist Joseph Ford. To learn and grow, we must reflect on our thinking and work. In the long run, the act of slowing down to reflect has the effect of permitting the group to speed up.

The ritual of *frequent debriefs*, which involve participants reviewing, playing back, and thinking retrospectively about how the group process is working (or not working), is essential to ongoing success. These debriefs can be scheduled into the workshop but are often initiated by the facilitator when she notices a conflict brewing, a task that is completed, the emergence of an important issue not previously surfaced, or some other significant group occurrence. Debriefing during requirements workshops allows the group to become more self-sufficient and productive more quickly.

Asking a group to reflect on its work and its interactions helps it to evolve more quickly through the natural progression of group formation. It also promotes internal and public commitment to both the products of the workshop and the processes used to arrive at them.

The following risks are associated with frequent debriefs:

- Negative feedback that troubles the group or facilitator
- Inability to use feedback to adjust the workshop process quickly
- Inexperience of the facilitator in conducting these kinds of debriefs

To use frequent debriefs effectively, you should implement these keys to success:

- Add quick process debriefs to the agenda.
- Hold periodic huddles with the planning team during the workshop.

- Reward workshop participants for their work by providing reinforcing positive feedback, having sponsors openly acknowledge the value of debriefing, and openly sharing the debriefing results with the rest of the organization.
- Conduct a final workshop debrief.
- Report on workshop results afterward.
- Share results with the rest of the organization.
- Survey stakeholders after the workshop (four to eight weeks later) for more feedback; devise improvement plans.

Note also the following interactions and trade-offs associated with frequent debriefs:

- A flexible structure works well with frequent debriefs.
- Frequent debriefing contributes to a project environment in which continual learning is valued.

Part Two demonstrates how these ingredients are integrated in your requirements workshop planning, design, and processes.

PART TWO

REQUIREMENTS WORKSHOP FRAMEWORK

C hapters 4 through 9 present a framework for planning and delivering requirements workshops. Each chapter represents an element of a workshop design framework that I call the *six P's*: purpose, participants, principles, products, place, and process.

Underlying this framework is a process that includes four high-level phases (plan, do, check, act), each with the stages shown in Figure II-1.

 A complete work breakdown structure, which includes detailed tasks for each stage of the process, is available on the book's Web site.

As you read the chapters that follow, this figure will reappear to guide your reading by highlighting the stage that's being explained.

 As you read more about the ingredients for a successful workshop, first described in Chapter 3, you'll see an icon similar to the one at the left.

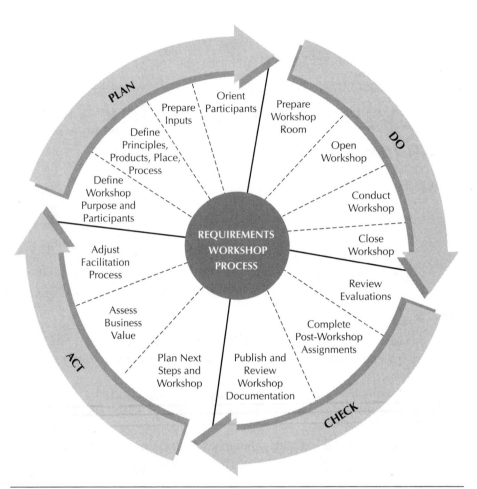

FIGURE II-1 THE REQUIREMENTS WORKSHOP PROCESS

4

PURPOSE: SHARING A COMMON GOAL

"It is not enough to just do your best or work hard. You must know what to work on."

—W. Edwards Deming

A workshop's *purpose* defines why it is being held. Having an agreed-upon workshop purpose is essential for you to begin designing your workshop. A concise statement of purpose is the starting point for defining the other elements: who, how, what, where, and when. You might think that the purpose of your workshop is obvious, but often it isn't. By asking questions of stakeholders, you often discover that the initial workshop purpose needs to be rethought.

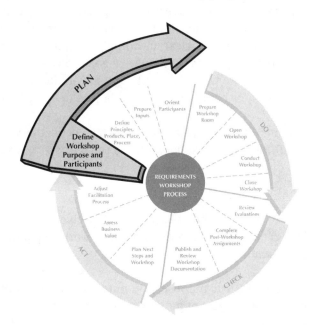

A *purpose statement* serves the facilitator in planning the session. As part of planning your workshop, you ask questions of the stakeholders and draft this statement; it, along with your other six P's (participants, principles, products, place, and process), is documented in an agenda and shared with participants before the workshop. (An agenda template is available on the Web site for the book. For more information on agenda design, see Chapter 9.) Knowing the workshop's purpose is also crucial for the participants: Shared purpose (see "A Shared Purpose" in Chapter 3) is essential for participants to become an effective working group.

Web
Site

Writing Your Workshop Purpose Statement

The basic format for a workshop purpose statement is that it have one to four sentences that state the reasons and justification for conducting a requirements workshop. Because it explains why you're conducting a workshop, it serves as a frame of reference for all your workshop planning.

Here's an example of a purpose statement for a scope-level requirements workshop: "Define the scope of XYZ project." This kind of purpose statement may be sufficient. Sometimes I suggest adding a list of questions to the purpose statement: "Who is involved? What will the system provide? What is provided to the system?"

Your purpose statement doesn't presuppose any particular requirements models as workshop deliverables. Rather, it clarifies to the participants and stakeholders why you're meeting. A clear, meaningful purpose statement sets a positive tone for the workshop. If you've done a good job of planning, the purpose won't change during the workshop, although the products may change—in format, degree of detail, or both—as the group begins to do its work.

You should display a copy of the statement in the workshop room on a wall poster. During the workshop, refer to the purpose as you facilitate each activity.

Don't Assume Anything

Beware of thinking that what you're first given as the reason for the workshop is the right reason. I have yet to define a workshop purpose that matched what I was first told.

To arrive at the true purpose, you must ask questions of multiple project stakeholders, with the goal of gaining an understanding of the real needs. This ques-

Shared Purpose

I have had the pleasure and honor of working on a really great team. We worked hard, had lots of fun, got the job done, and pleased our customers. Some people call this a "jelled" team. On our team, we were like a family. We had our problems, but we were respectful, passionate, forthright, sometimes argumentative, always trusting.

Perhaps you've shared this experience. If you have, you'll never forget it. You're probably smiling, inside or out, just remembering it.

One of the most important factors contributing to great teams is that everyone shares the same purpose. So it is with your workshop. If you've ever been on a team or attended a meeting in which your understanding of why you were doing this work, or having this meeting, didn't match another person's understanding, you know what I mean. Energy gets redirected from work to purpose-seeking. Conversation shifts from content to context. You spend time clarifying and debating purpose.

To have an effective requirements workshop, you must make your purpose crystal-clear to all the workshop players *before* everyone walks into the room.

tioning inevitably surfaces issues and problems that directly affect the workshop's purpose.

As the facilitator, you must become a diagnostician. You must diagnose the status of the project, the current state of the requirements, and the relationships among the players; you need to ask questions about the project's history, documentation, and models. (Later in this chapter you'll find sample questions to ask.)

When I asked one project manager what he viewed as the purpose of the workshop he was requesting, he replied, "To create a context diagram, stakeholders, use cases, business rules, an actor table, and an actor map." In other words, he answered the question in terms of products. I responded by asking many "why" questions. In the end, we agreed on this purpose statement: "To validate the scope and define high-level user requirements for the ABC project." The products actually turned out to be data requirements and business rules. A correct purpose statement allows you the freedom to tailor the products to the business problem and focus the workshop more tightly.

To focus on the purpose, ask, "What would the universe be like in order for this workshop to be unnecessary?" and work your way back to the purpose from the answer. You can also use the *ask why five times* technique to get at the root purpose. You ask "Why?" to each answer to the question "What is the purpose of the workshop?" and get successively closer to the core reason that the workshop is needed.

SEEK THE STORIES

To define a workshop purpose, you need to seek out stories from key project players.

One project team's business analyst asked me to facilitate a workshop to review, and then sign off on, the team's use cases. I began asking questions of him and the other key players—the software project manager, the business project owner, the subject matter experts supporting the users, the programmers, and the data analyst (see "Questions to Ask Stakeholders" at the end of this chapter). Each player had a different story to tell:

- The software project manager was worried that the customers might keep changing their minds (that's a new one, eh?).
- The business project manager was far from ready to sign off on the use cases.
- The subject matter experts thought that the requirements were hard to understand.
- The programmers had no idea how to begin—or even whether they *could* begin—coding from the use cases they currently had.
- The data analyst was concerned about the many gaps in his data model.

Each story was real and valid for the person telling it. Each story was like a thread in a tapestry that gave me a perspective of what was happening and what a facilitated requirements workshop might do for this group.

LINK WORKSHOP PURPOSE WITH PROJECT VISION

Remember that a workshop delivers work products needed by the project. Because the workshop's context is the project, the workshop's purpose must be linked to the project's vision or purpose.

The statement of the project's vision usually references the current business situation, the desired situation, the obstacles to achieving the desired situation, and the necessary changes—in other words, the business reasons for undertaking the project. Similarly, the workshop's purpose describes the business reasons for

STORIES WEAVE A TAPESTRY.

gathering the players together. The link between these two statements must be evident to all stakeholders. The examples in Table 4-1 illustrate these principles.

The workshop purpose should drive the workshop approach and the models to be used. In the first example in Table 4-1, identifying the workshop's purpose led the Acme100 participants to define the chief work product as use cases, which elegantly describe the user interactions. But use cases aren't always the best requirements model, so if we had mentioned use cases in the purpose statement, we might have wasted planning time—and potential workshop time—creating models that didn't fit the problem.

In the second example, the purpose statement led to a determination that a process map or UML activity diagram would do the trick, and that we could reuse the model as the basis for identifying changes needed for the Web page design. In addition, we decided that an as-is business process diagram of the current

TABLE 4-1 SAMPLE PROJECT VISION AND WORKSHOP PURPOSE STATEMENTS

Project Vision (Abbreviated)	Workshop Purpose
The Acme100 project will provide statistical analysis capabilities for a site's manufacturing data warehouse. It will also provide seamless access to important manufacturing data, robust and easy-to-use analysis and reporting tools for process improvements, cost reductions over manual information gathering, and, eventually, improved manufacturing yield.	Describe how users will interact with the current statistics software package when doing "what-if" analysis. Explore ways to capture these requirements and determine roles and next steps for continuation of the Acme100 project.
The GrateThing project will create a set of consumer information and marketing collateral for the launch of the GrateThing product on June 7.	Define user requirements for inbound call processing that will support product launch. Identify modifications needed to reuse the call flow requirements for the high-level Web page design.

product's customer support help desk, along with a list of the customers' problems and opportunities, would be the chief deliverable.

DEFINING PROJECT SCOPE

Every project must define its *scope*: what's "in" and what's "out." Scope breathes life into a project's business goals by broadly defining the who, what, when, why, where, and how associated with project goals and objectives. Scope determines the context for the user requirements effort.

If you think your project needs to define high-level or detailed user requirements in a workshop, check—and then double-check—with stakeholders about how clear the scope really is.

The expression *scope creep* (also known as *feature creep, creeping user requirements,* or *requirements creep*) has become part of the vernacular of software development. It means that new or expanded requirements have "crept" into the project after everyone thought the requirements had been defined.

Scope creep can be devastating to projects; it's one of the most vexing problems in software development and a chief cause of failed, late, and over-budget projects. Most projects are at risk of scope creep, so assume that your project will also suffer (or could suffer) from it.

BEWARE THE SCOPE CREEP MONSTER.

Workshops can help prevent scope creep. While you're gathering information from stakeholders, listen carefully for potential differences among the players in their understanding of the scope. If there are conflicting messages about what's in and out of scope, you may recommend that a team conduct a scope workshop rather than a detailed requirements workshop. Be clear with workshop stakeholders that without clear scope, a more detailed workshop cannot be successful.

One project team wanted to define detailed requirements for a package installation (see the SalesTrak case study in Chapter 11). The business sponsors were eager to get going. The software manager was concerned about which business requirements would be needed: The package had many functions, and he guessed the customer didn't need them all. Rather than jump into selecting from the list of product capabilities, I suggested that the workshop purpose be to define the scope of the requirements. Subsequently, in one workshop day, the participants defined a tightly focused scope. The business sponsors then decided to have users participate in a detailed requirements workshop to select specifics. You can imagine how much time would have been wasted hashing through details that weren't needed to support the business goals.

Scope workshops can't eliminate the risk of changing user requirements, a risk that is often present in businesses that are in a constant state of flux. However, a scope workshop tends to have a stabilizing effect on the degree of fluctuation. It also provides a forum for all the stakeholders to collaboratively define an understanding of the software product that should be built.

Note that even if you detect scope problems, you don't necessarily have to conduct a scope workshop. Instead, you might tell the team that a well-defined agreement on scope is a prerequisite for a high-level or detailed requirements workshop. You can have participants draft the scope in the form of models and text before the workshop and begin with that as a straw model. This is an area where pre-work can help you accelerate the workshop and prepare participants to dive into the details of requirements. (For more on this technique, see Chapter 7.)

IDENTIFYING THE WORKSHOP SPONSOR

Every workshop needs a *workshop sponsor* who has the authority and legitimacy to make the workshop happen. The sponsor's responsibilities include the following:

- Validating the workshop's purpose
- Ensuring that the right participants are present
- Engaging the facilitator and the recorder
- Kicking off the workshop and then returning for the show-and-tell (more on these in Chapter 9)
- Optionally, making workshop decisions

A workshop sponsor can be a software or business project manager, the project or program sponsor, or an analyst. The facilitator should *not* be the sponsor, though, because of conflicts of interest discussed in Chapter 5. In any case, be sure to clearly identify the workshop sponsor. You'll want your workshop sponsor to show up, even if she isn't an active participant, to demonstrate sponsorship to the participants and to legitimize the workshop's purpose.

DEFINING THE WORKSHOP PLANNING TEAM

You should define a small group of two or three stakeholders who will act as your *planning team*. The responsibilities of the team are to help you plan the workshop, identify whom you should talk to, handle workshop logistics, review any pre-workshop templates, and draft an agenda. They help you define and validate the six P's. The team's first tasks are to help you decide whom to interview in order to uncover the workshop purpose and to review a draft of the workshop purpose statement.

The planning team should include at least one business person and one software person so that you can get a balanced view of the needs and concerns of people in both areas. For example, for the Acme100 workshop, the team consisted of the software project manager, the business subject matter expert (SME), and an analyst. When you begin to delineate the specific workshop products, these varying views enable you to make suggestions about the requirements models to deliver in the workshop. Your planning team is also helpful during the session, giving you feedback and suggestions for changes during the workshop. The members of the team act as advisers to the facilitator.

For one high-level requirements workshop, the team lined up the right business attendees, provided me with project documentation, answered my questions about the project, and drafted scope documentation in both text and visual form

THE PLANNING TEAM HUDDLES WITH THE FACILITATOR.

using a context diagram and a list of functions in and out of scope. The team also acted as my focal point of contact for all interviews with project and workshop stakeholders, reviewed drafts of the agenda, and verified the decision rule (how decisions would be made in the workshop; see Chapter 6).

The planning team was immensely helpful to me during the session. I warned the members that I might need to huddle with them during breaks. Because one of the products was a conceptual data model, I also suggested that during the session, the enterprise data architect be added to our planning team. Several times during the two-day session, I huddled with the team to discuss how to reorder and streamline activities.

Sample Purpose Statements

The following subsections offer example purpose statements for various kinds of requirements workshops. (See Chapter 10 for detailed explanations of these strategies.) Note that the differences in these examples are in the level of detail. The examples include supplemental text that you might find useful.

Purpose for Horizontal Top-Down Requirements Workshop

Main text: Ensure that the stakeholders of the <name> project have a common understanding of the system to be analyzed and built. This common understanding defines the scope of the system—what's included and what's not included in the project.

Supplemental text: Clear scope can reduce project risk, enhance communications, and establish clear customer and user expectations. It also helps the workshop sponsor know whom to involve and how to efficiently expend resources for project analysis.

Questions to be answered (at a very high level):

- Who has a stake in the project?
- What's going to happen in the system?
- When will it happen, and what will result?
- What policies do we care about?
- What information will be provided by the system?

HORIZONTAL MIDDLE-OUT REQUIREMENTS WORKSHOP

Main text: Identify the major functions for the <name> project, and specify how users will interact with the system.

Supplemental text: High-level requirements provide a starting point for defining details.

Questions to be answered:

- Who will interact with the system?
- What are their goals in interacting with the system?
- What business rules must be enforced in the system?
- What information will they use to fulfill their goals?
- When, and how often, do they need to do things?

HORIZONTAL BOTTOM-UP REQUIREMENTS WORKSHOP

Main text: Specify details for how the <name> functions will work, and obtain closure on these details.

Supplemental text: We need detailed requirements to test our understanding of the system and also for the design, building, and testing of the software.

Questions to be answered (at a high level):

- What will the users' interactions with the system look like?
- What steps do they undertake to do that?
- What could go wrong?
- What data will be used?
- What triggers changes in the data?
- What business rules will be enforced in the system?

VERTICAL STRATEGY REQUIREMENTS WORKSHOP

Main text: Define the scope and specific details for a slice of important user functionality for the <name> project.

Supplemental text: Defining the scope of a subset of functions, and then defining associated details for those functions, will allow the project team to begin to build and test a small set of software. This will enable us to reduce risks earlier and clarify the actual requirements for the software more quickly.

Questions to be answered:

- Who are the highest-priority players who interact with the system?
- What do they provide to and receive from the system?
- What steps do they undertake to do that?
- What business rules are enforced in the system?
- What information will be used?
- What pieces of information are needed?
- What must be true about the information?

ZIGZAG STRATEGY REQUIREMENTS WORKSHOP

Main text: Define a small and comprehensive set of user requirements for the <name> project.

Supplemental text: Define a discrete set of user requirements that will allow developers to create a functional prototype for user and customer review. The requirements will provide a mix of depth and breath, giving us enough information to produce a mutual understanding of the requirements and let us build useful functionality and test the prototypes.

Questions to be answered:

- What user goals must be delivered in the first release?
- What business rules are enforced in the system?
- What will the flow of the screens look like?
- What are some sample uses of the system?
- What pieces of information does the system need to provide?

TIPS

- Don't assume that the first purpose you hear is the correct one.
- If the purpose of the workshop isn't to define scope-level requirements, make sure that the scope has been nailed down.

- Make sure that your workshop purpose is linked to your project purpose.
- Establish a workshop planning team to help you define your six P's.
- Be sure that your planning team has a mix of points of view.
- Seek multiple perspectives when defining workshop purpose.
- Keep your purpose statement brief and to the point.
- Omit specific workshop products from your purpose statement.
- Be sensitive to the people issues that might arise when you start asking questions about the project.

QUESTIONS TO ASK STAKEHOLDERS

The questions listed in the following subsections can help you determine your workshop's purpose. (If there isn't yet a specific project, substitute the word *problem* for *project*.) Select a subset of questions to ask each interviewee, and be sure to ask the same questions of multiple interviewees. You can begin your interview by saying something like this: "I'm here to gather information to plan a workshop for the <name> project. I got involved <explain>. I'm interviewing you to identify how to best plan for and design a facilitated workshop for this project. The primary outcome of our conversation will be a clearer definition of what the workshop purpose should be. It'll also help us determine who should attend, and what specific products we should create in the workshop."

As you read the following questions, keep in mind that you may believe you already know the answers to them (such as whether a vision or charter document exists). Your purpose in asking many of these questions is to verify your understanding, uncover conflicting answers from interviews or find out whether interviewees know the answers, and to learn what they think about various aspects of the current situation.

QUESTIONS RELATED TO PROJECT PURPOSE

- What is the purpose of the project that this workshop is intended to help?
- Does the project have clearly defined goals?
- Is the scope of the project clearly defined?
- Has the project been formally chartered?
- Who is the sponsor of the project?
- Who's sponsoring the workshop?
- Does a project charter or vision document exist? If it does, does it clarify business goals and project scope?

- Has a project structure (team roles, business user roles, steering committee, and so forth) been established?
- Does a formal business case (cost, benefits, barriers, risks) exist?
- To what extent did the business customer participate in building this business case?
- Has the business case been communicated to the organization? If so, how and to whom?
- Are there related projects? Does this project span multiple lines of business or departments?
- Is there a project plan? If so, how does this workshop fit into that plan?

QUESTIONS RELATED TO WORKSHOP PURPOSE

- What is the purpose of the workshop?
- How will that purpose help us achieve the project vision?
- What is the problem, issue, or need that you have that you believe a facilitated workshop will help you to solve?
- What's at stake in this workshop?
- What are your hopes and wishes for the workshop?
- How could the workshop impact other projects? How could other project work impact the workshop?
- In what ways might the team or organization help or hinder this workshop?
- What do you expect from the workshop?
- What specifically would need to happen in order for you to call the workshop a success? What would make the workshop a failure?
- Are there any problems that you foresee in pursuing this purpose?
- Do you have a time limit for the length of the workshop? Why? Why not?

Further Readings

FOR MORE INFORMATION

Avery (2001) offers practical wisdom for teamwork based on "team wisdom," highly productive and responsible work relationships. The author's useful tips and techniques include focusing conversation on the collective task and the shared focus (purpose) of the group's work in order to align individual interests with the task.

DeMarco and Lister (1999) is a witty and straightforward discussion about what successful software projects are all about. This is a must-read for software development leaders and managers. The authors' description of a jelled team emphasizes goal alignment (in other words, shared purpose) and getting the right people. They discuss how jelled teams experience joint ownership of the product, develop team chemistry, and have fun.

Johnson (1996) is a concise summary of the Standish Group's findings that successful projects depend on clear requirements and shared project vision.

Katzenbach and Smith (2001), the sequel to the authors' book *The Wisdom of Teams*, highlights the use of small teams with complementary skills, clear purpose, outcome-based goals, time-efficient processes, clear roles and responsibilities, and both mutual and individual accountability.

Pedler et al. (1991) provides practical tools for designing and creating an organization capable of adapting, learning, and developing. The book also offers exercises for helping a group to arrive at a collective purpose.

Senge et al. (1994) is a pragmatic guide full of examples of how to apply "systems thinking," popularized by Senge's previous book, *The Fifth Discipline*. Among the disciplines is shared vision, which builds a sense of commitment in a group.

Wiegers (1996) provides practical techniques for healthy software teams to use. Chapter 1 addresses one of a team's greatest challenges: sharing the vision of the final product with its customers.

5

PARTICIPANTS: ROLES PEOPLE PLAY

"Listen to see the world others see, not because it is right but because it is theirs."

—Unknown

Participants are the people who play roles in the workshop, from workshop planning to post-workshop follow-up. As you begin to develop the workshop's purpose, you and your planning team will have a better idea who can help to achieve it.

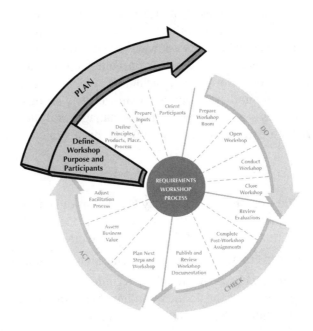

The main people who will participate are those who have the content expertise to define the requirements. Other people, such as sponsors, designers, developers, and stakeholders from related projects, can advise the planning team. These adjunct players can provide you with project and product background information that can help steer you toward particular requirements models and additional participants.

Workshop sponsors and project sponsors have stakes in the process and the outcomes of the workshop, and they should be physically available to the participants at the workshop. Technical staff who transform the workshop deliverables into other products—for example, code, test cases and scripts, user documentation and training, or design models—are also stakeholders who should participate in or observe the workshop, or at least be available to answer questions during planning.

WORKSHOP ROLES

Table 5-1 shows the various roles associated with a facilitated workshop as well as the names of generic job roles; people who play these roles may fill particular workshop participant roles.

Note that some of these generic roles appear in several places. A project manager, for example, might be both a workshop sponsor and a content participant or observer, depending on his knowledge about the business domain. Who will play which workshop roles depends on your project and your organization. For example, in one workshop I facilitated, the project manager was the recorder, whereas in another, the project manager was an observer. In another company, the business-savvy software project manager and the business's project manager were both participants because of their deep subject matter expertise.

Some roles are involved only during parts of the workshop process, or not at all.

- The workshop sponsor may be present only at the beginning and end of the session; she might also stop by to observe the session. (See my caveat on this in "Having Sponsors in the Workshop" later in this chapter.)
- Observers, with the group's permission, might come and go.
- You may choose not to fill the recorder role during the session, opting instead to have someone do the recording afterward. In that case, you need low-tech recording tools, such as sticky notes or sticky walls (adhesive applied to pa-

TABLE 5-1 WORKSHOP ROLES

Role	Responsibilities	Sample Roles
Workshop sponsor	Authorizes and legitimizes workshop	Project manager, requirements analyst, business analyst, business manager, product manager
Project sponsor	Authorizes and legitimizes project	Product manager, business manager, project manager, vice president, marketing manager
Facilitator	Plans and designs workshop; recommends appropriate requirements deliverables; leads process	Requirements analyst, business analyst, human resource consultant, project leader, data or rule analyst, developer, external facilitator
Content participant	Creates workshop products	Business user, product development specialist, business analyst, business technical specialist, data or rule analyst, business-knowledgeable developer or tester
Recorder (scribe, documenter, or technographer)	Records the group's work	Requirements analyst, administrative assistant, test analyst
Observer	Listens and learns	Project sponsor, workshop sponsor, any new software or business team member
On-call subject matter expert	Is available to answer or clarify spontaneous questions	Business analyst or user, business project manager

per or cards; see "Creating Sticky Walls" in Chapter 8). You'll also need a camera to photograph the workshop room walls, an infrared whiteboard, or a poster device that allows real-time capture of handwritten content.

Identifying the individuals who will fill each workshop role is a crucial early step. Actually, you're doing this as you're simultaneously defining the workshop purpose (see Chapter 4), principles (see Chapter 6), and products (see Chapter 7). Asking the right questions of different stakeholders gives you clues about who should be consulted during planning and who should be present during the actual session. (For good questions to ask, see "Questions to Ask Stakeholders About Participant Roles" at the end of this chapter.) Interviewing participants also helps to prepare them for the event.

The following sections describe these workshop participants.

THE WORKSHOP SPONSOR

The *workshop sponsor* champions the use of collaborative workshops, validates the workshop's purpose, ensures that the right people attend, engages the facilitator and recorder from inside or outside the organization, and provides guidance to the planning team on how it should make group decisions. In other words, the workshop sponsor legitimizes the requirements workshop.

A business manager or software manager often plays the role of the workshop sponsor, even if he did not initiate or champion the idea of conducting a requirements workshop. On one project, the business analyst contacted me to facilitate a workshop. The analyst was a vocal advocate of using requirements workshops and a key member of the planning team. However, she didn't have the authority to pay for the facilitator or for food, nor did she have the organizational influence to summon the right subject matter experts (SMEs) to the session. In that case, the software project manager acted as the workshop sponsor.

Occasionally, an involved project sponsor (see the next section) or product manager will also be the workshop sponsor. On another of my projects, the project manager both initiated the idea to use a requirements workshop and sponsored the workshop because she had the financial authority and organizational influence to make the workshop happen.

THE PROJECT SPONSOR

Whereas the workshop sponsor has the authority and legitimacy to make the workshop happen, the *project sponsor* has those same responsibilities for the overall project. You—and the entire project team—should know, without question, who this person is. In some organizations, the project sponsor and the workshop sponsor are one and the same; in others, the workshop sponsor may be far removed organizationally from the project sponsor.

You may need your project sponsor to line up the right participants by spreading the word to colleagues that they should let their people go to a workshop. Using the project sponsor's special influence and organizational clout is sometimes the only way that certain key participants will attend. This is why I recommend that you interview the project sponsor during your workshop planning.

The sponsor's unique, high-level perspective may help you to understand the context of the project and may also shape both the workshop design and workshop decision making.

In one of my workshops, the planning team was pleasantly surprised to learn that the project sponsor was delegating decision making about detailed requirements to the workshop participants. In another, the project sponsor decided to be a full participant in order to be the final decision maker about requirements scope (see "Decision Rules" in Chapter 6).

Who Sponsors Your Project?

Be practical about which person you deem project sponsor for the purposes of planning your requirements workshop. This can get complicated, especially in large organizations. There can be different types of project sponsors.

Executive sponsors are far removed from day-to-day project work, but they control the money. *Steering committees* act as advisers for projects with cross-functional impact. *Business project managers* work with the project on a daily basis; they may report to the executive sponsor or steering committee. *Product managers* or *marketing managers* are closely involved in the project, especially for commercial software projects.

You need the sponsors to ensure that appropriate people participate in the workshop. To identify the best level of sponsors, follow this guideline: *Go as high as necessary but as low as possible.*

In one company I worked with, the executive project sponsor had no contact with the project team except for status reports from the business project manager and occasional meetings with him. Because this manager was involved in the project almost daily and was responsible for managing the project's budget, we worked with him rather than the executive sponsor to ensure that the right participants were identified and lined up for the workshop.

Your project sponsor often must make decisions about scope and thus should be present in a scope-level requirements workshop. In some organizations, though, the project sponsor is far removed from the day-today project and won't attend the workshop. This is especially true for workshops delivering detailed requirements. In those cases, I recommend that the project sponsor kick off the workshop and then return for a show-and-tell activity (discussed later in this chapter). Simply showing up demonstrates sponsorship to participants and legitimizes the workshop purpose.

There are exceptions to this guideline. For example, on one project, Alice was the project sponsor. She was intimately involved in the project as a subject matter expert, and she was in the process of transferring her content knowledge to the business analysts who worked for her. For that workshop, it made sense for Alice to be both a content participant and the project sponsor.

HAVING SPONSORS IN THE WORKSHOP

If a workshop sponsor or project sponsor is not a participant, I invite him to stop by at any point and observe the workshop—but only under two circumstances. First, I ask permission of the participants to do so. If they believe the sponsor might be disruptive or that his presence might curtail their own ability to speak and act frankly, I will not invite the sponsor to appear. The second condition is that the sponsor not interrupt whatever workshop activity is going on—in other words, that he remain an observer.

During one workshop, the participants were deep into their work, creating requirements models on three walls. A sponsor peeked in the room and walked in, and then she stood in a corner watching in amazement. It was some five minutes before the participants noticed her. They glanced at her and went back to work. The next morning, one participant told me with pride that she had bumped into the sponsor near the elevator, at which time the latter commented on how impressed she was with the group's progress and intensity.

SPONSOR KICK-AND-CLOSE

The workshop sponsor or the project sponsor should kick off the workshop and return toward the end for a show-and-tell to close the workshop.

During the *kickoff*, the sponsor sets the stage for the group, taking no more than 10 minutes. A good kickoff speaker is also a bit of a cheerleader. If the group is unfamiliar with using process roles (such as the facilitator and recorder), the sponsor should also review these roles.

Here are some topics you might prepare the sponsor to convey:

- Why we're here (in other words, the workshop's purpose)
- What we need to deliver
- An appropriate sense of urgency

- Hopes for the group to work collaboratively, build synergy, speak frankly, and follow the decision rule process (see "Decision Rules" in Chapter 6)
- How the sponsor will support the group and its deliverables

The *show-and-tell* is a presentation (lasting one hour or less) by the workshop participants on their deliverables: models, actions, issues, and decisions. The presence of a sponsor at this event reinforces her support of the group's work. Better yet, sponsors inevitably gain a deeper understanding of the project and can also learn about potential obstacles to project success.

Many times, I've heard participants explain to sponsors that conflicting management priorities, lack of closure on business issues related to their requirements, or even the way user groups are organized are potential barriers to successful delivery of the requirements.

The show-and-tell has several benefits for participants.

- Knowing that the sponsor will show up at the end of the workshop provides additional incentive to do the work and do it well.
- Preparing for show-and-tell allows participants to review, summarize, and evaluate their own work. It serves as a mini-retrospective about content that begins the important closure process for the group.
- Delivering the show-and-tell imparts a sense of personal and group accomplishment. This sense of accomplishment, along with the mutual support of the group, promotes frank and open information sharing with sponsors—many of whom are usually inaccessible.

All these are powerful reasons to make the show-and-tell a regular part of your workshop agenda.

CONTENT PARTICIPANTS

Content participants, whom I'll call simply *participants* from this point forward, arc the stars of requirements workshops. They provide background information to the planning team, create the content, stay fully engaged throughout the workshop, and take on follow-up actions after the workshop.

These participants are primarily direct users and subject matter experts. The latter have information and knowledge about the business domain and understand the tasks that direct users perform using the software, all in the service of business goals. This means that you should consider including *indirect users* (or *secondary users*) who will come in contact with the system's outputs, such as files and reports, or system by-products such as decisions. Also consider involving *content advisers* (or *tertiary users*), such as legal and regulatory experts who have relevant information about the requirements. If you can't get direct users to attend and you use surrogates instead (see the next section), you risk slowing the requirements process and obtaining flawed requirements.

Participants don't just "show up" for a requirements workshop. They must be actively engaged in the process from conception through workshop follow-up.

Specifically, they must do the following:

- Understand the project's purpose or at least the requirements problem they are gathered to solve
- Understand the workshop's purpose within the context of the project
- Provide background information to the facilitator before the workshop
- Review the agenda and ask questions about it as appropriate
- Complete any pre-work assignments
- Attend any scheduled workshop orientation or briefing meeting
- Be fully engaged during the workshop
- Abide by agreed-on workshop guidelines for participation (see Chapter 6)
- Provide suggestions for improving the workshop process
- Follow up on post-workshop actions and tasks

Business management might be reluctant to free up key people for user requirements workshops, in the belief that they're vital to the day-to-day operation of the business. Ironically, this is a sure way to identify key participants. These people are experts, often managing the work of junior people, carrying a heavy workload, handling complex day-to-day issues, or bearing some combination of these responsibilities. It is precisely their knowledge and experience that you need in the workshop.

Be wary of allowing participants to appear occasionally or only at certain times. Providing a brief presentation to the group is one thing, but content experts should participate in the entire process. For one thing, you can't accurately predict when a topic will be covered; workshops are structured but flexible.

PARTICIPANTS WIZARDS KNOW THEIR STUFF!

More importantly, integrating a new participant is not just a matter of saying, "Hi, this is what we're doing now" and expecting the newcomer to catch up. The group creates multiple models, each of which provides a different view of the requirements. Each workshop activity builds on the preceding one, a process that increases the participants' knowledge and skills. In addition, occasional participants also miss out on the "forming" that naturally happens in every group session (see Chapter 6). Adding a new person means restarting that cycle, and that slows down the group.

Having key people participate in a well-planned, results-driven workshop saves time in the long run. The alternatives—elicitation techniques such as one-on-one interviews, surveys, review meetings, e-mails, conference calls, and collaborative software tools—are the next best choices. Gathering the right people together at once compresses the feedback and correction loops that you need when you use these alternative approaches. It also increases the quality and reliability of the requirements because workshops integrate the collective needs of users. This is an important consideration for geographically distributed teams.

Workshops for Distributed Teams

A typical objection to using workshops to elicit requirements is that distributed software and user groups must travel, and that raises the cost of the project. Vendors of collaborative software tools pitch travel savings as a legitimate reason for using their products, and they have a point. These tools have their place *once the team knows how to collaborate*. That can be accomplished only with face-to-face work, and a requirements workshop provides the structure, and the flexibility, to help the team learn to collaborate.

When should you invest in a real-time workshop for a distributed team? Consider these situations:

- The stakes are high for the project.
- The organization has a history of inefficient requirements gathering.
- There is a history of poor-quality requirements.
- Relationships among team players are less than stellar.
- The team needs to work over a series of releases.

A project ultimately saves time and money when more complete and correct requirements are delivered. After an initial requirements workshop, the group can decide to integrate distributive technologies such as conference calls, videoconferencing, e-mail, or one of the myriad collaborative software products on the market (for online resources, see the Web site for this book).

SURROGATE USERS

A *surrogate user* (or simply *surrogate*) is a stand-in, someone taking the place of an actual user. The surrogate may be someone who has previously performed the role of the user or whose job includes understanding user requirements through site visits, market analysis, or user or customer data provided by marketing or support departments (such as help desks or production support groups). For commercial software, the product manager or marketing representative often plays this role. For business software developed in-house, surrogates might be assigned without regard to their actual expertise.

When you use surrogates for high-priority stakeholders, it's a good idea to budget extra time and resources to accommodate rework, delays, or errors in requirements. You can handle this in numerous ways.

- A risk plan forces you to explicitly surface and address risks associated with having surrogates rather than direct users as participants.

SURROGATE USERS SUBSTITUTE FOR ACTUAL USERS TO HELP DEFINE
REQUIREMENTS.

- Assign pre-work that requires surrogates to interact with and gather information from direct users.
- Integrate direct users into post-workshop requirements reviews. This technique gives them a chance to correct gaps in content while simultaneously encouraging them to stay connected with the project.

On one project, the manager of insurance claims told me that there was no way that her most experienced claim analysts could fully participate in requirements workshops because they were critical to day-to-day operations. We addressed this well before designing the workshops, during a project charter workshop involving the project management team. The members agreed that requirements workshops would be our primary requirement elicitation technique.

I set aside an hour to address workshop risks. The participants listed, and then ranked, project risks according to probability and impact. Unavailability of the claims analysts was top on their list. Next, I asked them to work in subgroups to arrive at risk mitigation strategies to handle this risk. Several useful ideas came out, including scheduling shorter workshop days centered in the middle of week, off-loading cases to other analysts (thereby stretching their skills and giving them new opportunities), and adjusting month-end plans to account for slightly lower throughput. In the end, facing the issue head-on proved useful to everyone.

In another project I was involved with, people at the corporate home office acted as surrogates for their globally distributed direct users. Before our workshop, they devised a communication plan for keeping the direct users informed about the requirements. The surrogates posted all the workshop deliverables on a project Web site, held walkthroughs of the deliverables and then prototypes, and provided "screen cams" that simulated scenarios defined in the workshop.

Workshop Risk Plan

Your workshop planning team should develop a risk mitigation plan that identifies problems you're likely to encounter in delivering a successful requirements workshop. You should disclose workshop risks to your workshop sponsor. Typical problems include the following:

- Having surrogates instead of direct users
- Not having sponsors kick off or close the workshop
- Having participants who are on call for problems outside the workshop
- Not having access to participants during planning
- Needing extensive pre-work to be completed by participants

If the risks include the use of surrogates, the risk mitigation plan should state clearly who will serve as surrogates, how they will work with direct users to get information they might not know otherwise, how direct users can be involved in the requirements process, and alternatives to using surrogates.

Seeing this information, sponsors sometimes choose to support at least limited involvement by actual users, such as having them attend prototype reviews or requirements document reviews or employing multiple workshops of shorter duration. Your sponsor may need to be involved in implementing your risk mitigation plan.

ENSURING ATTENDANCE

When sponsors are reluctant to allow users or SMEs to attend workshops, you can make a financial case for the savings gained by getting the right people together at the same time to define your requirements quickly. "Making the Case to Management" in Chapter 12 describes ways you can gather data from workshops and feed it back to help sell the approach. Once the sponsors understand the business value of requirements workshops, they're apt to ensure that the right people are present.

THE RECORDER

The *recorder* documents the group's work as it proceeds. This person is sometimes called the *scribe, technographer,* or *documenter.* (Note that more than one person may be playing this role.) The recorder's primary responsibility is to ensure that the group's work is captured correctly for use during and after the workshop. This documentation serves both the short-term and long-term memory of the group. Workshops are high-bandwidth: A lot of complex and detailed information can be discovered in a short time. Subsequently, details discussed during the workshop can be forgotten an hour later.

Participants' short-term memory is refreshed by repetition and visual cues. The recorder's job is to have those cues at hand, enabling participants to refresh their memories quickly and correctly. Long-term memory requires documentation of the workshop so that people can reference such things as the decisions made, the people present, and specifics related to deliverables. This information might be needed days, months, or even years later.

The recorder also relieves participants of the job of typing and writing during the workshop, freeing them to be fully engaged in exploring the requirements content. He can enter the information into a word processor, draw in a visual modeling tool, write on flip charts, or use an automated tool to efficiently capture content. What the recorder is capturing should be in full view and, if handwritten, legible. He should stop the group to clarify information as it's being recorded. Using simple technologies such as a laptop with a word processor, a requirements management tool, and a drawing tool can enhance a workshop immeasurably.

At times, you can use several recorders. In one workshop I facilitated, the data modeler acted as recorder; he captured the business participants' conceptual data model in the modeling tool and their text business rules in a homegrown repository tool. At the same time, the project leader used a laptop to capture all other group work (issues, actions, and summaries of each activity) in the agenda document.

Not all requirements workshops need an explicit recorder. The recorder can collect all the work prepared by participants on posters, cards, or sticky notes from the workshop room when the workshop is finished. She can then enter that information into a document or drawing tool. In that case, you still need to clarify who'll do this work. (To help with transcription errors that might occur, I also recommend taking photos of the room before the material is taken down.)

You can also use tools that capture the content of a whiteboard or posters into a computer as images. These images can be routed around or posted to a project repository, such as a Web site or project database. (For online resources for capturing deliverables posted around the workshop room, see the Web site for this book.)

Participants should review the recorded information soon after the workshop. In multiday workshops, you should begin each successive day with a review of the prior day's documentation. Having a printer and a laptop in the room for the recorder accelerates this process and allows for real-time corrections. After the final session, participants should get notes and models within a day or two, depending on your requirements schedule. Corrections or clarifications should be filtered through the recorder and sent to all participants.

The recorder can be anyone who might benefit from learning about the requirements but who is not a content expert and therefore doesn't need to be an active participant. This can include project leads, testers, documentation analysts, developers, or newly hired business analysts. Remember that the workshop contents, and contributions made by individuals, are viewed as *group* contributions. For this reason, it's important that the recorder document without attribution to specific persons. Anonymity enhances group ownership of the deliverables.

Technography

Technographers are a special type of recorder who act as co-facilitators. They decide which data to display and how to display it, capture content interactively, and help the group to stay on the same page and navigate through information (DeKoven, 1999a). They use projected computer output or collaborative software to enter, display, and rearrange contributions in real time.

A significant benefit of using a technographer is that the documentation is immediately corrected and available. If subteams produce deliverables, you can use multiple technographers; when the subteams converge to share their work products, each technographer projects the information for all participants, correcting it as needed.

For online resources about technography, see the Web site for this book.

THE FACILITATOR

The *facilitator* is responsible for planning and designing the workshop and then leading the group through its activities. Key aspects of this work include managing group dynamics and providing an environment in which the group can deliver its work products. As facilitator, you use conflict, disagreement, and differences as opportunities for clarity, understanding, and ultimately a higher-quality product.

As facilitator, you aren't a participant but a *process leader*. Explicitly, and with permission from the group, the facilitator influences the flow of the group's work, maximizes participation, minimizes individual domination and interruption, and guides the group toward closure. The facilitator takes initial direction from the workshop and project sponsors, but once the workshop purpose is understood, the facilitator serves the entire group of participants. He should be someone who is acceptable to the participants and is substantially neutral with regard to the content.

FACILITATOR AS PLANNER AND DESIGNER

The facilitator takes the primary lead in designing the workshop process. This involves a number of tasks, including the following:

- Interviewing stakeholders
- Assisting the planning team in determining the workshop's purpose
- Reviewing or recommending participants, the recorder, and observers
- Selecting appropriate requirements deliverables
- Ensuring that sponsors are invited to kick-and-close and are prepared for these activities
- Optionally, helping lead a workshop orientation meeting
- Creating and testing pre-workshop tools such as templates or checklists
- Arranging the appropriate sequence of activities and tasks for the group to perform
- Integrating doneness tests into these activities (see "Define Doneness Tests" in Chapter 7)
- Helping the group to determine its decision rules (see "Decision Rules" in Chapter 6)
- Selecting workshop opening and closing activities

The facilitator doesn't participate in decision making but instead guides the group along an agreed-upon decision-making process.

In addition to knowing how to design a group process, you as the facilitator, or at least one other member of the planning team, must have knowledge about the meaning and interrelationships among the workshop deliverables—the requirements models—as well as a high-level understanding of the business domain.

The Facilitator and Decision Making

In traditional meetings, the person in charge of the project or deliverable is the decision maker who holds the ultimate power. (This person also usually runs the meetings.) Playing the dual role of controlling content and process puts this decision leader in a conflicting situation. It's like driving your car in heavy traffic in an unfamiliar city: You must constantly follow the map and look for directional signs for your next turn while simultaneously scanning other cars for trouble and controlling your car's speed and direction. Inevitably, the leader will miss points in the discussion while thinking about the next turn—or even miss the turn while focusing on the discussion.

When the same person manages the content along with the process, the result is often lackluster participation, low morale, and incomplete communication. For this reason, requirements decision makers should not serve as facilitators.

Your job as the facilitator is *not* to get the group to agree; it's to help the group establish an environment in which all the participants share their knowledge and perspectives in order to make decisions using an agreed-upon process. In other words, the group makes its own decisions.

Using a participatory approach to decision making leads to more sustainable decisions. The facilitator provides process expertise to enable everyone to communicate. This includes constructive debate, differing opinions, and new information. Chapter 6 discusses how the facilitator can assist the group with decisions by using the Decide How to Decide collaboration pattern.

Knowing about the business content helps you to recommend the right combination of requirements models and also to ask good questions. However, being too close to the content can be a barrier to the process role because there's a tendency for you to add content or lose track of your role as process leader.

When you're unfamiliar with the business domain, your "dumb" questions often end up exposing assumptions that could otherwise result in incomplete or unclear requirements. Use your lack of content knowledge as an asset. Make an effort to obtain a basic understanding of the business domain by reading existing project documentation and asking the planning team to explain the essentials. Because of the importance of business terms, you should also become familiar with basic terms that participants will use in the workshop. (These should also be listed and described in the project glossary.)

FACILITATOR AS PROCESS LEADER

The facilitator as process leader is performing a high-wire balancing act. You must maintain a healthy balance among awareness of self, of others, and of context.

As the facilitator, you must be aware of the following:

- Your effectiveness in the facilitator role
- Your personal opinions about the group and its work
- The needs and dynamics of the group and of the individuals
- The needs of the project and the organization in which it operates

As the leader of the process, you're responsible for the following:

- Monitoring agreed-to group behavior and guidelines for participation
- Assisting the group in using its agreed-upon decision-making process
- Attending to the pace, pulse, and process of the workshop
- Providing feedback to the group members about their behavior and progress

THE FACILITATOR MUST PLAY MANY ROLES.

- Summarizing and clarifying comments by participants
- Monitoring scheduled versus actual time taken by activities
- Observing the group process and deciding when and how to intervene
- Challenging assumptions
- Ensuring that the group content is being captured in written or graphical form or both
- Making content suggestions when the group is stuck

FACILITATOR OBSERVATION AND INTERVENTION SKILLS

One of your important facilitation skills is *observing*. A keen observer sees what is happening and puts it in the context of the individual participants, the group, and the project.

Intervention is the ability to decide whether and when to make a comment, suggestion, or recommendation to the group to shift the current process. A facilitator can intervene in numerous ways:

- Stopping the conversation ("Let's stop and talk about what is going on right now")
- Asking permission to make a recommendation ("I'd like to make a suggestion for the group at this time")
- Making an observation to the group and then being silent ("I'd like to make an observation" or "I'd like to share a pattern that I'm seeing in the group")
- Making an observation and then testing its validity ("Did I hear [or see] that correctly?")
- Making an observation and then asking the group to take its own corrective action ("What would you like to do about this?")
- Making an observation and then asking a direct question that focuses attention on the consequences of the observation ("I noticed this. How do you want to handle this if it happens again?")
- Discussing the observation or recommendation with the planning team during a break
- Asking one person or a subgroup to bring up something that was discussed in the smaller group work

To decide whether you should intervene, consider whether the behavior you're concerned about will, in your judgment, prevent the group from achieving its purpose, or whether it violates the group's own principles for interaction (see "Basic Ground Rules" in Chapter 6). If the participants don't seem to be aware of either of these, you as the facilitator must intervene. You can, however, delay intervening to allow the group time to correct itself or to test whether your observation is correct in the first place.

Knowing about the past, present, and future of the group and its project guides your choices about intervening. For example, if you know that the group or project hasn't openly surfaced disagreements, such as those that often occur around requirements scope or priority, you'll be more assertive in your observations to help them openly confront their disagreements. If you know that most of the participants will continue together in another workshop, you should incorporate activities that allow them to examine their interactions (see the Self-Reflect collaboration pattern in the Appendix).

OTHER FACILITATOR CONSIDERATIONS

If your candidate facilitator doesn't have expertise in both facilitation and requirements models, you have some options. Two people can provide the needed expertise on your planning team: a facilitation (group process) expert and a requirements model expert. If those competencies are not available in your organization, you can outsource to an external consultant who has one or both of these proficiencies.

If you use an external facilitator or requirements expert, make sure that your arrangement includes mentoring your own staff to simultaneously develop your own in-house expertise. A competent external requirements facilitator will want to mentor her client while also helping you deliver your requirements efficiently. She should ask you about the means by which her success will be measured. Look for consultants who have requirements workshop experience (and check references!). You might prefer people who are certified facilitators (see "The IAF" in Chapter 12). This certification is an indicator, but not a guarantee, that the person has the basic skills and experience you should expect.

SHOULD YOU HIRE AN OUTSIDE FACILITATOR?

There are times when you might need to have an external facilitator for your requirements workshop. These are circumstances when either you do not yet have the internal expertise or your project might benefit from an outside, neutral facilitator because of conditions such as these:

- Stakeholders do not trust the skills, abilities, and neutrality of the internal facilitator.
- Your organization has a history of ineffective meetings and decision-making processes.
- Time is of the essence, and an outside facilitator can get to the heart of matters quickly.

An external facilitator can lend credibility to the requirements workshop process and can help teams work through difficult relationships that otherwise might be obstacles to the project's success. When projects aren't going well, stakeholders and team members can more easily talk to an outside, objective person. An external consultant also lends credibility to using techniques and processes that some team members want to use but don't have the clout to implement.

A neutral external facilitator helps establish an environment of equity. The facilitator is expected to solicit input from all participants, regardless of level or status. He intervenes during the workshop when organizationally superior participants dominate the discussion, cut people off during discussion, or respond negatively to the ideas and suggestions of less powerful participants.

It's sometimes easier for an external facilitator to do the following:

- Get a good handle on the true story.
- Be honest with management that it has problems with requirements.
- Introduce techniques such as using a decision rule (forcing sponsors to "decide how to decide," as discussed in Chapter 6) and quality assurance checklists to help them check their requirements.
- Openly point out that "real" users were needed for workshops.

Hiring an external facilitator is also appropriate for projects in which multiple stakeholders are vying for priority treatment of their requirements. In these situations, a neutral person's mere presence tends to reduce overt competition. Furthermore, rivals tend to share their contentions with the facilitator during the workshop information-gathering stage, and that allows the facilitator to prepare activities that help the group arrive at defensible decisions. See Chapter 9 for techniques that help groups prioritize requirements. The Appendix describes two collaboration patterns that are particularly useful in this context: Decide How to Decide and The Sieve.)

OBSERVERS

Observers are interested parties who watch, listen, and learn. An observer benefits by learning about the project's content, the workshop process, or both.

Look for opportunities to involve testers, developers, trainers, and marketers as observers. Get permission from the group for observers to be present, especially if sponsors are observers (see "Having Sponsors in the Workshop" earlier in this chapter).

In one requirements workshop I facilitated, new business analysts observed the workshop so that they could get on board with their new jobs more quickly. On another project, a manager who had no content expertise observed to learn about the business rules. Her silent presence also served another purpose: to demonstrate support for the group's work. On yet another project, project leaders who planned to use workshops for related projects attended ours to learn about how the process worked. For a fourth project, I requested that training experts observe so that they could understand the potential content and format of the training manuals they were slated to design.

Although observers are passive during workshop activities, they can certainly interact with participants at breaks or lunch. These are opportunities for observers to ask clarifying questions, query the facilitator about the workshop process, and form relationships with participants with whom they might interact later in the project.

Facilitating is hard work; you can't always see everything that's happening in the room. Observers can help a facilitator by observing group dynamics. I often ask for observers' help in this regard. I ask for feedback, during breaks or lunch, on behaviors such as whether any participants appear puzzled, concerned, or uninvolved. Asking an observer about the group's energy level gives me information about when to modulate the action by adding energizers, using small groups more or less often, or querying the group directly about how to enhance productivity.

Observers should be seated in the back or to one side, out of the way. Their roles—to learn, to demonstrate support, or both—should be described at the beginning of the workshop. During your pre-workshop interviews or in an orientation meeting, ask the participants how they feel about observers being in the room, particularly if you suspect that the presence of observers might cause controversy or divert the group.

Prepare your observers to be active listeners and watchers by giving them questions to answer as they watch and listen. Here are some good questions to ask:

- Were all the participants engaged in the process?
- Were there points when the energy level seemed particularly high? If so, what was happening?
- Was the facilitator prepared? How do you know?
- What surprised you? What puzzled you?

For more observer questions, see the Web site for this book.

Dealing with Runaway Observers

Despite your best efforts to prepare observers for their passive roles, some people turn out to be "runaway" observers—difficult to control and needing attention. These runaways can be disruptive and can put the group at risk by diverting focus from the work at hand. In these cases, the facilitator must take a firm hand on behalf of the participants.

In one of my workshops, Anne, an observer and a knowledgeable data analyst, kept interrupting business participants as they mapped out as-is use cases. She kept correcting their work and offering what were, in her view, better processes. The participants' responses to Anne indicated that she was distracting them. I politely asked her to withhold her comments until they finished.

Her behavior persisted, so I spoke with her privately during a break; I suggested that if it was too difficult to be silent and listen, perhaps she might elect to not return to the workshop room after the break. Instead, I offered, she could review the work after the fact and make her suggestions through one of the planning team members. Luckily, she opted not to return after the break, and she took no offense to my request.

In another workshop, I had to escort a runaway observer away from small groups of business participants who were modeling at the wall. Despite several private conversations, during which I asked him to leave these people to their tasks without disruption, he persisted until I firmly gave him a final warning: Leave them alone or leave the room, alone. This did the trick.

ON-CALL SUBJECT MATTER EXPERTS

Occasionally during a workshop, it's critical that you obtain highly specialized or technical information from on-call subject matter experts. You may need them for a short time, perhaps only minutes. Participants should prepare these on-call SMEs for a possible phone call during a workshop break or a request for a brief "guest appearance."

In one workshop I facilitated, a participant phoned a colleague during a morning break to ask a specific question. She had an answer, on her voice mail, within two hours. She shared the information with the group, and it enabled them to reach closure on one of their deliverables. In another workshop, a knowledgeable SME was asked to step into the workshop room and answer a few questions. Her presence for those five minutes helped this group agree on a key scope issue.

At other times, you might need for an SME to share important information relevant to the group's work. He might explain a business process or walk through a model or user interface. This should be a prearranged, highly focused, and time-limited activity.

In one workshop I facilitated, we arranged for a business expert to help us for an hour. He walked through the current system interface using a live connection. We projected the application screens onto the wall as he navigated through the system, explaining how he did his work. We asked him to conduct his walkthrough using sets of goals (use cases) that the participants had drafted earlier in the day. As the expert navigated through the screens, participants asked him questions to clarify specific steps and business rules.

The expert spent 45 minutes with the group and then left. After this, the participants modified and expanded their use cases and business rules; the interface designer created a prototype immediately afterward. The same expert came to another workshop several days later, this time to interactively walk through the prototype and provide corrections and feedback on the flow of the screens and the system's underlying business rules.

Identifying on-call SMEs ahead of time saves time during a workshop. Ask participants to identify these people and to let them know that their expertise might be needed. Address this with participants toward the end of your participant interview, in a workshop orientation meeting, or in the section of your agenda titled Participant Pre-Work. (See Chapter 9 for more about workshop agendas.)

TIPS

- Be clear about who the workshop sponsor and project sponsor are.
- Interview as many potential participants as you can.
- If it appears you'll have surrogates instead of direct users, devise a workshop risk plan.
- Don't rely on distributed collaborative technologies before the group has had the chance to gather face-to-face.
- Use a neutral facilitator.
- Use observer and recorder feedback to adjust the facilitation process.
- Arrange for on-call subject matter experts to fill in the blanks of participant knowledge.

QUESTIONS TO ASK STAKEHOLDERS ABOUT PARTICIPANT ROLES

The following questions can help you determine workshop roles. You can preface these questions by saying, "The next set of questions will help us identify the players we need to have a successful workshop."

- What is your role in the organization and this project (or these requirements)?
- Who should participate in the workshop? Why?
- Who are the people who can represent the needs of direct users of the system?
- Whom do you view as decision makers about the scope, correctness, or completeness of the requirements?
- Are there people who might benefit from observing, but not participating in, the workshop?
- What is the history of this group of people?
- Given the list of potential workshop participants, is anyone missing?

FOR MORE INFORMATION

Berry (1995) engagingly argues that being a "smart ignoramus"—having an honest lack of knowledge about the problem domain—can lead to asking good questions and testing assumptions that might not otherwise be surfaced. This supports the value of having a facilitator who's familiar with, but not steeped in, the business, and also having participants who can ask honest, clarifying questions of business experts.

Doyle and Strauss (1976) describe, in three helpful chapters, how to be a good facilitator, recorder, and group member.

Gause and Lawrence (1999) explain how critical it is to incorporate users into the requirements and design phases of the software development process as a means to reduce the risk of delivering the wrong product or of delivering the right product at the wrong time.

Chapter 4 of Wood and Silver (1995) briefly describes JAD roles and explains how to select a JAD team.

6

Principles: Ground Rules for the Workshop

"Planned participation promotes productivity."
—Lynda Baker

Principles, which I also refer to as *ground rules* in this chapter, are guidelines for group participation. Ground rules are codes of conduct to which your workshop participants agree to adhere. Groups need interaction precepts to maintain socially acceptable behavior (norms) that promote workshop goals: delivering the predefined work products in the allotted time.

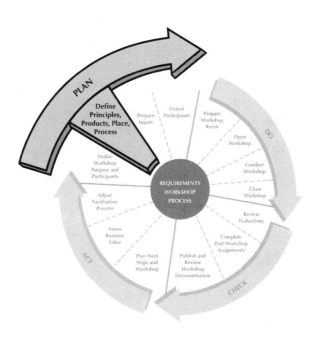

Ground rules serve as a process guide for the facilitator and the participants. They serve as a tool for detecting and correcting unhealthy group interactions and evolving toward productive and healthy interactions. Just as significantly, participants learn to check, and reflect on, their experience in comparison to their ground rules; then they adjust their interactions to make their experience a more productive and satisfying one.

FORMING, STORMING, NORMING, AND PERFORMING

Groups invariably develop *norms*, which are standards for interacting. Figure 6-1 illustrates a widely recognized cycle with which norms are associated.

Forming involves groups finding common goals. This process is well served by early identification of your workshop purpose (see Chapter 4). *Storming* involves members openly disagreeing, which under healthy circumstances strengthens the

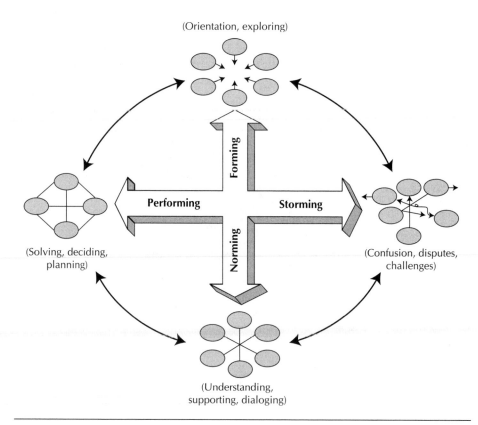

FIGURE 6-1 THE GROUP DEVELOPMENT PROCESS

group and promotes deeper understanding and diversity. *Norming* is the process of finding ways, both healthy and unhealthy, to interact. During *performing*, the group is task-oriented and focuses on producing its agreed-upon work products.

Numerous group development experts suggest a final stage, *adjourning*, in which the group acknowledges its work, reflects on its collaboration, and says goodbye. See Chapter 9 for tasks and questions associated with these stages of group development.

Norms can be healthy or dysfunctional. Examples of healthy norms include waiting for someone to finish speaking before making your own comments, being on time, sharing relevant and necessary information, volunteering to take on a task that you have the skills and knowledge to complete, and respecting confidences shared in the group.

Most of us have experienced dysfunctional group norms. Examples include withholding important information, speaking disrespectfully about others (inside or outside the room), and being unwilling to take on tasks that help the group's goals. Unhealthy norms are unproductive to the group's process, are barriers to delivering quality products, and can make the group experience painful.

Norms emerge spontaneously or explicitly. Under ideal circumstances, healthy norms can emerge spontaneously. When you have less than ideal circumstances, explicitly defining guidelines for participation promotes healthy group dynamics. Without those guidelines, individuals make assumptions about and interpret others' words and behavior, something that results in miscommunication, a poor group process, and low-quality group products.

The solution, as embodied by the collaboration pattern Is There a Norm in the Room? (see the Appendix), is to explicitly establish guidelines for participation—ground rules that are congruent with both individual and group needs.

BASIC GROUND RULES

Ground rules should be specific, visible to everyone (posted in the room), derived with group input and then agreed to by all group members, and malleable (in other words, adaptable as needed throughout the workshop). Ground rules should follow some basic principles regarding their creation and use. To prepare yourself for your role as facilitator, consider devising your own ground rules for your role as facilitator (see "Ground Rules for the Facilitator" in Chapter 12).

Participants can use a list of generic ground rules as the basis for collaborating in a manner that enhances productivity, increases participation, and honors individual contributions, experience, and knowledge. Here are some examples.

- All participants' inputs are equally valued.
- Participants are expected to share all relevant information.
- The sessions will start and end on time and will start on time after breaks.
- Only one conversation will go on at once (unless subgroups are working on a topic).
- The group is responsible for the deliverables.
- Discussions and criticisms will focus on interests and not on people.

Ground rules concerning common courtesy—such as keeping cellular phones in vibrate or display-only mode and not answering the phone while in the workshop—may not be appropriate for all participants. Some participants have work roles for which they're on call, and they must respond to phone calls immediately. Suggest a compromise, such as turning the ringer off or leaving the room to answer the call. Don't spend valuable group time debating the options.

Ground Rules for Ground Rules

Because ground rules are norms about behavior, I offer these rules about your ground rules themselves:

- Co-create ground rules; make them explicit.
- Every workshop should have ground rules.
- Ground rules are monitored by the whole group, for the group. The facilitator is there to guide the process of deriving and checking the group's ground rules.
- Display the ground rules so that they're visible to everyone.
- Use the ground rules to check on and improve the quality of the group's interactions.
- Ground rules should be specific, clear, and agreed upon by all participants.
- Use no more than 10 ground rules.
- Ground rules can be changed at any time as long as you abide by the ground rules listed here.

Your group may wish to include ground rules that use jargon widely used in your company or team culture. For example:

- Speakers should "cut to the chase."
- "Off-target" discussions are limited to five minutes but are recorded as issues.
- "Headline" your comments.

"Cut to the chase" means to speak briefly and directly; "off-target" means topics that aren't relevant to the current activity; and to "headline" is to provide a summarized, short version of a comment. Using such phrases is fine as long as everyone understands their meaning.

Ask questions to uncover potential ground rules. Examples: "What does this mean?" "How can I recognize that we're violating this ground rule?" "Is anyone here unfamiliar with this ground rule?" (For more examples, see "Questions to Ask Stakeholders About Ground Rules" at the end of this chapter.) Make sure that the ground rules are clear to everyone. For example, saying "Be respectful" is vague. In one organization it might mean "Don't interrupt when someone else is talking," whereas in another it might mean "Don't withhold relevant information."

Ground rules essentially communicate the message "Let's work well together." With the help of your planning team and the participants, select five to ten applicable rules, including your decision-making ground rules (see "Decision-Making Ground Rules" later in this chapter). Remembering more than ten rules can be difficult, and they have less impact. (See the Web site for this book for a comprehensive list of possible workshop ground rules.)

You might need to include special ground rules (see the next section) or culturally aware ground rules. When you're planning to work with the same group in another workshop, or if the group will continue to work together on the project, it's especially important to consider integrating some of the values-based ground rules used by developmental facilitators. Both types of special ground rules are discussed in the next section.

SPECIAL GROUND RULES

Project pressures, politics, prior workshop experiences, or group history may make it necessary to include ground rules to address specific circumstances.

Knowing your participants and the history of the project can help you suggest ground rules that can save time and energy by avoiding discussion of topics that are out of scope or irrelevant.

In one workshop I facilitated, the group was delivering a migration strategy for standard business rules. Some members of the group had participated in a prior series of workshops that delivered a logical data model. We added a special ground rule: "We will not review the completed and validated data model from the prior workshop." When questions arose about the data model, I simply walked to the poster where the ground rule was written. One participant, a veteran of the data modeling workshop, volunteered to explain the specific data model question to other interested participants during breaks.

In another workshop, I was warned by numerous participants that much debate and energy had been spent to arrive at project scope. We added the ground rule, "We will not discuss or debate scope because it has already been agreed upon." Indeed, at several points on the first morning, I found myself asking, "Is that a project scope issue?" (The answer was "yes" each time.) I pointed out, "Our ground rule tells us that we won't discuss scope any further. Would you like to add a 'parking lot' item about this and move on, or just move on?" (For more on the parking lot, see Chapter 9.)

VALUES-BASED GROUND RULES

If you'd like to explore ground rules in a systemic, and thereby deeper, manner, consider the skilled facilitator approach developed by Roger Schwarz. His work is based on a theory of group facilitation that contains a set of four core values in addition to ground rules. The values are as follows: valid information, free and informed choice, internal commitment, and compassion. The first three come from the work of Chris Argyris, who's known for his work in the areas of organizational learning; Schwarz added the fourth value. These values are the basis of the following 10 ground rules*:

1. Test assumptions and inferences.
2. Share all relevant information.
3. Use specific examples and agree on what important words mean.
4. Discuss undiscussable issues.
5. Focus on interests, not positions.

---

* Used with permission by Roger Schwarz, Roger Schwarz & Associates, http://www.schwarzassociates.com.

6. Explain your reasoning and intent.

7. Combine advocacy with inquiry.

8. Jointly design next steps and ways to test disagreement.

9. Keep the discussion focused.

10. Use a decision-making rule that generates the level of commitment needed.

Schwarz and many others consider these ground rules to be central to both basic and developmental facilitation. Basic facilitation helps a group to solve a substantive problem (such as defining requirements for software). In developmental facilitation, a group also learns to improve its process.

Unlike behavioral ground rules, such as "start on time" or "one conversation at a time," Schwarz's ground rules help the group identify dysfunctional group behavior, serve as a teaching tool for developing effective group norms, help guide the facilitator, and allow groups to set new expectations for how they will interact with each other.

Culturally Aware Ground Rules

Participants may come from various corporate cultures, work groups, cities, or countries. Each may have different norms for acceptable group behavior. In your pre-workshop interviews, be sure to ask questions to explore these norms. For example, in some cultures, such as in Italy, it's not uncommon for more than one conversation to occur at a time. In Asian cultures, saying "yes" means that you're listening and you understand what's being said, whereas in the United States, it means "I agree."

Nonverbal behaviors can also have cultural significance. For example, failing to make direct eye contact in the United States is often interpreted as a sign of deceit or insecurity; in Asian cultures, silence is an indication of respect, and not, as often in the United States, of agreement. Also be aware of cultural differences in decision making and sharing information. Different cultures have different frames of reference for decision making. For example, people in Latin American cultures prefer making individual decisions, whereas the Japanese commonly use consensus, and many Americans value delegation. You also need to be careful with regard to food (some people don't eat meat or certain types of meat) as well as energizers and other serious play activities.

Also keep in mind that these generalizations may not be valid in your situation just because some of your participants are from a particular culture. When you have multicultural participants, take extra time before and during the workshop to test your assumptions about these cultural norms and the usefulness and validity of each ground rule. Explore cultural differences and engage participants in a discussion about those differences when you determine ground rules early in the workshop. This approach allows everyone to communicate about communicating.

INTRODUCING AND TESTING GROUND RULES

One of your workshop opening activities is to agree on the ground rules. (See "Opening the Workshop" in Chapter 9 for more on workshop opening.) Prepare participants for this task by providing a draft list of ground rules for them to review before the workshop. For questions you can ask during your pre-workshop interviews, see "Questions to Ask Stakeholders About Ground Rules" at the end of this chapter.

If your planning team is well acquainted with the participants, ask the team to draft a list of recommended ground rules. At a minimum, inform participants that you'll be collaboratively addressing the guidelines they'll use during the workshop. The Web site for this book contains more information about how to elicit ground rules, test them during the workshop, and evaluate them afterward.

It's the participants' responsibility to adhere to and monitor the ground rules, with your guidance. If the ground rules become the facilitator's and not the group's, you've lost an important tool for increasing the participants' ability to interact effectively. Worse, you become an enforcer rather than a guide.

During your workshop's opening activity, ask whether all participants will agree to "call" one another on ground rule violations. Some people might be reluctant, especially if their bosses or a high-level manager is a violator or if their cultural norms conflict with speaking out. Include periodic ground rule checks to promote appropriate process checks on the ground rules. Ask, "What can you do to take ownership of these ground rules?" and "What do you want to do if someone violates a ground rule?" This approach allows the group to reflect on how to self-monitor its behavior.

Seek ways to help workshop participants interact effectively by asking, "What should I do, as the facilitator, to help you honor these ground rules?" and "What role do you want me to play in regard to these rules?" One workshop group asked me to point out violations as they occurred. Another asked me to schedule times during which to review the ground rules.

Once the group has experience with *self-reflection* (examining its own interactions for the purpose of learning and improving), you can ask the participants to consider how they can transform their successes into future work together. This is a good way to conclude the "next steps" portion of your workshop closing activity. (See Chapter 9 for more on workshop closing.) The Self-Reflect collaboration pattern provides the rationale for this technique (see the Appendix).

If participants have had difficulty working together in the past or if emotions are running high around the topic of requirements and their priorities, you'll need to invest more than 10 minutes to arrive at your ground rules during your workshop opening. Unless people are comfortable with sharing information and feeling safe with one another, your entire workshop plan, no matter how great it might be, will not be effective. By surfacing hidden agendas, discussed next, you should know about these kinds of issues ahead of time.

HIDDEN AGENDAS

Hidden agendas are needs, wants, or motivations closely held by one or more participants. A hidden agenda can have a healing nature or a harmful nature. Healing ones arise from hopes and wishes that are restorative, as exemplified by the following people I've worked with:

- The project sponsor who wanted all the participants to leave the workshop enthusiastic about the project
- The project leader who wanted the business sponsor to understand that real users should be involved in the detailed requirements definition
- The tester who hoped that others would be respectful of his contributions to the project
- The business analyst who hoped that other business participants would be willing to stay involved during acceptance testing

When you learn about healing hidden agendas, consider sharing them as intangible workshop products (see Chapter 7). Build activities into your agenda, such as energizers or brief team-building activities, to promote them.

Energizers are ways for participants to share their personal backgrounds, interests, or hobbies. For example, in one group in which several participants shared their healthy hidden agenda of "more teamwork," I included a short activity in which they lined up in birth order (month and day, not year!). Then they shared with one another "the riskiest thing I've ever done in my life." In another group, several participants wanted others to leave the workshop more willing to take on project tasks in the future. I included several short, fun energizers getting them to interact on a more personal level, laugh, and find out more about one another's special talents.

Harmful hidden agendas arise when people withhold information, are vying for power, or feel isolated—they believe their contributions, skills, and opinions aren't valued by others. A hidden agenda is often unspoken but still known to one or more people. This agenda is usually *undiscussable*, which means that everyone knows it, but it seems too dangerous for them to talk about it openly. Examples include "Our boss doesn't tell us anything" (I wish she would), "Our customers don't want to take ownership" (I want them to), and "This system could make my job obsolete" (and "they" are hiding this information from me).

Harmful hidden agendas can disrupt or interrupt the credibility of the workshop process—let alone the project—and can prevent individuals from freely partici-

HIDDEN AGENDAS CAN BE HEALING OR HARMFUL.

pating in the workshop. You must uncover hidden agendas by directly asking stakeholders and participants about them during interviews. Any hidden agendas that aren't surfaced ahead of time will emerge during the workshop. If you're prepared for them, you can reduce their harm and handle them more easily during the session.

Be sure not to inject your own hidden agendas. For example, a pet peeve of mine are meetings, workshops, or seminars that don't start on time. I believe that the ground rule "start on time" is an important way to communicate mutual respect for people's time and also to lend a sense of urgency and order to a workshop. However, I must get agreement on that ground rule from the participants. I ask participants or the planning team whether that ground rule is acceptable in their culture. If some people violate it by norm but there's agreement that this ground rule will be helpful to the group, I ask the workshop sponsor or project sponsor to tell people that the workshop will start on time. (Having the sponsor also inform participants that she will be there for the workshop kickoff—discussed in Chapter 9—helps to drive the message home, too.)

Numerous seminar and conference attendees have shared with me their experiences of having a leader with a hidden agenda attempt to use a workshop to get a group to agree with a decision that he has already made. You can discover this by skillful interviewing. Explore the decisions that need to be made during a workshop and advise the decision leader (see "Decision Rules" later in this chapter) to choose a decision-making rule that promotes participation and commitment.

DECISION-MAKING GROUND RULES

A critical success factor for your requirements workshop is the ability to reach closure on the requirements you are creating.

Closure means locking down a deliverable and knowing it's "done." This means making real-time collaborative decisions during workshops. For the most part, you strive to reach closure. At times, however, issues and new understanding arise in a requirements workshop and result in a lack of closure. That is especially true when you discover missing requirements and don't have the right people or resources in the room to get the answers you need. In those cases, during your workshop closing be sure to specify who needs to do what to reach closure (for more on the workshop closing, see Chapter 9).

Collaborative
Closure

Doneness tests (see "Define Doneness Tests" in Chapter 7) provide guidance to a group for making a decision, but they are not a substitute for a lucid, well-understood decision-making process. To implement decisions successfully, people need to be truly committed. When groups collaborate effectively, they establish norms for decision making; these norms become part of the workshop ground rules.

Decision making in the business world is often complex and fraught with dangers. It's complicated by factors such as these:

- How quickly the decision must be made
- Individual hidden agendas
- Group history and culture
- Groupthink (group members think it's more important to agree than to state their areas of disagreement)
- Knowledge held by the decision maker
- Fear of retribution for making a "wrong" decision
- Insufficient or incorrect information

The decisions involved in a software project affect the professional lives of numerous stakeholders: users, designers, builders, testers, managers, marketers, customers, and others. Software projects aren't immune to the risk that decision makers don't involve the stakeholders impacted by the decision or that they make decisions based on insufficient information. Requirements workshops provide an early quality gate for making sound decisions that can have enormous downstream effects on a software project. Defining decision-making ground rules before the workshop helps to crystallize workshop products, promote appropriate participation, and accelerate the requirements process itself.

PRODUCT AND PROCESS DECISIONS

Decisions in your workshop are both product- and process-related. Product-related decisions are about the deliverables of the workshop, and they involve the specific requirements the participants create together. The work products vary according to your workshop design strategy (see Chapter 10). For example, if you're using a vertical, who-first workshop design strategy, the decisions will be about closure on the actors, events, use cases, business rules, and parts of a logical data model or class model created in the workshop. Process-related decisions define who will do what by when, and how the results of that work will be communicated to the group. These decisions are most often decided during the workshop closing (see "Closing the Workshop" in Chapter 9).

In a requirements workshop in which sound decision making is used, participants leave the room with an agreement about the requirements they worked on. For example, each might say, "We decided to accept use cases 5 and 10, but we didn't close on use cases 9 and 11 because we didn't have correct business rules for them. Also, we agreed to accept use cases 3, 6, and 7 with revisions that we made during the workshop." Process decisions are reflected in comments such as "Jim and Ava are going to research business rules for use cases 9 and 11, and Jim's going to send us all an e-mail by Friday with a list of business rules in template format for those use cases. We'll meet on Monday at 9:00 A.M. to review them and attempt to reach closure on them." To achieve this degree of clarity after a workshop, you must use sound, collaborative decision-making ground rules.

COLLABORATIVE DECISION MAKING

In requirements workshops, users, customers, and suppliers all hold stakes in the decisions about the requirements deliverables they're defining:

- The stakes of direct users or external customers (such as buyers of shrink-wrap or packaged software) involve having the requirements represent their real needs. In this way, they can feel confident that their software development partners understand what the software should do to solve their business problems.
- The stakes of the internal customers or buyers of software development services involve defining requirements that satisfy cost and schedule constraints.
- The stakes of the builders, such as developers and testers, involve obtaining requirements that are good enough, respectively, for use in designing and prototyping and in building test scripts and test cases.

Group decisions are generally superior to those of even the smartest individual. When people participate in decisions in which they have a stake, commitment tends to be higher and the decision is generally more successful. Because the requirements you deliver from your workshop have important consequences, and because they require support by all team members, the best course is to use a collaborative decision-making process.

The characteristics of a *collaborative decision* include the following:

- The stakeholders participate in the decision-making process in a way that meets the needs of the individuals and the group.
- The decision includes the diverse views of all stakeholders.
- The decision enhances the group's ability to continue to work together effectively.

Collaborative decisions address all the *legitimate concerns* of participants: concerns that have possible consequences "that might adversely affect the organization or common good or that are in conflict with the purpose and values of the group" (Saint and Lawson, 1994).

With a *noncollaborative* decision, stakeholders aren't consulted, or their input is obtained without inquiry into the reasoning behind their thinking. To avoid this, stakeholders who will use, design, test, and implement the requirements should be present at the workshop and involved in making decisions about the requirements. As you plan your workshop and define its decisions and decision-making process, ensure that your list of participants includes the people who must implement the decisions. For example, if your workshop is delivering use cases, business rules, and a data model, you'll want to have people who work with the products downstream—such as architects, developers, testers, data administrators, quality analysts, and database administrators—present as observers.

When you make important decisions about requirements in a noncollaborative manner, you risk making poor decisions that are difficult to sustain. And without a *decision rule*—an agreed-upon way of making decisions—people are vague about when, and even whether, a decision has been made; they delay taking action, and that results in the waste of valuable time and money.

DECISION RULES

The first step in collaborative decision making is for the decision leader to determine the rule by which you will make the decision—the *decision rule* (Kaner et al., 1996). The *decision leader* is the person who has the authority to implement the decision or to obtain resources to implement it, and the responsibility to ensure that the decision is supported in the organization. This person should reside as high as necessary, but as low as possible, in the organization chart.

In scope-level requirements workshops, the decision leader is often the business sponsor or business project manager. In high-level and detailed-level workshops, the decision leader is often the business project manager or leader who is close to the content and can balance known project constraints.

The decision leader needs the input of other stakeholders who can provide informed and valid inputs about any requirements decision. In making a decision, the decision leader must account for the fact that the people who must implement the decision should be consulted. For example, although a business subject matter expert might be the decision leader for the use cases, business rules, and data model, to reach closure that person will want to be sure that the data administrator agrees to the data model under consideration. The use of decision rules and an explicit decision-making process clarifies this process. I describe this process in the collaboration pattern Decide How to Decide (see the Appendix).

Various kinds of decision rules exist; Figure 6-2 shows some examples.

- *Majority Vote* involves the group in making decisions by counting the number of votes for two or more options. The option with the highest number "wins." This rule enables fast decisions, and it's efficient when large groups are involved. On the other hand, some people will always lose (something that can create an adversarial atmosphere), choices may not be based on valid information, and the quality of the decisions is often not high. It's best to use this rule when the decisions are trivial, the stakes are low, and the options are clear.

- *Delegation* involves the appointment of one person to make decisions. This rule also enables fast decisions, and the accountability is clear. On the other hand, the appointee may not have the necessary expertise, there may be insufficient buy-in and commitment from the other participants, or the resulting decision can undermine the authority of the person in charge. It's best to use this rule when you need to make decisions quickly, the delegate actually holds the authority, or the decisions aren't very important.

- *Negotiation* involves compromise on a middle position that incorporates the most important positions of all sides. This rule requires a lot of discussion, which tends to increase the thoroughness of the decision making. On the other hand, everyone loses something along the way, and it can increase the adversarial nature of an already polarized group. In addition, the quality of decisions is often not high. It's best to use this rule when there aren't any viable alternatives because of the contentiousness within the group.

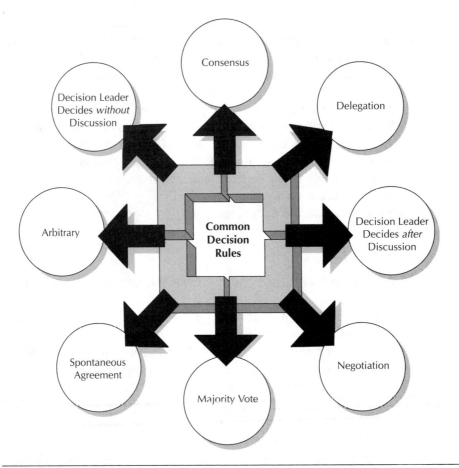

FIGURE 6-2 COMMON DECISION RULES

(Used with permission. Adapted from Sam Kaner, *The Facilitator's Guide to Participatory Decision Making,* 1996, New Society Publishers, www.newsociety.com)

- *Spontaneous Agreement* occurs when participants quickly and sponta-neously arrive at a decision without considering the decision factors. This rule results in quick and easy decisions. On the other hand, there's no discussion about possible consequences and impacts, and there's a risk of groupthink, which occurs when people feel pressured to agree (see "Group Dysfunction" in Chapter 9). It's best to use this rule when the de-cision has minimal consequences and needs to be made quickly or when discussion and sharing of preferences aren't important to the quality of the decision.

- The *Arbitrary* decision rule involves making decisions by some arbitrary means, such as flipping a coin. This rule provides for fast and efficient low-stakes decisions. On the other hand, it devalues the importance of the decisions. It's best to use this rule when the decisions are unimportant, they don't have long-term consequences to participants, and they must be made quickly.

- *Decision Leader Decides* without *Discussion* involves the decision leader making a decision without consulting any of the other stakeholders. This rule provides for fast decisions while clarifying who's in charge. On the other hand, the quality of the decision may be compromised if the leader doesn't know about possible consequences, and she misses an opportunity to learn about surrounding issues. There's also a risk of insufficient buy-in and commitment from those affected by the decision. It's best to use this rule when decisions must be made in the face of a crisis and they're being made by a competent, knowledgeable leader whom the other stakeholders trust.

- *Decision Leader Decides* after *Discussion* involves the decision leader making a decision after consulting with the other stakeholders. This rule enables those stakeholders to provide input, and that promotes commitment on their part while also clarifying who's in charge. On the other hand, not all stakeholders share responsibility for the decisions. It's best to use this rule when the leader has knowledge and expertise about the topics of the decisions, he wants to make the decisions collaboratively, and there's a need to balance decision quality with speed.

- *Consensus* involves "a state of mutual agreement among members of a group where all legitimate concerns of individuals have been addressed to the satisfaction of the group" (Saint and Lawson, 1994). Using this rule builds trust, creates high levels of support for and commitment to the decision, considers the impact of the decision, enables more sustainable decisions, and promotes learning because it requires deep listening and inquiry. On the other hand, it generally takes longer than other rules, it requires stakeholder knowledge and expertise, and the quality of the decisions can be low if the participants don't have all the relevant information. It's best to use this rule when the decisions are important and they require the commitment of all stakeholders.

An effective decision-making ground rule takes into account the need for participation and balances that with the need to reach closure in a timely manner. The two decision rules that work best for making medium- to high-stakes decisions, such as those you make about requirements during workshops, are Consensus and Decision Leader Decides after Discussion.

REACHING CLOSURE

To be effective, the two collaborative decision rules called out in the preceding section need a mechanism that tests the degree of agreement among the group members. This mechanism must be understood and accepted by everyone. To make this happen in my workshops, I use a four-point degree of agreement scale, shown in Figure 6-3, based on Kaner's original eight-point scale (Kaner et al., 1996).

By polling all the participants, you can find out where each one falls on the degree scale in terms of indicating how strongly he or she agrees with the proposed decision. For example, someone might make the proposal, "Accept this use case as is." To have consensus, everyone participating in the decision must be in the "zone of agreement," which means 1 or 2. All those who designate themselves as 2s must share their concerns. Further discussion may result in modifications to the proposed decision.

To achieve consensus, the group must continue to work on the proposed decision if there are any 3s or 4s. However, if the decision rule is Decision Leader Decides after Discussion, the decision leader can choose to make the decision at this point or ask for more discussion. In requirements workshops in which you're making decisions, use this scale to check for the degree of agreement. Start by identifying the decisions to be made in the workshop. The easiest way to start is by listing the specific requirements models you plan to deliver and assuming that each of these will require at least one decision. You might bundle logical groupings of requirements for a single decision; for example, you should make a decision for a use case along with its related business rules, data attributes, and draft prototype screens.

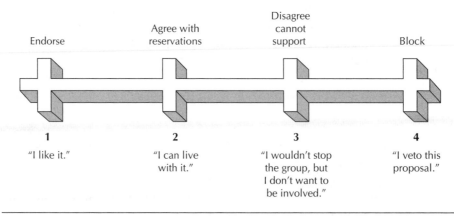

FIGURE 6-3 DEGREE OF AGREEMENT SCALE (BASED ON KANER ET AL., 1996)

When your group is ready to consider a specific proposal during the workshop, clarify the proposal. Next, poll each person. The process you should use depends on how controversial the proposed decision appears to be. For example, you might poll the group anonymously if the decision is controversial; if it isn't, you can ask everyone to hold up an index card labeled 1, 2, 3, or 4. If you think participants would benefit from hearing a final comment on the proposal, ask them to explain their reasoning in one minute or less.

Workshop participants repeat this process for each decision, taking one minute or less for each round. If there are any 2s, ask those individuals to share their reservations. This process creates a group norm for decision making.

Steps for Collaborative Decision Making

1. Before the workshop,

   - Identify each decision to be made.
   - Identify the decision leader for each decision.
   - Have the decision leader pick the decision rule.

2. During the workshop opening activity, have the group practice the decision-making process (steps 3–6) and then decide whether you will use this process during the workshop.

3. Close discussion around a requirements model or a set of related models.

4. Clarify the proposed decisions.

5. Poll the group using the degree of agreement scale.

6. If the decision rule is Consensus, participants will need to vote 1s and 2s; for any 2, ask the participant to state his or her concerns. If the Decision Leader Decides after Discussion rule is in effect, ask the decision leader whether he is ready to make a decision. If not, find out what he needs to make the decision, and facilitate a process to get to that point.

Test the decision rule process at the beginning of the workshop. The next section describes a real-world example.

Defining your decision-making ground rules promotes effective team collaboration. The team tends to make timely, high-quality decisions and to successfully follow up on them. Participants learn from divergent perspectives, listen to one another's interests, make reasonable choices, and come to closure. Good decision-making groups seek inclusive decisions that merge the best of all available options.

Perhaps just as important, if the decision turns out not to be the best one, these teams have the ability to recognize it and recover. They've learned how to balance the content of the decision with the process of arriving at it.

A Real-World Example

I facilitated a two-day requirements workshop involving a purchasing application for a global consumer products company. The application was being designed for use by some 120 users in 60 countries. The participants were the software and business teams responsible for delivering the system.

I interviewed the potential participants to gauge their needs and perspectives and to define the workshop's purpose. I also inspected the work products: drafts of 12 use cases representing user requirements. For each use case to be modeled in the workshop, the group had to decide its disposition: We had to be able to answer, at the end of the workshop, "What's the disposition of this use case?" The team also needed more requirements models to supplement the use cases, so we added business rules, prototype screens, scenarios, and a high-level data model to the list of workshop products.

After I determined the workshop's purpose, my next step was to work with the decision leader to select the decision rule. Pamela, the business project manager, was responsible for representing the needs of this customer base. She and her two business analysts would test and support the application and train users after it went live in seven months. Pamela "owned" the requirements; she had obtained the funding and would continue to play this role. It was Pamela's responsibility to make the decision rule.

Pamela initially selected the Consensus decision rule, which meant she was seeking agreement among her analysts. Because the software participants didn't have the content knowledge or authority to fully contribute to this decision, choosing this rule made sense; but I was concerned about the time needed to achieve consensus. I knew there was a risk that we wouldn't cover all the use cases in a single workshop. Offsetting that concern was the fact that Pamela was a subject matter expert. After she went through the modeling and reviewing activities and received input from her team, she would likely be able to make good decisions.

I told Pamela about my concerns with regard to time. She reconsidered and chose Decision Leader Decides after Discussion. She realized that polling her team members for their degrees of agreement would give her sufficient data for making a decision.

At the beginning of the session, I explained the decision rule choice and the process, and I also polled the group to check their degrees of agreement on using it for this workshop. The participants all specified 1s, so we proceeded to use this decision rule for each use case. In the end, using that rule accelerated the flow of the session. Although Pamela didn't accept all the use cases, it was clear which ones she did, what modifications were needed, and who had to do what in order to reach closure. Within a few days, that same group reached closure on the requirements and proceeded with design and development.

TIPS

- Solicit ground rules before the workshop.
- Get agreement on the ground rules at the beginning of the session.
- Ask questions to uncover hidden agendas.
- Be sensitive to the need to define culturally diverse ground rules.
- Define decisions to be made in the workshop.
- Use a collaborative decision rule and decision-making process.
- Be sure that all stakeholders in decisions, or their representatives, are involved during or after the workshop.
- Continually check on the validity and utility of the ground rules during the workshop.

QUESTIONS TO ASK STAKEHOLDERS ABOUT GROUND RULES

The following questions can help you to determine workshop ground rules. You can preface these questions by saying, "The next set of questions will help us determine what guidelines for participation, or 'ground rules,' will help us interact effectively during the workshop."

- How would you describe the group atmosphere?
- Are any topics off-limits?

- Are there any skeletons in the closet?
- What has been tried that failed?
- Do you have any hidden agendas for this workshop? Do you believe that others have any hidden agendas for this workshop?
- Are there any questions about ground rules that I should be asking but haven't yet asked?

See the Web site for this book for more questions about ground rules.

FOR MORE INFORMATION

Bens (2000) is a practitioner's guidebook loaded with techniques, tips, and tools. Chapter 6 provides a discussion of effective decision making; it addresses the pros and cons of various options.

Fisher and Ury (1981), a best-selling book about negotiation, has useful guidance about how to help people focus on interests, not positions, and how to use objective criteria to evaluate and invent options.

Kaner et al. (1996) provides practical, high-level guidance useful to both new and experienced facilitators. Chapter 16 outlines the degrees of agreement (there are eight in all); Chapter 17 provides a solid discussion of how to reach closure in groups.

Nutt (1998) describes the author's research into business decisions, many of which were made by software organizations. He found that the most successful decisions are those in which a decision leader gathers sufficient information and then enables the stakeholders in the decision to make the decision, rather than trying to persuade them or issue edicts.

Schwarz (1994) is an in-depth work on values-based facilitation; based on Argyris's work, it brings together theory and practice. Although Schwarz's approach is aimed at developmental facilitation, which focuses on helping group process, the rich information in this book is valuable to all professional facilitators.

Strachan (2001) offers an excellent discussion of core values for the facilitator: integrity, mutual respect, and authenticity.

Saint and Lawson (1994) presents a concise yet comprehensive guide to consensus. The authors' definition of consensus is the best I've found. They present useful options for closing decisions and tips for the facilitator.

7

PRODUCTS: ENDING WITH THE BEGINNING

"You can't have everything. Where would you put it?"
—Steven Wright

Your workshop *products* include inputs and outputs. The outputs include requirements and supplemental deliverables such as statements of issues and follow-up actions. The inputs are any materials that jump-start workshop activities and prepare participants: posters, templates, documents, workshop activity instructions, draft or predecessor requirements models, and the results of participant pre-work (see Figure 7-1).

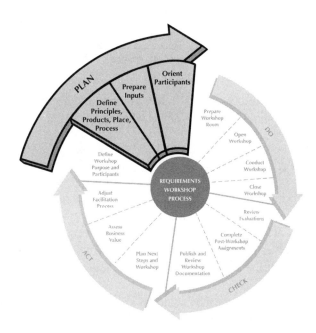

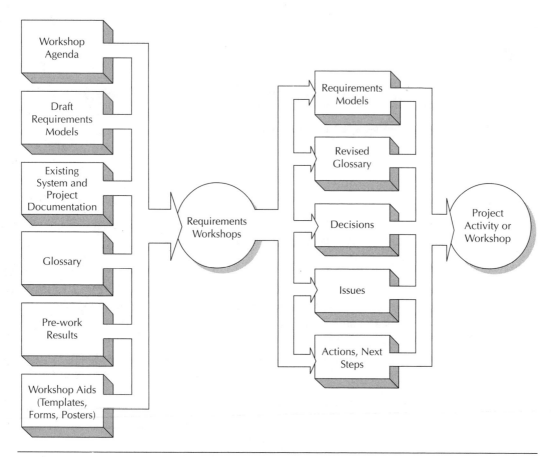

FIGURE 7-1 WORKSHOP INPUTS AND OUTPUTS

I discuss output products first because they are the basis for deciding which inputs you should use for your workshop.

OUTPUT PRODUCTS

Your primary output products are the requirements models created by the participants. (Later in this chapter I discuss intangible workshop products, such as decisions about the state of the requirements.) Along with your core requirements deliverables, you'll create supplemental deliverables, such as posters or documents that list actions or next steps, issues, and decisions.

In some cases, you may want to create supplemental workshop products to accelerate follow-up activities. In one workshop, the participants created a communication plan for organizations to be affected by the software. In another workshop, the participants identified risks and then created a risk mitigation plan and a post-workshop implementation plan. As part of an activity to jump-start their requirements modeling work, another group created a set of posters depicting a vision of what work would be like after the system was in place.

Although this book focuses on the core deliverables—the requirements models—you should consider how supplemental deliverables can dovetail with project activities and help the team to communicate effectively. Creating visually rich supplemental deliverables is fast and efficient.

MAKING DELIVERABLES VISUALLY RICH

To add visual value to deliverables, either the facilitator or the participants can use a variety of visual tools in addition to the diagram-oriented requirements models. Table 7-1 shows some formats for framing information and ideas graphically.

TABLE 7-1 VISUAL DELIVERABLES

Visual Product	Uses	Limitations
Poster	Display visions, draw themes or concepts, show agenda	Describes single point or concept
List	Brainstorm steps, define issues and expectations, identify parking lot items, name next steps	Hard to compare listed items
Clusters, affinity groups	Group related items, find themes, analyze options, associate items	Doesn't show dynamics; categories may be unclear
Arrows, flows	Cause and effect, sequence, logical progression	Implies sequence that could be incorrect
Grids, matrices	Define missing elements, clarify choices, compare choices	Can compare only a few items at a time
Drawings	Visions, stories, road maps, history, plans, business concepts	Fear of not being skilled enough to draw
Mind map	Ideas, categories, text and image groups, hierarchies	Complex to read
Circles, wheels, mandalas (circles symbolizing unity)	Unifying concepts, unstructured relationships, layers of relationships	Doesn't show details or sequence

Note that a *mind map* is an unstructured diagram that shows groupings of ideas and concepts associated with a central theme or topic (Buzan, 1989). A mind map starts with a central image or idea, which forms a focus for both eye and brain. It then branches out organically, with each branch representing a grouping or category.

The requirements models created by participants are sources for other project activities (such as design, testing, and coding) and for additional workshops (if you decide to produce requirements iteratively in a series of workshops). For example, outputs such as detailed use cases, business rules, and sketches of screens would be inputs to design and coding. You can use high-level requirements models—such as context diagrams, event tables, stakeholder classes, and use cases produced in a workshop that follows the horizontal, or "width first," workshop strategy (see Chapter 10)—as inputs to another workshop that adds more depth to those models.

To determine which requirements models to deliver, you need to do the following:

- Select model views that are aligned with the business problem domain.
- Use multiple models to increase the quality of your requirements.
- Mix text models with diagrammatic models to increase the speed of requirements definition and promote mutual learning.
- Pick multiple views and focuses (see "Model Focus" in Chapter 2) to enhance the quality of your requirements.
- Define the appropriate level of detail for each selected model.
- Iteratively deliver the requirements.
- Prioritize the requirements deliverables.
- Decide whether you should partition requirements across multiple workshops.
- Clarify your doneness tests for delivering "good enough" requirements in the workshop.

The following subsections explore these topics.

SELECT MODELS ALIGNED WITH THE BUSINESS PROBLEM

Model views—behavior, structural, dynamic, and control—provide differing perspectives of user requirements (see "Model Views" in Chapter 2). Even though each business problem is unique, the generic set of heuristics presented in Table 7-2 illustrates how the business domain influences the types of requirements models that most strongly express user requirements.

This table is intended to be representative, not inclusive. No one view can express user requirements completely, so it's important to draw from several views. For example, if users are handling the ordering task, behavior models are useful.

TABLE 7-2 HEURISTICS FOR SELECTING REQUIREMENTS MODELS

Model View	Sample Domains	Suggested Models
Behavior	Operations, administration, inventory management, payroll, hiring, order processing, billing, accounting	Actor map and table Context diagram Domain model Event table Glossary Process map Prototype Scenarios Use cases Use case map
Structural	Data query and analysis, data extraction and reporting, customer relationship management	Business policies Business rules Context diagram Domain model Glossary Prototype Scenarios
Dynamics	Workflow problems such as document management, materials management, procurement, logistics, configuration management, imaging, loan management, credit application management, demand management, contract negotiation	Event table Glossary Process map Prototype Scenarios Statechart diagrams Use case map
Control	Logistics, claim adjudication, mortgage loan underwriting, financial risk, fraud detection, product configuration, power usage, clinical diagnosis, credit checking	Business policies Business rules Decision table/decision tree Event table Glossary Scenarios

At the same time, they're interacting with business concepts and domains such as orders, cancellations, and customers, which are best captured in structural models. As you can see from the table, a glossary should always be part of your requirements deliverables; in fact, a draft glossary should always be an input product (see "Draft Models" later in this chapter).

As you learn more about the models and use them in workshops, you'll begin to recognize which ones are more useful for the business problem you're trying to solve.

One project team asked me to review its requirements workshop plan. The business problem was to create a flexible hierarchy of salespeople and commission schemes to be used globally. The group's plan called for using use cases almost exclusively. I asked them a few questions, such as, "Who will directly interact with the system?" "How frequently will they interact with it?" "What kinds of decisions do you want the system to make?" "What information does the system use?" Their answers told me that little human interaction was needed and that the core characteristic of their business problem was to establish and manage commissions, salespeople, and zones (global groups). The problem was best expressed not with behavioral models but rather with structural and control models. Consequently, we refocused the model orientation from use cases to a data model, business policies, and business rules.

USE MULTIPLE MODELS

No single user requirements model can fully express the functional requirements for your project. A solution is to use multiple models (see the Multi-Model collaboration pattern in the Appendix).

Delivering multiple models increases the comprehensiveness of your requirements because each model reveals aspects of another. In addition, you can use one model to test the correctness of another. (Chapter 9 describes how to weave testing into the workshop flow.) This testing is aided with the use of a list of model quality assurance (QA) questions devised before the workshop (see "QA Checklist " later in this chapter). Possible questions include the following:

- For each event in our event table, is there at least one associated use case?
- Which use case would handle this scenario?
- For each use case step, have all the business rules been defined?
- What data is needed to support this business rule?

The specific questions depend on which models you deliver and their degrees of detail, but you can see how one model acts to trigger elements of another model. As illustrated in Figure 7-2, using multiple models allows you thread one model to another within a single workshop.

A structural model (such a context diagram or the glossary) relates to a dynamic model (such as the event table); a behavioral model (such as a process map) provides clues for a control model (such as business policies). Figure 7-2 also illustrates the concept of "chunking" the workshop deliverables into iterations (see "Iteratively Delivering Requirements" later in this chapter).

You can arrange the sequence of your models differently, depending on what you have as a starting point (see "Draft Models" later in this chapter). An example is presented later of a variety of sequences for arriving at business rules.

MIX TEXT AND DIAGRAMMATIC MODELS

Plan for participants to deliver a combination of both text and diagrammatic requirements models. Weave both styles of products into your process design (see Chapter 9). Text models are more precise and contribute to accuracy; diagrammatic models are fast to create and understand, something that promotes overall speed in the process. The two styles also work well with regard to our two-sided brains, with the right side being more adept at dealing with things that are visual and random and the left side being stronger at linear and analytical tasks.

To put it a different way, a picture may be worth a thousand words, but the question is, Which thousand, and what do you mean by them? You need words to answer that.

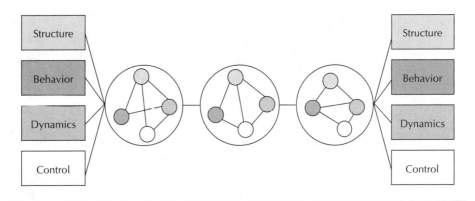

FIGURE 7-2 THREADING MULTIPLE MODELS THROUGH A WORKSHOP

Consider mixing text with diagrams for each view you deliver. For example:

- Use case text and a use case map
- An actor table and an actor map
- A glossary definition and a data model

Some models are strictly text-based and require visual models in order to elicit them. Business rules and business policies are good examples. You won't get too far asking business people, "What business rules do you need?" Instead, you need visual models that will call up the business rules. One way to overcome this problem is to represent business rules using a decision table or decision tree. Another way is to start harvesting business rules using other models. The BestClaims case study in Chapter 11 provides an example of using a visual model (a statechart diagram) to drive the specification of business rules.

Models for Harvesting Business Rules

You can use all or part of a model to thread to another model. For example, a single step of a use case gives you a thread to the data attributes needed by a data model and also to the business rules that must be enforced within that step. To arrive at business rules, you can use a variety of sequences, including the following:

- Use case → events → business policies → business rules
- Use cases → actors → domain model (class model or data entities) → business rules
- Actor → decisions → business rules
- Actors → use cases → domain model → business rules
- Events → domain model → business rules
- Events → use cases → business rules
- Events → domain model → life cycles → business rules
- Domain model → events → life cycles → business rules

MIX FOCUSES AND VIEWS

Draw from various requirements model focuses (who, what, when, where, why, and how) as well as views. Here's a typical combination:

- Use cases are a behavior view focused on *how* work gets done.
- An actor map is also a behavior view, but it focuses on *who* does the work.

- A data model or class model is a structural view focused on *what* information is needed.
- Business rules are a control view focused on *why*—the decisions that software needs to make.

Eliciting a combination of models with different focuses helps you to detect requirements errors. In one of my workshops, for example, the use cases that were created made the customer realize that at least 20 business rules needed to be defined more precisely before the requirements could be closed. The model view can trigger creation of additional models that provide more focuses. For example, if you choose a behavioral view of your requirements (say, use cases), you can use those use cases to harvest related models.

DEFINE THE LEVEL OF DETAIL

Decide how precise each requirements deliverable should be (see Table 2-4 in Chapter 2).

Scope-level models are particularly important when there's a high risk of scope creep or conflict among users about requirements, or when the requirements aren't precise enough to support the start of design work. In that case, if users and developers expect to make the transition to design at the end of a workshop that delivers that level of detail, you'll have many unhappy project team members.

A useful strategy for moving from scope-level or high-level requirements down to detailed-level requirements is to use iterations. This involves working together to deliver a set of models at roughly the same level of precision, checking their quality, and then moving down to the next level of detail. This approach is a top-down horizontal strategy (see "Building a Horizontal Strategy: The Top-Down Approach" in Chapter 10). Iterating in a top-down manner can accelerate the group's mutual understanding of the requirements and reduce rework within the workshop.

But you may not always want to elicit your requirements models in that top-down order. If your project has a well-defined scope, the team should be ready to jump into high-level requirements. In some cases (particularly if you're replacing an existing system), you'll start at a lower level of detail, with prototype screens and use case steps. At other times, you'll iterate among the levels in a zigzag strategy (see "The Zigzag Strategy" in Chapter 10).

Each project is unique. To decide the best way to elicit user requirements in workshops, you'll need to consider factors such as team size, location, degree of customer and user involvement, past history with software development, existing documentation and software, and team modeling experience.

ITERATIVELY DELIVERING REQUIREMENTS

As you consider each requirements model you want to deliver, begin to partition the model into its component parts. For example, divide a detailed use case into its name, header information (such as the triggering event, event response, and initiating actor), and use case steps. Next, group elements from your various models at about the same level of detail.

Figure 7-3 shows how a use case and its related requirements can be grouped in an iterative fashion.

Although this example shows four iterations, you can use two or three iterations. This example moves from the high level to the detailed level, following what I call the vertical, how-first strategy (see Chapter 10), in which you drill down within one focus. Note that if you choose this strategy, time will constrain how many use cases (and related requirements) you can deliver.

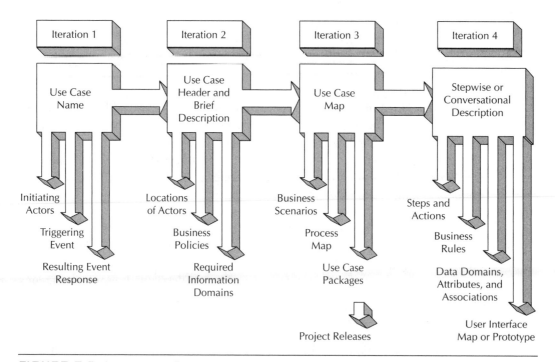

FIGURE 7-3 ITERATIVELY DELIVERING REQUIREMENTS IN A WORKSHOP

In iteration 1, participants begin with a named use case; they then define the initiating actor, the triggering event, and the event response. In iteration 2, using the prior set of requirements, participants complete the use case header using a use case template (see "Templates" later in this chapter). They do this by writing a one-paragraph description of the use case, adding the locations of the actors, listing the associated business policies, and modeling the high-level domain model (class model or data entities).

In iteration 3, participants create a *use case map* to visually lay out the predecessor-successor relationships among the use cases. (Creating a *process map* puts the use cases in the context of the workflow, giving the team the big picture of the set of requirements. This map also allows the users to understand how the use cases can fit into their workflow. This work is accelerated if a process map has been created before the workshop.) Participants logically partition use cases into packages, which in turn they'll use to define releases or increments for delivery.

In iteration 4, the participants add detailed use case steps, define business rules for each step, list data attributes needed by the steps and their rules, and sketch prototypes for each use case.

At the end of each iteration—which should take one to three hours, depending on the number of use cases—participants should test the quality of the models they've delivered (see "Define Doneness Tests" later in this chapter) in order to reach closure on that set of requirements before moving on to another set.

Using a "divide and conquer" approach helps you to avoid workshop scope creep—getting off-track during the workshop by moving up and down to different levels of detail. It also gives you a basis for ordering group activities. You also save time by eliminating the step of cleaning models up.

Chapter 9 describes ways to assign work to subgroups, iterating among individual, subgroup, and whole group activities for maximum efficiency.

PRIORITIZE THE DELIVERABLES

It's not possible to predict exactly how long it will take to deliver each model. Knowing what's important *before* you begin the workshop will help you to adjust the agenda during the session. Decide with your sponsor and planning team which of the planned requirements models are the most critical and which can be skipped or skimmed if you run out of time.

Know whether you need to deliver *more* models with *less* precision or *fewer* models with *more* precision. This will influence the number of QA activities you build into the schedule. For one set of workshops I facilitated, the products included business rules, a data model, and life cycles for a well-defined scope. The work was to be done in four- to six-hour sessions within a four-week time frame. Anticipating that we might not complete all the deliverables, I needed to know which was more important: volume or quality. I asked the workshop sponsor what she wanted from the workshops: *more* business rules, or fewer, but *more correct*, business rules. She chose quality over volume. For that reason, I designed an agenda that added scenarios as a deliverable and also incorporated a process for testing each set of business rules with those scenarios before moving on to another set of rules.

Estimating Time

There is no magic formula for knowing how long it will take to deliver your requirements in a workshop. You must consider people factors and product factors.

People factors include how "formed" the group is as you begin (see "Forming, Storming, Norming, and Performing" in Chapter 6). Newly formed groups need more time before they can be productive, whereas a group that has worked together will be able to get down to business more quickly.

Product factors include how "done" you need your requirements to be and how much of a head start you have before the workshop. You'll need more time if your requirements must be very precise and well tested or if you don't have models to serve as a starting point. Chapter 9 has generic guidelines for workshop timing by model.

I can offer a general heuristic from my years of experience: List the deliverables you think the group can deliver in the workshop, and then divide your expectations by 3. The result will be a more realistic estimate. For example, if you think you will deliver a revised glossary, stepwise use case descriptions, prototype screens, and a high-level data model, you're likely to deliver one-third of the content for each deliverable. This is why it's important to prioritize your requirements deliverables before the workshop.

Wise Groups

Once participants have a good understanding of their requirements and are working well together, you should consult them about which ones are most important to work on together. Well-formed groups are very wise: The participants know what to do together and how to compensate for time pressures. For example, one group I facilitated decided to work through four high-priority use cases and then trust two of the participants to draft the remaining ones and return for a workshop to review, revise, and approve them.

PARTITION REQUIREMENTS ACROSS WORKSHOPS

If you're under tight time constraints or if your group is new and will need time to form, consider delivering your requirements iteratively across multiple workshops. An advantage of this approach is the efficient use of group time; participants take on post-workshop tasks, and the group uses that work as input to later workshops.

After one workshop in which we created high-level requirements, the participants went back to their business areas to ask questions of their colleagues and management so that they'd be prepared to provide details about the use cases and assess their priority. In another workshop, a list of business policies became the basis for research by a business analyst to determine which policies could be changed along with the new system. In yet another workshop, we used the high-level data model created by the participants to conduct data mapping for two possible software packages; in that way, we were able to provide details for selecting a software package in the next workshop.

Figure 7-4 shows an example. Each workshop delivers a predefined set of related requirements. These requirements then serve as inputs to another workshop occurring soon thereafter. I like to schedule iterative workshops no more than five working days apart.

There are numerous ways to arrange your session. You can conduct daily morning sessions and leave afternoons for post-workshop tasks, as described in the HaveFunds example in Chapter 11; you can use multiday workshops within a one- or two-week period, and so on. Use a schedule that optimizes the availability of people without exhausting them. Try to include time off between tasks that you will use to jump-start the next workshop.

DEFINE DONENESS TESTS

Doneness Tests

A *doneness test* consists of one or more criteria that you use to determine whether a particular deliverable is "good enough" to reach closure on. Your doneness tests will be more or less precise depending on three factors:

- The project's size (the number of people being coordinated)
- The criticality of the systems being created
- The priorities of the project (whether, for example, human lives are at stake or simply human comfort)

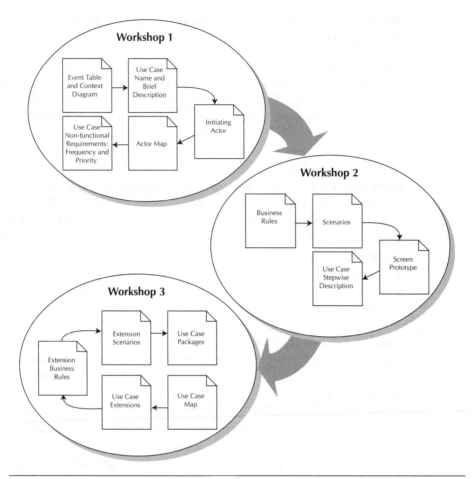

FIGURE 7-4 PARTITIONING REQUIREMENTS ACROSS WORKSHOPS

As Cockburn (2001) aptly points out, more correctness and documentation are needed by projects with a large number of team members producing critical systems using nondiscretionary funds. A "light" set of models would not do in that situation. If, however, you're building an application for internal consumption with a medium risk of monetary loss if you deliver defects, your doneness tests can be looser.

Different stakeholders have different views of doneness:

- A customer might want to deliver the requirements and end product as quickly and cheaply as possible. Perhaps you need only do some scope requirements and a prototype. The desire is to deliver relatively little detail for fewer requirements models.

- A user might be concerned with usability, so you'd focus on translating requirements associated with *who* and *how* focuses—such as actors, actor maps, prototypes, interface navigation diagrams, use cases, and use case maps—into more precise requirements.

- A software designer or architect might be most interested in building a robust product. She would want requirements models that cross multiple views and focuses, thus offering a broader understanding of the whole project rather than only the current release.

Each of these perspectives presents a special challenge to the requirements facilitator, who must help the team determine the most appropriate doneness tests for the short term while also considering the long-term goals of the project and the needs of the various stakeholders.

Your doneness tests can involve the use of a tool or a process. Available tools and processes include the following:

- A QA checklist for testing the models (see the next section)
- Scenario- or prototype-based reviews integrated into your workshop process (see Chapter 9)
- Matrices for analyzing one model or model element against another
- Metaphors for testing doneness

QA CHECKLIST   A *quality assurance (QA) checklist* is a series of questions, usually stated in binary format, about a requirements model or its elements, along with questions about how one model cross-checks another. For example, if you're producing an actor table, use cases, and the glossary, these questions would apply for each use case:

- Is the use case named as an actor's goal?
- Does the use case name start with a strong action verb?
- Does the use case name include a meaningful object?
- Is the object in the use case name defined in the glossary?

The Web site for this book offers other QA checklist questions.

Using QA checklists provides more benefits than may be immediately obvious. The very process of creating and agreeing on the checklist helps the team—users, software team, perhaps even sponsors—to clarify and define expectations for each deliverable clearly and precisely. As with using reviews during a workshop (see Chapter 9), checklists push participants to create high-quality requirements in the first place. The checklist forces you to begin with the end in mind.

In one workshop I facilitated, the group created scope-level requirements in the form of an event table and a context diagram. I divided the group of 14 people into subgroups. Each subgroup received a copy of the same checklist.

As a facilitator, I've discovered that participants give you what you ask for. My experience is that taking a testing attitude toward deliverables helps workshop participants to find more defects and find them earlier. So I told them, "Find errors in what we created."

Each subgroup indeed found defects, which were shared with the larger group and corrected. For example, the group forgot that it had to get periodic updates from an employee database, and it realized that it would need someone to play the role of approving certain types of queries to sensitive data. After that, the group continued the workshop by defining detailed requirements for each event within the scope.

MATRICES *Matrices* can help you to detect incomplete and extraneous requirements; they also serve as a useful tool for checking doneness. Participants can also create complete matrices to detect missing or extraneous requirements.

In the matrix in Table 7-3, participants fill in the cells to indicate which actors initiate which use cases. An actor without an associated use case (such as Actor02) indicates either an extraneous actor or a missing use case. Perhaps having two initiating actors might be fine (as in UseCase01); or perhaps it indicates that the actors are truly the same and that you might benefit from having a more generic name for an actor.

TABLE 7-3 Sample Matrix for Doneness Testing

	Actor01	Actor02	Actor03	Actor04
UseCase01	x		x	
UseCase02				x
UseCase03			x	
UseCase04	x			

METAPHORS

A *metaphor* is a symbol, image, or figure of speech. You can use a metaphor as a loose form of doneness testing. In one workshop, we used a bull's-eye. I created a poster with a bull's-eye showing concentric circles with the label "100%" in the center. The sponsor and planning team declared before the workshop that the goal was to achieve 80 percent doneness for the models. At the end of each workshop day, I gave each participant a colored sticky dot and asked each of them to place the dot on the bull's-eye to represent where he believed our requirements deliverables were at the moment.

Each day, over four days, participants placed different dots on the bull's-eye. Each day, they got closer to the center. I also used each day's bull's-eye in leading a brief discussion about what they needed to do to get closer the next day.

Metaphors can also include wishes in the form of lists, scenarios, or visions. In one of my workshops, participants wrote stories of an ideal future, describing their work environment after all their requirements were met. In another, participants provided a list of ideal reports they could get if their requirements were met. For yet another, participants drew posters of their ideal operational environment.

Each of these metaphors serves as a doneness test because you can ask participants to return to their original metaphors or visions after they create their requirements to see whether their vision has been achieved.

DONENESS TESTING AND DECISION MAKING

No matter which doneness tests you use, they're not a substitute for your decision rule and decision-making process (see "Decision Rules" in Chapter 6). Your doneness tests check only the desired level of quality of your requirements, so you must follow up with your agreed-upon decision-making process. If a doneness test tells you that you have "uncooked" requirements, you can still make a decision on how to proceed.

In one of my workshops, the decision maker was the business project manager; he was also a subject matter expert. He decided to reach closure on a set of use cases, prototype screens, and business rules even though some of the QA answers indicated that the models were not complete. By following the decision-making process, he learned that the participants, including the software team, supported the current states of the models despite the flaws. He made the decision to declare them good enough, and we moved on to another set of requirements.

Combining Pre-Work with Doneness Tests: An Example

For one workshop I facilitated, plant managers needed to provide high-level data requirements for financial analysis. There were many complaints about the existing data: It was inconsistent, incorrect, late, and more. The primary deliverable for the workshop would be a data model, supplemented by the questions that managers would need to ask to run their plants, streamline operations, and meet operating targets.

Using a spreadsheet, I created a template in which they would enter their plant-management questions along with the business reasons for the questions, the decisions they made based on the answers, and a list of specific data attributes they would need. During the workshop, a review of those questions led to the discovery of high-level data entities and attributes.

We also asked the plant managers to bring to the workshop a list of the top three reports they used to help run the business, and a list of their top five "wish list" reports.

Their pre-work served as doneness tests for their data requirements, which in the workshop were listed on wall posters. In subgroups, the managers responded to these questions:

- Can you get the top three reports using the questions you've created? (If not, write a new question.)

- Can you get the top three reports with the data shown on the walls? (If not, add all the missing data to the entity—we called them data groupings in the workshop—to which it belongs.)

- Will your wish list reports answer the questions you've created? (If not, add one or more new questions to get answers.)

- Will your wish list reports be answered with the data shown on the walls? (If not, add all of the data to the appropriate data grouping.)

INTANGIBLE OUTPUT PRODUCTS

In addition to the tangible deliverables, your workshop should deliver *intangible* outcomes, including decisions, enhanced knowledge, and increased motivation.

Stopping to test for closure—in other words, to make decisions about the state of your requirements—sounds, on the surface, as if it would take valuable workshop time. Actually, it speeds up a workshop. Forcing an explicit decision creates tension as you talk about what is missing, wrong, or important. It requires you to analyze related details. It emboldens communication.

Making decisions explicit requires the group to define ground rules for achieving closure (see "Basic Ground Rules" in Chapter 6). Reaching closure requires that you combine your doneness tests with the use of a decision rule process.

The technique is simple: You explicitly define what needs to be decided during your workshop, and then add those decisions to the list of output products. Ask the workshop sponsor or project sponsor to remind people about it during the workshop kickoff. Typical decisions include the following:

- The scope of the project as represented by the requirements
- Which requirements, as represented by use cases, will be delivered for the current release
- The detailed requirements and their priorities for the next release

You also need to know whether other intangible outcomes are desired, such as people leaving the workshop with increased knowledge or motivation. These can be the healing hidden agendas discussed in Chapter 6. If you specify these outcomes, you must design workshop activities to incorporate ways of addressing them (see Chapter 9).

Note that this might prompt you to revise the list of workshop observers (see "Observers" in Chapter 5). When one intangible outcome is to increase the software team's knowledge of the business, for example, include developers and testers as observers. For one project, one desirable intangible outcome was for analysts and the project leader to become knowledgeable about how to conduct a requirements workshop. We included them as observers; I gave them a list of questions to keep handy while they observed. After the requirements workshop, we also conducted a debrief and an action planning workshop to help them incorporate, in their own projects, what they learned from observing.

When you ask questions about intangible outcomes, you might uncover hidden agendas. When I asked one project leader about intangibles, he told me that the team members were discouraged by prior requirements efforts and were concerned that they wouldn't learn anything new. He wanted to enhance the team's motivation. We decided that it was important for the project sponsor to kick off the workshop and for subject matter experts, not surrogates, to attend.

In another project, the sponsor wanted to increase team members' motivation. In addition to having him kick off the workshop, I facilitated a brief activity in which each person shared his or her professional development goals.

INPUT PRODUCTS

Once you've planned your workshop outputs, it's time to determine what input products you need. Using a set of well-thought-out input products speeds up your workshop and helps groups reach closure.

Input products include a variety of materials that prepare participants for the mental work they'll do, provide tools for jump-starting workshop activities, give guidance for creating higher-quality requirements models, and serve as doneness test resources. Input products can include the following:

- The workshop agenda
- Draft requirements models
- Systems and user documentation
- The results of pre-work
- Templates
- Workshop aids

The following subsections discuss each of these kinds of input products.

THE WORKSHOP AGENDA

The *workshop agenda* is an ordered list of activities planned for the session. The agenda, which you send to all the participants before the workshop, should also include your other P's: purpose, participants, principles, products, and place. (See Chapter 9 for tips on designing your agenda; an agenda template is available on the book's Web site.)

DRAFT MODELS

Use predecessor requirements models or draft output models to jump-start your modeling work. For example, if you're creating use cases in the workshop, you can use an actor table or an actor map as a mechanism to help you create a list of use cases. By using focus questions about the predecessor model (for example, "What goals does this actor have for interacting with the system?"), you can elicit another related model. (See "Using Focus Questions" in Chapter 9 for more about focus questions.)

You can also use predecessor and draft requirements in performing doneness tests on models. For example, a list of scenarios created before the workshop can be used in testing use cases. To test for doneness during the workshop, you can use pre-work such as user-created scenarios and prototype screens created by the software team by walking through them in parallel with use case steps.

A draft version of a model provides the basis for an activity to fix or finish it. For example, you can use a draft event table or context diagram during an activity in which the group reaches closure on scope. A rough version of a statechart diagram gives you a starting point for generating more states, which in turn triggers events and business rules.

At a minimum, *you should create a draft glossary before a requirements workshop*. The terms in the glossary are the semantic basis for all your user requirements; the definitions are themselves fundamental business rules.

I like to ask one person to be the *glossary guardian,* the person in charge of keeping the glossary up-to-date during the workshop (see illustration on page 163). The job of the glossary guardian is to listen for business terms that haven't been defined or that might need to be clarified. Allow everyone to tune in to terms; challenge each participant to also play the role of glossary guardian. (To make it fun, I sometimes announce a reward for anyone who stops the group when a term needs to be defined or clarified. Reverse rewards can work, too, if you make them humorous—for example, getting "banged" with a rubber hammer if you use a term without explaining it.)

Data modelers make excellent glossary guardians because they naturally think in terms of words and their connections, and they often seek precise definitions of business terms.

UNIVERSAL MODELS   An alternative or supplemental draft model you can use as input is a *universal model*. This generic business model is documented in books or available for purchase from consulting companies.

Universal models tend to be abstract. They use generic business terms (*business party, transaction, event, agreement*) that you can use as starting points for modeling activities. For example, if the universal model is represented as a data model, participants can list examples of each concept in the model or list subtypes to jump-start the modeling of their own domain model.

SYSTEMS AND USER DOCUMENTATION

It's a good idea to have documentation available that might be useful during the workshop. This includes the project charter or vision statement, organization charts, operating procedures and guidelines, reference manuals, user documentation, help desk documentation, user job aids, training manuals and documentation, and systems manuals and documentation. Identify each document that might be useful, and be sure that someone is responsible for bringing it.

PRE-WORK

Pre-work involves specific assignments for participants to complete before the workshop. Examples of pre-work include filling out a template that lists steps to complete a task, naming business rules in a specific format for a set of use cases, listing stakeholders and their functional areas, reviewing and commenting on a set of draft use cases, reading the project charter, listing key inputs needed by users, and drawing a poster that depicts an image of the future after the requirements have been met.

Asking participants to complete pre-work has one or more of these benefits:

- It mentally prepares participants for the type of thinking they'll do in the workshop.
- It provides research information and starting points to one or more workshop activities.
- It forces participants to seek information from other experts who might fill gaps in their subject matter expertise.

Specifying some kind of pre-work signals that the requirements workshop isn't an ordinary meeting.

Pre-work is essential when you're operating under a tight time frame, when users are surrogates and not real subject matter experts, when participants hail from different business areas, or when you'll be working with detailed requirements. Your workshop schedule must take into account the time for preparing pre-work. For example, you may need to create a template with instructions (see "Templates" next).

Designing pre-work is one thing, but how do you get participants to complete it? Your sponsor and your planning team can help. For example:

- Have the pre-work assignments made by the sponsor or an influential planning team member.
- Provide information at least one week before the workshop.
- Conduct an orientation meeting to brief participants on how to complete the pre-work, particularly if their assignments are complex.
- Ask the workshop sponsor or project sponsor to send e-mail or voice mail to the participants requesting that they complete their pre-work.
- Have the pre-work responses sent to the workshop sponsor or a planning team member rather than to the facilitator.

Workshop Orientation Meetings

Under certain circumstances I like to arrange orientation meetings before workshops.

In one workshop I facilitated, participants came from around the globe. They had pre-work assignments and would be gathering in a central location for the session. Many of them had never participated in a requirements workshop, and few of them knew one another. We arranged a videoconference orientation meeting kicked off by the project sponsor. In this meeting, we reviewed the workshop agenda and clarified how to complete the pre-work. We also discussed important issues such as what to wear and how they would access their voice mail on breaks during the workshop. This 45-minute meeting helped to break the ice before the live workshop.

Here are some circumstances under which you should consider holding an orientation meeting:

- Participants have pre-work assignments that may involve completing templates or doing complex research.
- Participants don't know one another.
- Participants would benefit from hearing suggestions for what materials to bring to the workshop.
- You are meeting over a period of days or weeks.

Keep the meeting short, and be sure you have the project or workshop sponsor kick it off to set the stage.

TEMPLATES

Templates are standardized formats that you use during workshop activities to structure the contents of an output product. Templates can be used for building the requirements models, prioritizing requirements, creating related deliverables (such as an action plan or a communication plan), debriefing the workshop, and assessing the team climate (if you incorporate team-building activities into the workshop).

Creating templates forces your workshop planning team to think deeply about project-specific deliverables. It also helps participants to make the best use of their workshop time, and it helps you to provide precise, clear instructions about workshop tasks.

Business Rules Templates

Business rules come in many forms and categories, including terms, facts, constraints, factor clauses, and action clauses. There's no agreement on a standard set of categories for business rules—nor should there be, because the rules should fit the business problem. Some business problems are more business rule-*based* (for example, insurance underwriting), whereas others are more business rule-*constrained* (such as payroll). Business rules are vital for high-quality requirements, and they also provide useful links to other requirements models.

You can capture your business rules as free-form statements generated by business people, but these statements tend to be ambiguous and not rigorous. Each free-form business rule may decompose into numerous rules. You must untangle each statement and resolve its internal inconsistencies. Also, it's hard to trace such unstructured statements to other requirements models, and they create change control headaches. If the rules are smaller and more discrete, you can more easily manage change. To capture business rules atomically, it helps to have a business rule template designed for the purpose.

A *business rule template* presents standard, precise syntax for writing business rules. The template should be designed so that the resulting business rules are declarative, atomic, distinct, independent statements. The very process of tailoring a template to a particular business problem is beneficial because it requires you to understand the problem in great depth. This means working directly with business customers to design and tailor the template.

Examples of useful business rule templates include the following:

- Each <business term> may <verb phrase> <business term>.
- When <event|condition is true>, then <action>.
- If <condition true>, then <condition true/conclusion>.

You can use your templates during the workshop to guide participants in writing business rules.

For one workshop, I worked with the planning team to settle on a template for the use cases. For another, I created a business requirements matrix template for use during the workshop. For yet another, I designed a simple form for capturing scenarios. In another case, I devised a template for scenario testing our use cases and data model. In several workshops in which the subsequent software product had cross-functional impact, I used a communication plan template. For most workshops delivering precise business rules, a business rule template is also critical.

Your template should include instructions (or it should be supplemented by a document work aid that has instructions) and perhaps examples of how to properly complete the template. Templates can be created as word processing documents or can be drawn on posters. If your recorder acts as a technographer (see Chapter 5), she can input the group's work into a word processor. You can then display or print the contents of all completed templates for participants to refer to or review during the session.

Templates help to ensure that you get high-quality, consistent information from participants. This is especially critical when you use multiple subgroups working on different requirements for the same model at the same time during the session, a technique discussed in Chapter 9. Templates also force you to clarify doneness tests because you must describe what each deliverable should look like. If you can visualize what the group members must deliver, it's easier to design the collaborative processes to get them there. Templates also help you to give precise instructions to the group during the workshop.

You can supplement the template with a completed example (see "Examples" later in this chapter), which helps participants understand the models they need to create.

WORKSHOP AIDS

Workshop aids are tools for conducting activities in the session. These aids include static posters for participants to reference, sample models, instructions or tips to use while working on the models, worksheets for documenting changes to models, and materials and supplies.

POSTERS   *Posters* are charts that are visible in the room. Create your posters before the workshop, and place them on the workshop room walls using tape, pins, or tacks or by using sticky poster paper (posters on a pad with the top back prepared with repositionable glue). You should prepare posters with the following titles:

- Workshop Purpose
- Workshop Products
- Workshop Agenda (the flow of activities)
- Issues or Parking Lot (titled and left blank)
- Input Products
- Actions (titled and left blank)
- Decisions (titled and left blank)

Tips for Working on Posters

- Print in thick, CAPITAL letters.
- Write straight up and down.
- Use plain block letters (not script).
- Avoid black, except for numbering charts.
- Use these colors for text: blue, brown, purple, green.
- Use these colors for highlighting: orange, red, yellow, pink.
- Be faithful to people's own words.
- Use white space liberally.
- Consider using the symbols shown in Table 7-4.

EXAMPLES Sample models use a "begin with the end in mind" philosophy: They show participants what the end product should look like by providing simple but correct examples. I've found these examples useful for almost every re-

TABLE 7-4 POSTER SYMBOLS

•	Bullets (centered dot) to help items stand apart
☆	Stars for noteworthy items
○	Circles to connect ideas and draw attention to items
▭	Borders to frame a page or blocks of text
→	Arrows for sequences, cycles, and merging

quirements model that employs a template, including use cases, business rules, and scenarios. To create examples that are relevant to the problem, consult with your planning team or other subject matter experts. Even an example that's wrong, but is correctly written or drawn, is useful for participants.

INSTRUCTIONS AND TIPS   Prefabricated instructions or guidelines can help you save time during the workshop. Tell participants what they need to do for each workshop activity, and also give them written instructions (paper handouts or on posters). This method gives everyone a reference point for completing activities.

Provide instructions, especially early in a workshop, for subgroup activities (see Chapter 9). For example, instructions might stipulate that there should be a time-keeper, a recorder, and someone to make sure that the content of the work follows a template format.

It's a good idea to include tips for creating high-quality models. In one workshop, I gave participants a list of good verbs to use in their use case names. In another, I provided a list of verbs for them to use for data model relationships. These kinds of tips help save workshop time.

WORKSHEETS   Your recorder can use worksheets for tracking the disposition of and changes to requirements models. When your recorder uses a laptop with a word processor or spreadsheet program, you can project the changes on a screen or print them for reference. In several workshops that delivered use cases, I found a use case completion worksheet helpful (see the Web site for an example).

A note of caution: Don't assume that your readers will be able to understand your workshop aids. Test any input products you create—instructions, examples, tips, worksheets— before you give them to participants. Ask planning team members and a few of the participants to review the instructions and see whether they understand them. Then, during the workshop, review the instructions and ask for clarifying questions.

MATERIALS AND SUPPLIES   Materials and supplies include all the physical things you'll need to run the workshop: items such as name cards, posters, cards or sticky notes, color markers, paper cutters, side-hole punches, a printer, and binders. (A generic list is available on the Web site.)

Set up binders with dividers in which participants can store all the paper documents they'll work with during the session. I like to supply tab dividers already labeled for things such as purpose, principles, and agenda. The binders can also hold copies of modeling tips, activity instructions, templates, and examples.

After the workshop, participants can use the binders for reference and for storing hard copies of requirements and workshop and project information. Binders save people time by helping them to avoid searching through large sets of documents. They also help participants stay organized during the workshop, and using them sends a message that their work warrants a special storage place.

THE WORKSHOP REPOSITORY

The *workshop repository* is where you store the soft copies of your workshop products, pre-work, and post-workshop products. You might use a project Web site, a requirements management tool, a network folder, or a combination of these. Remind participants before, during, and after the session about the repository. Arrange access for them, allowing them to deposit any pre-work there.

TIPS

- For your workshop deliverables, use a combination of text and diagrammatic models.
- Select requirements models that align with the problem domain.
- Use multiple views and focuses.
- Partition each requirements model into parts; group parts at the same level of detail.
- Prioritize your expected deliverables.
- Be realistic about how much participants can deliver.
- Design or use templates for your requirements deliverables.
- Provide examples or draft models for participants to use as starters.
- Assign pre-work to participants.
- Define doneness tests for each requirements model you plan to deliver.
- Use multiple workshops integrating the best practices listed here (see the example in Figure 7-5).

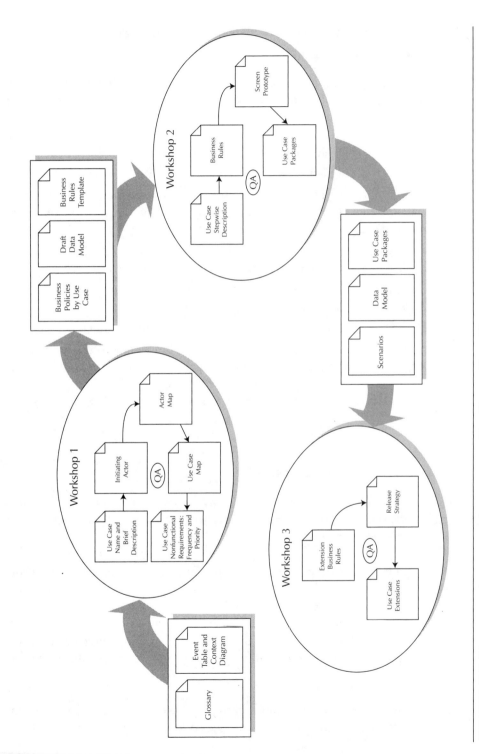

FIGURE 7-5 WORKSHOP ITERATIONS INTEGRATING PRE-WORK, POST-WORK, AND QA

QUESTIONS TO ASK STAKEHOLDERS ABOUT PRODUCTS

The following questions can help you determine workshop inputs and outputs. You can preface these questions by saying, "The next set of questions will help us determine what products to deliver during the workshop."

- What deliverables do you expect to produce in the workshop?
- How much detail should each deliverable have?
- What criteria will you use to determine that the deliverables are complete, clear, and correct? How will we know that they have the quality you expect and need?
- Would you rather have more requirements delivered at a higher level of detail, or fewer requirements with more detail?
- What products are needed as input to the workshop? How much lead time do we have to pull together input products?
- Who can review the instructions for the group activities that we'll create?
- Where will the workshop materials be stored (a workshop repository)? Do we need to do any work to create this repository?

See the Web site for the book for more questions about workshop products.

FOR MORE INFORMATION

Boehm and Basili (2001) summarize 10 ways to reduce defects in code, including peer reviews and perspective-based reviews (such as using scenarios to walk through your requirements).

Boehm and Hoh (1999) describe a technique for analyzing and negotiating conflicts in requirements.

Brooks (1995), a classic on the human aspects of software engineering, points out that eliciting requirements is the most difficult part of building software. The author emphasizes the need to continually refine and iterate requirements with customers.

Buzan (1989) provides insights and techniques, based on research on the human brain, for tapping into the right and left sides of our brains.

Cockburn (2001) presents wisdom on how software teams work best. Chapter 4, on methodologies, provides an excellent discussion on how you must tailor your methodology for each project, including the types of work products and their precision.

Cohen (1995) provides a step-by-step guide to quality function deployment (QFD), a systematic methodology for deriving and evaluating product features from both customer and designer points of view. The key technique, the "voice of the customer," is explained along with Kano's understanding of quality from the customer's perspective.

Chapter 9 of Highsmith (2000) discusses workstate lifecycle management, in which teams iteratively deliver components (from requirements to code and tests) in a predefined state, rather than focus on workflow.

Howell (1995) is a useful reference for a variety of visual tools you can adapt for your supplemental workshop deliverables. Included are tools for representing text information in provocative and interesting ways, such as circles, continuums, workflows, t-charts, and a variety of worksheets.

THE GLOSSARY GUARDIAN KEEPS THE GLOSSARY UP-TO-DATE DURING THE WORKSHOP (SEE PAGE 153).

8

PLACE: BEING THERE

For *same time–same place* collaboration—the topic of this book—it's important to ensure that the physical space for your workshop is conducive to group work. In addition to finding a place of suitable size, you'll need to attend to other logistical issues, such as access to wall space, equipment you'll use during the workshop, and food. And remember to accommodate people's needs during breaks, such as bathrooms and phones.

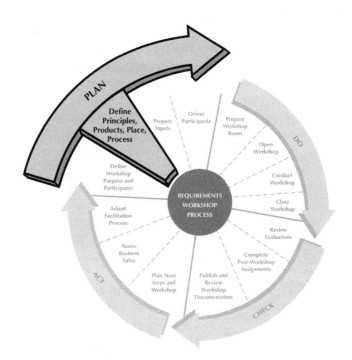

WORKSHOP LOGISTICS

Logistical concerns for a workshop may appear mundane, but attention to these details is vital for a successful workshop. For one 16-person requirements workshop I facilitated, our large room easily accommodated three full walls of posters and storyboards, an area for refreshments, and even separate "breakout" rooms for small-group activities. Lunches and snacks, nearby bathrooms, and several phones in a gathering area outside the room made our multiday workshop much more pleasant than it otherwise would have been.

Shared Space

Table 8-1 lists the factors you should consider when scouting a workshop location.

Requirements workshops lasting a day or longer are best located offsite. As Table 8-2 suggests, participants' focus is generally better when they're offsite.

Having a workshop offsite also communicates the importance of the collaboration because it involves physical separation from the normal work venue. A group member's home can be a low-cost alternative to renting offsite space. In one of my projects, the software project leader volunteered her finished basement, which had plenty of wall space, for our workshop. This provided a warm and welcoming environment away from the pressures of the office.

Participants can help you to make the best of any room. If the layout is unexpected, ask them to help arrange the room. This makes the room theirs and gets them collaborating right away. I also ask for one person to volunteer to be the "temperature monitor." Her job is to adjust the thermostat or act as the focal point for contacting the building's maintenance workers if necessary to get the room comfortable. During the workshop opening, I ask for a volunteer and then request that everyone make any room temperature requests of that person.

Know what kind of wall space you will have. For one of my workshops, the business analyst was pleased to tell me that she had secured an offsite location used for business meetings and known for its setting and elegant interior design. When I inquired about wall space, I found out that there was virtually none; columns were spaced along the meeting room walls, and one side had a series of windows. It would be impossible to lay out sticky walls (see "Creating Sticky Walls" later in this chapter) for modeling our user requirements.

I arranged to rent four large wallboards with rollers. Without those, we wouldn't have been able to accomplish our workshop goals.

TABLE 8-1 PHYSICAL LOCATION CONSIDERATIONS

Factor	Comments and Suggestions
Location	Offsite locations help people to focus on the workshop. Be sure to suggest "business casual" dress. It's good to have a place nearby for posting messages for participants to check during breaks.
Size	The room should be large enough for people to move around the walls and work in small groups, have space for refreshments, and comfortably accommodate participants, observers, and visiting sponsors. If possible, find a location with separate breakout areas nearby so that small groups can work quietly together.
Wall space	There should be at least two walls with enough space to place static posters (such as Ground Rules, Purpose, Products, and Agenda posters) as well as contiguous wall space for modeling work (for example, at least six or more feet wide and four or more feet wide).
Equipment	There should be at least one phone outside the room. (Pull the plugs or turn off ringers to prevent incoming calls to any phones inside the room.) Make sure that adequate outlets exist for the recorder's laptop and printer.
Seats, tables, and ergonomics	Comfortable chairs make for comfortable minds. Ensure an even room temperature (68°F is best) and adequate lighting, and block any intrusive noise from nearby rooms. Each chair should have sufficient table space for writing and reviewing handouts.
Food and drink	Food always draws people, and allowing people to break bread together is a simple and powerful way to build trust. Provide refreshments for all workshops that will last at least two hours. In mid-afternoon, avoid high-sugar items (cookies, cake, candy); instead, supply low-fat carbohydrates such as pretzels and popcorn. For sessions that span lunch time, provide lunch, and be sensitive to the dietary needs of your participants.
Access to on-the-fly subject matter experts	If you're onsite, you might want to choose a location near your SMEs. With their prior permission, this makes it easy to invite them for a brief appearance at the workshop to answer questions. Another option is to ensure telephone access for participants to phone on-call SMEs (see "On-Call Subject Matter Experts" in Chapter 5).

TABLE 8-2   ONSITE VERSUS OFFSITE LOCATION CONSIDERATIONS

Plus or Minus	Onsite	Offsite
+	▪ More convenient for participants ▪ Less costly ▪ Less travel hassle ▪ More control over logistics and access to materials	▪ Change in venue relaxes and opens up participants ▪ Less opportunity to get caught up in daily tasks ▪ Better food (usually)
–	▪ Interruptions from co-workers ▪ Tendency to run back to desks ▪ Difficult to separate mentally from daily tasks	▪ Costlier ▪ Difficult to arrange early room setup

ROOM SETUP

One of the most important elements of a room is the seating pattern. The ideal pattern is a U shape in which the open area faces away from the entrance door. For maximum viewing, place your screen (for projecting from a laptop or overhead) in the corner. This arrangement also preserves the most wall space.

Although the most common arrangement is a U-shaped room with tables in front of participants, other setups are possible (or necessary because of constraints on room size and shape). These include clusters of tables in "rounds," which you arrange to simulate a U. With this arrangement, it's critical to position the tables and chairs so that all participants can see one another. (The last section of this chapter contains a checklist of things to remember when you set up your workshop room.)

CREATING STICKY WALLS

Your walls should have at least six to eight feet of continuous flat surface area for posting cards, sticky notes, and posters. It's here that you'll place butcher paper (or paper rolls) and flip charts. You can also use large bulletin boards or pin boards. (See the Web site for the book for links to products you might find useful.)

Sticky walls provide a ready-to-use surface for posting cards for your modeling work. (Use 5-inch x 8-inch or 4-inch x 6-inch index cards (stock weight); they come in a variety of colors.) To make a *sticky wall*, line a wall with poster paper (you can get it in 50-yard rolls, 48 inches wide), and then spray the paper with *repositionable* or *remountable* spray (use 3M or a comparable brand). This makes a tacky surface to hold the cards and lets you reposition them as you like.

Use cards as tools for representing detailed elements of requirements, such as data items, use case names, use case steps, parts of business rules, and so on. As they work, the participants will be creating, sorting, clustering, removing, and combining cards using the Wall of Wonder collaboration pattern (see "Wall of Wonder" in Chapter 9). A sticky wall supports this activity with minimum interruption.

PREPARING THE WORKSHOP ROOM

Prepare your sticky wall before the meeting. Because the smell of the spray bothers some people, I spray the wall at least half an hour before our start time. Having the room prepared before participants arrive allows you to be available to meet and greet them and perhaps attend to other details, such as putting out marker pens, arranging tables, and posting wall posters (such as Workshop Purpose and Products). It also communicates to the participants that you are prepared—and that you care.

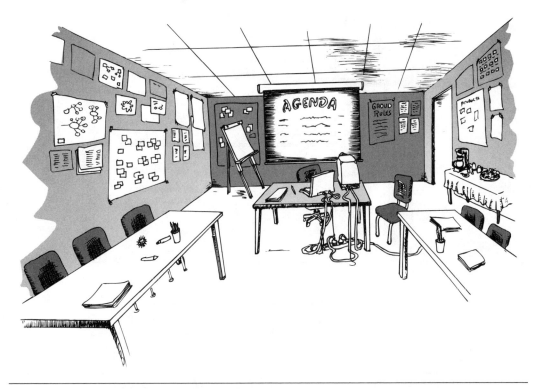

THE WORKSHOP ROOM SHOULD BE INVITING AND EFFICIENT.

DIFFERENT TIME AND PLACE OPTIONS

The requirements workshops described in this book are face-to-face meetings in which participants are in the same place at the same time. However, you can vary these two dimensions—time and space—to provide other collaborative experiences.

Time can be *synchronous* (everyone's present at the same time) or *asynchronous* (participants aren't meeting at the same time). Space can be the same when people are physically *co-located*, or it can be *distributed* (participants are in different locations).

Figure 8-1 shows ways to hold workshops with various time and place combinations. These include options ranging from using industrial-strength collaborative technology tools (discussed in the following subsections) to setting aside a *war room*, a room where the team can place project artifacts at any time.

In same-time meetings, a facilitator is needed. Technography can be extended for different-place workshops as well. In different-time meetings, you don't need a

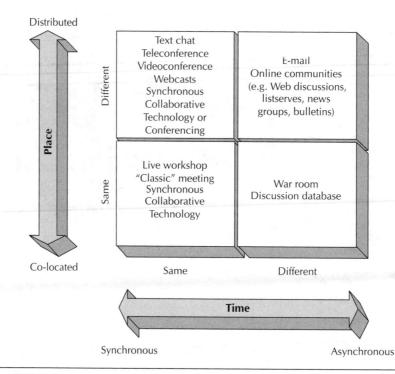

FIGURE 8-1 TIME AND PLACE MEETING OPTIONS

facilitator except to provide planning and design of the meeting content and rules for the process. As discussed later, though, the successful use of collaborative technology does require skilled facilitation.

Technography for Different-Place Workshops

Technography facilitates same time–different place workshops by making the technographer responsible for documenting the group's work (see Chapter 5). Participants meet at the same time, but they gather via the Internet to see their work and enter ideas, and they use the telephone in a teleconference. The technographer acts as a bridge between the group process and the technology. At the direction of the participants and the facilitator, the technographer enters and records contributions in real time.

Technography relies on simple technology: a laptop, a word processor, and a browser. Note that the technographer can perform these same tasks in a same time–same place setting to similar effect via the simple addition of a computer display device that projects the images from the technographer's monitor onto a screen.

VIDEOCONFERENCING

Videoconferencing—a same time–different place technology—isn't appropriate for requirements workshops. Aside from the obvious risks of technical difficulties, such as transmission delays and audio problems, the absence of body language and eye contact in videoconferences creates low *bandwidth* (the capability for information to flow quickly and concurrently). These delays interfere with the creativity and learning that are the hallmark of well-run requirements workshops.

Perhaps more importantly, in a videoconference, participants can't interact directly with their requirements models. The human interactions that occur when people manipulate their models and prototypes are essential to product innovation and group convergence.

Videoconferencing, however, can be effective for reviews of workshop deliverables and are a good way for participants to reconnect after a workshop. The group can use a videoconference to present revisions to workshop deliverables, discuss actions taken to complete requirements, and share results of post-workshop research. To be successful with videoconferences, you must plan carefully and use predefined protocols. Some suggestions are available on the Web site for the book.

COLLABORATIVE TECHNOLOGY

Collaborative technology is a catchall term for computer-aided facilitation. Related terms, including *groupware, meetingware, electronic meetings* (EMs), *group support systems* (GSS), and *computer supported collaborative work* (CSCW), refer to software tools that aid collaborative work. Each of the products in this class of software is unique in perspective and approach, but each aims to support groups in collaborative tasks. Among their strengths is the capability to promote participation through anonymity and to present immediate documentation.

Synchronous collaborative technology requires special rooms in which tables contain embedded computer screens and keyboards; the tables are arranged in a U shape. Videoconferencing capabilities might also be present when some participants are co-located and others are in different locations. You can use any of several collaborative technology tools with either co-located or distributed participants.

Most collaborative technology tools have software capabilities to design and structure the agenda as well as participant capabilities such as capturing items from brainstorming, filtering, categorizing, ranking, combining, and voting. Like face-to-face facilitators, experienced collaborative technology facilitators use common collaboration patterns.

ThinkLets

Experts in collaborative technology have codified a set of small interactive structures, called thinkLets, that combine technology and techniques. A *thinkLet* is a pattern of thinking that is similar to the higher-level collaboration patterns discussed in this book and cognitive patterns studied by knowledge engineering methodologists.

The patterns of diverging, converging, organization, elaborating, abstracting, evaluating, and moving toward consensus are all ways of thinking. Each thinkLet contains the components of specific hardware and software technology and their configurations, along with a script describing the sequence of events and instructions for the group.

For example, the *LeafHopper* thinkLet promotes divergent thinking by allowing individuals to concurrently hop around a variety of related topics, a technique that keeps everyone interested while enabling the capture of a wide variety of information. For more information on this topic, see the reference section at the end of this chapter.

If you use collaborative technologies for same-time same-place workshops, the need for physical materials such as flip charts, sticky notes, sticky walls, and cards is minimized or eliminated. The primary mode for generating, categorizing, summarizing, sorting, and ranking is the software product's interface.

The implications of collaborative technology are not only technical but also social. It exists within a socio-technical environment. Seasoned facilitators realize that focusing exclusively on the technical issues is a sure route to an expensive failure.

Table 8-3 summarizes the key pluses and minuses of collaborative technology.

TABLE 8-3 COLLABORATIVE TECHNOLOGY PLUSES AND MINUSES

Plus or Minus	Element	Explanation
+	Levels the playing field	Anonymity reduces or eliminates dominance or power plays among individuals, allowing minority views to be heard. Anonymity mitigates conformance pressure (groupthink) and encourages participation by everyone regardless of organizational level or personality style (including people who are less comfortable speaking in groups).
+	Speed and immediacy of documentation	Participants enter responses simultaneously, accelerating documentation. Members don't have to take turns to "speak," so information is gathered quickly. All information is immediately available, as is a permanent record of group memory.
+	Focused discussion	Activities focus on one topic, issue, or decision at a time. This forces the facilitator to get the sequence right and participants to choose words carefully and get to the point.
+	Enables larger groups to collaborate	Groups of 16 or larger are more easily managed, and that tends to bring in more knowledge, information, and skills.
–	Loss of human contact and nonverbal cues	Participants and the facilitator don't have behavior cues as they do in the context of live facilitation, and that makes it difficult to detect misunderstanding, boredom, and disagreement, which are often communicated visually.

Table continued on next page.

TABLE 8-3 CONTINUED

Plus or Minus	Element	Explanation
–	Harder to build a team	Team building, an important by-product of requirements workshops, enhances trust and strengthens communications. The opportunities for team building activities with collaborative technology are limited.
–	Takes more time to build common vocabulary	Shared vocabulary takes longer to achieve because of the loss of visual and verbal cues and the lack of immediacy associated with real-time conversation. A common vocabulary is critical for defining high-quality requirements.
–	Need for high degree of structure and planning	The software requires a process that uses a prescribed set of tools.–
	High degree of dependency on facilitator	Quality is highly dependent on the skills and experience of the facilitator; in live workshops with mediocre facilitators, participants can compensate by taking on aspects of the facilitation role.
–	Dependency on technology working right	Things can (and do) go wrong.
–	Potential alienation, FUD (fcar, uncertainty, and doubt) factor	Some individuals are reluctant to do something unfamiliar, especially when it involves technology. Compound that with dealing with the content: work problems, issues, or plans that may be loaded with controversy.
–	Harder to reach closure over distance	Different-place participants have more difficulty converging to a decision than do same-place participants. The increased difficulty might be due to limitations in bandwidth; give-and-take negotiations are more rigid and structured.
–	Enables free riding	Anonymity allows some people to avoid contributing.

COLLABORATIVE TECHNOLOGY VARIANTS

A variant of collaborative technology is *electronic polling*, which supports simple numeric or binary input. These polls are most useful for large groups to gather specific data. Like videoconferencing, discussion databases can be useful for pre- or post-workshop reviews and information sharing provided that the databases are well managed and well organized.

COLLABORATIVE TECHNOLOGY: A CAVEAT

Although collaborative technologies can be useful, there are important issues.

- With distributed facilitation, planning, leading, and managing participation for the sessions require more attention than with face-to-face facilitation.
- Results tend to be highly dependent on the effectiveness of the facilitator.
- When collaborative technology is in use, conflict resolution and session management tend not to be as effective as they are in face-to-face, JAD-like sessions.

No matter which type of collaborative technology you use, planning is essential. Technology is only a tool for the facilitator—and *technology will only make a bad process worse.* Used properly by a skilled facilitator, however, these technologies offer a practical way to augment the shaping of requirements.

If you're interested in pursuing different time–different place tools, remember to do the following:

- To build trust, consider having an initial same-time same-place scope workshop or high-level requirements workshop. At the end of the workshop, participants should agree on how they will collaborate in your virtual world.
- Learn the tool—and practice, practice, practice (and test, test, test!).
- Invest in the ergonomics needed for same-time same-place collaborative technology events, including appropriate lighting, seating configuration, and work space.
- Use the same six P's framework to plan your different-time or -place session, clearly defining purpose, participants, principles, products, and process just as you would for a face-to-face workshop.
- Adapt your ground rules. Changes may include respecting the need for anonymity and not discussing individual contributions outside the session when anonymity was used during the session.

 ## TIPS

- Arrange for a room with sufficient wall space and room space for the participants. Set up the room at least an hour before the workshop.
- Use an offsite location for longer workshops.
- Visit the room if you haven't seen it, or have someone describe it to you.

- Provide refreshments.
- Be sensitive to the dietary needs of your participants.
- Appoint a planning team member or participant to monitor the room temperature during the workshop.

PLACE CHECKLISTS

The following list provides guidelines for finalizing your workshop place.

- Get approvals for expenditures (room, food) if necessary.
- Reserve the room.
- Order refreshments.
- Create a map and instructions to the site, if it's offsite.
- Notify participants about the location.
- Create posters for the workshop room (see the following checklist).

Following are guidelines for preparing the workshop room.

- Put a welcome sign or poster outside the room.
- Call your food services supplier to tell them where to place the food.
- Post your Workshop Purpose, Workshop Products, Agenda, and Ground Rules posters.
- Arrange tables in a U shape.
- Set up your sticky wall or wall areas for sticky notes.
- Set up your recorder area.
- Set up and test your laptop and printer.
- If there's a phone in the room, set it to "no ring" or pull the plug.
- Set up a table in the corner for food and refreshments.
- Set out cups with black and colored marker pens around the tables.
- Post blank posters you'll use, such as Parking Lot, Actions, and Decisions.
- Arrange for chairs in the back of the room for observers.

FOR MORE INFORMATION

Boehm et al. (2001) describes how to use collaborative technology in conjunction with the WinWin method, which stakeholders use to resolve conflicting requirements.

Briggs et al. (2001) presents the rationale for the delightful miniprocess patterns known as thinkLets, as well as a detailed example of their use in collaborative technology sessions. The latter includes script comments by the facilitator. Although the example in the article is connected with specific software tool functions, these same patterns are part of the collaboration patterns discussed in this book.

Carmel et al. (1992) describes the mixed results the authors found in comparing real-time JAD sessions with "electronic" JAD (in other words, use of collaborative technology). The electronic JAD sessions had less discipline, less success in resolving conflict, and less overall session management but also more participation. The authors conclude that the facilitator needs to be a JAD facilitator first and only secondarily an electronic meeting facilitator.

Schrage (2000) makes a compelling case, based on research into business innovation, for using simulations, prototypes, and models in product design. Teams who "play" with some representations of reality—such as diagrams, running code, and sketches—arrive at innovative products, but this play must include customers.

Chapter 16 of Wood and Silver (1995) provides an overview of some forms of collaborative technology. It also discusses caveats, cautions, and do's and don'ts.

PROCESS: PLAN THE WORK, WORK THE PLAN

"Plan to be spontaneous tomorrow."
—Steven Wright

Y ou should design your workshop process to include structured sets of activities that let the group deliver the workshop products in a logical sequence. This chapter is your road map.

Flexible Structure

The basic structure of a workshop is simple: Open the workshop, conduct group activities, close the workshop (see Figure 9-1). Along the way, you will use the inputs created beforehand; integrate quality checking of deliverables; and incorporate techniques that energize, engage, and encourage participation. Awareness

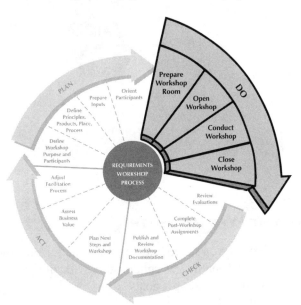

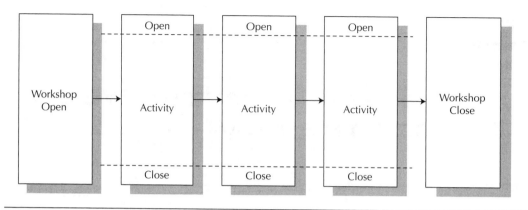

FIGURE 9-1   STRUCTURE OF A REQUIREMENTS WORKSHOP (BASED ON KANER, 1996)

of group dynamics will help you to keep the process on track and productive. Any structure you design should allow you to be flexible and change course during the workshop.

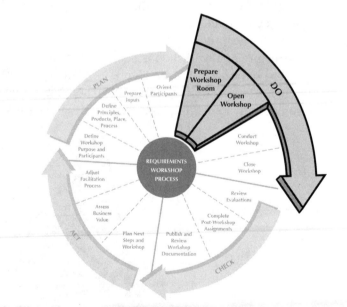

OPENING THE WORKSHOP

The way you start a workshop sets the tone for the whole event. Begin in a way that helps participants get comfortable with the process and gain further commitment to the workshop's goals.

By the time the participants arrive, the room should be ready (see Chapter 8 for guidelines). Starting your workshop on time tells people that you value their time, that you'll take time limits for breaks seriously, and that there's work to be done. Give people a two-minute warning, and then ask them to take their seats and write their names on name cards.

Each workshop should begin with a set of rituals. You can adapt your own, but there are some essentials to include:

- Have the workshop sponsor or project sponsor do a welcome and kickoff (see "Sponsor Kick-and-Close" in Chapter 5).
- Explain the roles of the facilitator and the recorder.
- Review the workshop's purpose and products.
- Review (and revise, as necessary) the ground rules, including those about decision making.
- Explain the workshop process and describe how each agenda item will be handled.
- Review any time constraints.
- Tell everyone about the essentials: food, bathrooms, breaks.
- Conduct an opener (discussed next).

You can present this information if you're the facilitator, the workshop sponsor, or a planning team member, or a combination of people can present it.

THE OPENER

The workshop *opener* (also known as the *icebreaker* or *warm-up*) is a starting activity that allows participants to get acquainted and begin the forming process (see "Forming, Storming, Norming, and Performing" in Chapter 6). Openers help foster participation, open-mindedness, and a sense of safety with the workshop process.

You need to decide whether the opener will be purely for participants to introduce themselves and have some fun or will incorporate a learning point about the workshop content or deliver a workshop product.

When the group members already know one another, there is little ice to break. If your opener is purely introductory, it should last about one-sixteenth of the total workshop time (for example, half an hour for a full-day workshop). If your opener also makes a point about the content of the workshop, it can last twice as long.

In one scope workshop, I used an "information hunt" opener. After having the participants randomly form subgroups, I asked each person to quickly gather different information about the other participants and the project and then share his or her findings. I gave them topics such as the types of contributions each participant could make, their greatest concerns about defining the project scope, and their hopes and wishes—as well as concerns and fears—about the workshop. After they gathered, prepared, and presented the information to one another, I facilitated a brief discussion about the opener. As a result, the participants adjusted some of the ground rules we had devised before the workshop and then were ready to start their first activity.

Trust

Another way to open the session is to ask participants to create their own ground rules. I've asked participants in several workshops to form small groups and then list, on cards or posters, ground rules that would help them have a productive workshop. You can use a storyboard process to finalize the ground rules (see "Wall of Wonder" later in this chapter).

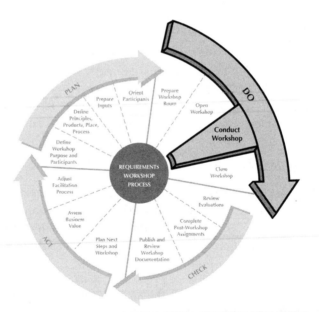

DESIGNING ACTIVITIES

An *activity* is a process that transforms inputs such as draft models, templates, and examples into outputs (see Figure 9-2). Each activity should specifically address a topic or deliverable: define system context, define events within scope,

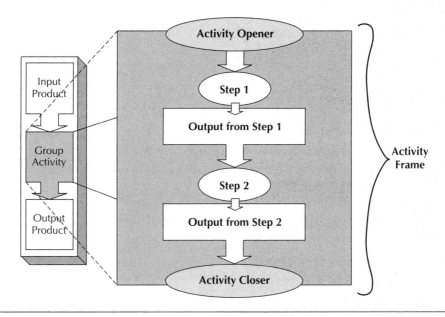

FIGURE 9-2 STRUCTURING AN ACTIVITY

name use cases, specify business rules, and so on. Deliverables from one activity are used as inputs to the next.

Knowing which models the group should deliver, and how precise each model must be, helps you to find connections among them and decide on a sequence. With a well-designed workshop process, you'll be able to handle any changes that arise. In the end, *structure permits flexibility*. The subsections that follow provide guidelines for designing activities.

SEQUENCING ACTIVITIES

Because requirements models are connected in numerous ways, you may have numerous possible starting points and sequences. In one of my workshops, the deliverables included business and temporal events, data entities, entity states, and business rules. These models are connected in a variety of ways: Events trigger business rules; business rules are enforced for one or more entity states; business rules require data entities; entity states and business rules both require data. Figure 9-3 shows an example of how these models thread together. You can essentially pick one model (say, events or entity states) and follow the thread to another model.

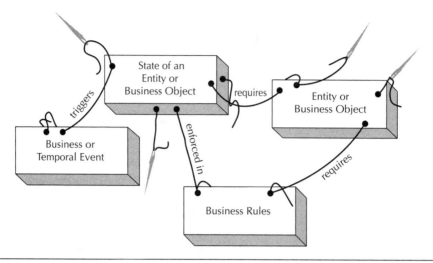

FIGURE 9-3 HOW MODELS THREAD TOGETHER

To decide where to start, identify your most complete or clearest input model. In one workshop, the planning team and I had drafted a set of entity states, so we began the modeling process with states. For another workshop with similar deliverables, our inputs were a list of metrics about field sales results and sample marketing and sales reports. Because the metrics named data and because a data model is a collection of related data attributes, the first activity was to list data attributes.

If your inputs don't include other requirements models or at least the beginnings of models, start with project goals, visions, objectives, or any other available visual or textual information about the business need. For example, if you're facilitating a scope workshop, you can use the project goals or objectives to ask questions such as these:

- Who are the stakeholders associated with this goal?
- Which of these stakeholders need to interact directly with the system?
- What are their goals in interacting with the system?

These are focus questions that help you to define stakeholders, actors, and use case names (see "Using Focus Questions" later in this chapter).

One common pitfall associated with activity planning involves overloading a workshop with too many activities and deliverables. To avoid this problem, consider which tasks might be done before and after the workshop. When you're unsure which sequence of activities would work best, try a test run with your planning team before the workshop. If the process doesn't seem to be working while you're in the workshop, stop the activity, check with participants about how it's going, and then adjust the sequence as necessary.

FRAMING ACTIVITIES

Every workshop activity should be framed with explicit start and end points (see Figure 9-2). The few minutes you spend doing this gives participants a context for their work together and allows them to make the transition into a new activity or reach closure on a completed one.

Start each activity by telling participants what has just happened, what's about to happen, how the next activity relates to the workshop's purpose, and what process you'll use to build the deliverables. To explain the process, begin with a mini-tutorial (discussed next), provide directions for the process, and then ask your starting focus questions.

When you explain the process, show participants any available examples, templates, draft models, and aids (see "Workshop Aids" in Chapter 7). Give specific directions. Have directions written on a poster, or project them on the wall from a word processor, in full view as you explain them. Ask whether anyone has questions about the process.

End each activity with closure on the deliverables. Review what the group has accomplished; then ask for proposals on the deliverables and apply your decision rule process.

MINI-TUTORIALS

Pre-work

It's often useful to provide a one- or two-minute mini-tutorial about the requirements model (or partial model) that participants are about to work on. This technique allows them to learn more about the model, practice, and gain confidence in using it.

Show them an example or two that are relevant to their business. To test participants' understanding of the examples, ask them questions. In one of my workshops, one subgroup was about to generate a list of states for a data entity. After that, the participants were to name business rules associated with the states and any attributes needed by each state. I showed the members of the subgroup a simple statechart diagram displaying the states Ordering, Filling, and Shipping. I asked them what other states their products might be in; they responded with several states and also data attributes. This gave me the chance to clarify the differences and relationships between states and data attributes. When one participant suggested Back Ordering—a substate of Ordering—I took the opportunity to demonstrate the concept of substates.

Be careful not to overwhelm participants with too much information about the models or to use obtuse modeling semantics that aren't relevant to their immediate task. In one workshop, most participants were business people unfamiliar with the data model they were about to create, and the planning team advised me that using technical terms would put them off. For that reason, I provided a one-minute overview of a data model without using the terms *entity*, *cardinality*, or *optionality*. For another workshop, the planning team opted not to call use cases by that name, instead calling them "user goals."

ELEMENTS OF A WORKSHOP ACTIVITY

Each activity can be decomposed into a number of elements, including steps, step inputs, techniques used in each step, and step deliverables (see Figure 9-4).

The *steps* of an activity include specific tasks that the group will do and focus questions you might use for a step. For example, if your activity is to define use cases for the next release and as input you have a list of customer wants from the prior release, the steps might be as follows:

1. Define use cases.
2. List use cases.
3. Cluster similar use cases and remove duplicates.
4. Agree on criteria for narrowing the list of use cases.
5. Apply the criteria to the list.
6. Review the proposed list of use cases for the next release and the criteria for selecting them.
7. Apply your decision rule process.

Participants will operate in one of three modes: working individually, working in a subgroup, or working as part of the whole group (*plenary*). In the beginning steps of an activity, ask participants to work individually to list items such as data attributes or use cases. This allows them to think alone before forming subgroups.

FIGURE 9-4 ELEMENTS OF A WORKSHOP ACTIVITY

Define the *content* of the deliverables for each activity, and then determine the specific *format* for each deliverable. Examples of formats include *subject+verb+object* for describing business events, and *time to <verb+object>* for describing temporal events. This should be easy if you've carefully defined your workshop products. See "Output Products" in Chapter 7 for more about deliverables, and "Input Products" in that chapter for information about products that serve as *inputs* to activities.

Techniques are group methods such as listing, a brainwriting pool, role playing, gallery review, and walkthroughs. (For more information about these techniques, see the references at the end of the chapter.) These techniques help groups to generate, specify, categorize, prioritize, and select models and modeling elements. Techniques also incorporate collaboration patterns such as the Wall of

Sizing Your Subgroups

I prefer workshop subgroups with no more than three people (*triads*). Triads get the work done faster, and each person is likely to contribute when everyone gets to interact with everyone else. In addition, the number of pairwise (one-on-one) conversations is reduced, something that also saves time. With three people in a subgroup, you have three possible discussion pairs. Add just one more person, and the group would need six pairs of conversations. You can see the trend.

Of course, dyads (groups of two) are the fastest subgroups. At the beginning of a workshop, dyads are helpful because they allow the two people to get comfortable with each other. However, if you have more than six or eight people in your workshop, dyads often aren't feasible, and that's why I generally strive for three in each subgroup.

You can't always get triads, though. With a larger group (13 to 17), subgroups will probably need to comprise four or five people. To offset the timing problems associated with larger subgroups, I try to wait until the group members as a whole have some experience and familiarity with one another before using subgroups of four or more. This method makes it more likely that the participants will seek everyone's input and challenge one another, as "performing" groups tend to do (see "Forming, Storming, Norming, and Performing" in Chapter 6).

Wonder and Divide, Conquer, Correct, and Collect. These patterns are discussed in later sections in this chapter.

You also need to estimate the time to allow for each step or activity and decide whether the group can do all the planned activities within the allotted time (see "Estimating Activity Time" later in this chapter).

 A template to help you design your workshop activities appears on the Web site for this book.

SAMPLE WORKSHOP ACTIVITY

Figure 9-5 shows the steps for defining high-level use cases with use case names and brief paragraph descriptions. Table 9-1 presents a supporting activity template that assumes a group of 12 participants.

After the facilitator explains what use cases are and provides an example, the participants list use cases for some of the actors on the actor table and the actor map, which were created in a prior activity or a pre-work assignment. Each sub-

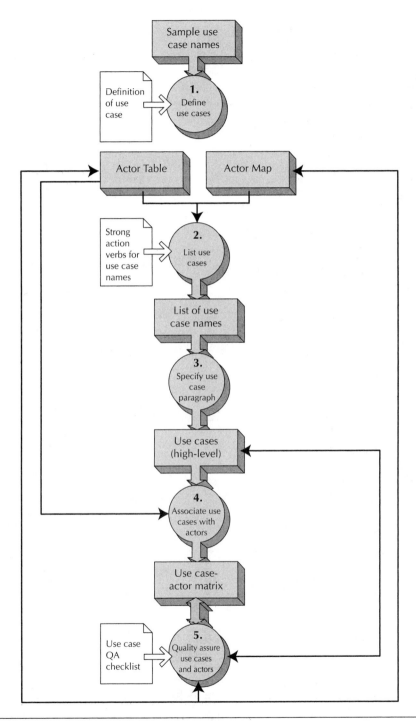

FIGURE 9-5 SAMPLE STEPS FOR AN ACTIVITY

TABLE 9-1 SAMPLE ACTIVITY TEMPLATE

Steps	Tasks	Inputs	Focus Questions	Interaction Format	Deliverable Content	Format
1. Define use case (3 minutes)	Explanation by facilitator or planning team participant	▪ Definition of use case ▪ Sample use case names	N/A	N/A	N/A	N/A
2. List use cases (10 minutes)	a. Partition actor maps to subgroups. b. Each subgroup lists use cases for their assigned actors. c. Subgroups converge on list.	▪ Draft actor table ▪ Draft actor map ▪ List of "good verbs to use" when naming use cases	What goals does <actor> have in interacting with the system?	Individual and then subgroups	Named use case	Sheet of paper; then one use case per post
3. Specify use case paragraph (7 minutes per use case)	Write a paragraph.	Use cases list from prior task	What must happen for the actor to achieve the goal?	Subgroups	2–4 sentences per use case	Large post
4. Associate use cases with actors (10 minutes)	Post each use case on the wall next to the actor who initiates it.	Actor map posted on wall	Which actor initiates which use case? [Make another copy of any use case that is initiated by multiple actors.]	Subgroups	N/A	Use case posts next to actors in the actor map
5. QA use cases and actors (15 minutes)	a. Review the QA checklist. b. Subgroups swap use cases and apply the QA questions to the use cases and actors on the wall. c. Review as whole group.	Use cases posted on actor map	Using the QA checklist, can you find errors, omissions, or unclear or extraneous use case or actor information?	Subgroup and then whole group	Revised actor names, revised use case names, revised use case paragraph descriptions, removed actors or use cases	Posts updated

group (here, there are four subgroups of three people each) writes a brief paragraph description for a set of use cases. (The estimate assumes that each subgroup will work on three use cases.) Each subgroup also maps use cases to actors using posts or sticky notes, and then the subgroups perform quality checks on one another's work using a QA checklist.

Typically, this activity requires less than one hour. At the start of each step, the facilitator should tell participants how long they have to complete the step. It's important to try to stay within those times if at all possible. Naturally, some steps will take more or less time than others. As the workshop progresses, participants become more familiar with one another and their own requirements, and they become more adept at working together and better able to complete steps quickly.

ESTIMATING ACTIVITY TIME

To estimate times for activities, you must consider the number of deliverables and how many elements you might need to elicit for each element, keeping in mind that groups won't be productive right away.

Table 9-2 provides guidelines for estimating the time required to produce requirements models. These guidelines assume that the models have medium complexity and volume and that each model has a starting point (such as a draft model).

The information in the table is based on my own experience with groups of 7 to 16 participants.

Allow some time—say, 5 to 15 minutes before and after each modeling activity—for the activity start and end steps. Because this isn't an exact science, you should keep track of how much time you actually used for each activity, and then use this information to adjust your estimates going forward.

The same general heuristic for deciding how many products you can deliver applies to how many activities you should include in your design: Take the total you think you can do and divide by 3. Select those activities and deliverables that are most important; save the rest to do as time permits.

USING FOCUS QUESTIONS

Focus questions are queries you use to direct participants' attention to a specific topic at the start of each workshop activity. For the facilitator, *questions are the*

TABLE 9-2 GUIDELINES FOR ESTIMATING ACTIVITY TIME REQUIREMENTS

Requirements Model or Portion	Interaction Format	Duration
Relationship map	Whole group	2–3 hours
Details on relationship map	Subgroup	1 hour per partition
Process map (with triggering event and event responses predefined)	Subgroup	1 hour per map
Context diagram (first cut) and event table	Whole group	1–2 hours
Detailed flows (in and out) on context diagram	Subgroup	1 hour per partition
Business and temporal events	Whole group	1 hour
Conceptual data model (entities and identifiers)	Whole group or subgroups	6 hours
Use cases (names, brief description, headers)	Individuals and subgroups	20–30 minutes each
Actor table and actor map	Subgroups and whole group	1–2 hours
Data entities (including attributes)	Subgroups	1–2 hours per data entity
User interface prototypes, along with necessary data	Subgroups	1 hour per screen or report
Statechart diagram for data entity or class (with only event transitions) along with associated attributes and business rules	Subgroups	30 minutes to 1 hour per state
Detailed use cases and associated data attributes and free-form business rules (stepwise or conversational format, with a list of use cases and actors as a starting point)	Subgroups	1 hour per use case
Use case map	Whole group or subgroups	1 hour
Scenarios (for testing detailed user requirements)	Subgroups	30 minutes per scenario

Focus Questions

answer. Clear, concise, and well-timed focus questions allow participants to find their own answers. Focus questions are useful as a way to start any workshop activity, not just modeling tasks. For example, they're helpful for a group that is developing an iteration plan or a set of project risks or defining elements of a project vision.

Immediately follow each question with a specific task that the participants must do, such as listing use case names on a card, sorting sticky notes with data attribute names into groups, prioritizing use cases, writing a short paragraph to describe a scenario, or matching business rules with use cases.

When the activity's outcome is to produce a requirements model, well-chosen focus questions direct participants' thinking to one or more elements of the model. For example, in modeling the external agents (actors) on a context diagram, you could ask, "Who or what provides information to or receives information from the system?" or "Who or what must interact with the system?" When you are ordering elements in a model, your question might direct the participants to a sequencing task: "In what order will a user do these steps?" You should also be prepared during the workshop with examples for each of your own focus questions; this can help jump-start people's thinking in a concrete way.

Choose focus questions for user requirements modeling based on your workshop design strategy. If you're starting with a middle-out, how-first vertical strategy, your first question might be, "What goals will users have when they interact with the system?" (Chapter 10 discusses the various strategies you can use in planning workshops.) After participants list these goals, your design strategy might be to move on to actors, so you'd ask, for each goal (which is a use case), "Which role has this goal?"

A requirements workshop, like any facilitated workshop, benefits from the artful use of a variety of questions. The Web site for the book contains a list of useful focus questions.

IMAGINE THIS . . .

A powerful way to energize, focus, and motivate participants—and also to help them make the transition into a new activity—is to precede your focus questions with an image. An *image*, as the word implies, paints a picture—in our case, a picture of a future that may or may not happen. The image allows the participants to visualize something concrete. It centers their attention on the focus question that immediately follows.

For example, if you're asking participants to list data attributes for a use case called Register Vehicle, you might say, "Imagine you're sitting at your desk, about to register a vehicle, and you've got all the forms, manuals, documents, sticky notes, and other materials you need all around you. What are all the pieces of information you reference as you register the vehicle?"

Other Types of Focus Questions

The facilitator and participants can use other kinds of focus questions to help modulate group dynamics, expand or contract the discussion, and move the group toward closure. Well-placed questions help create an environment in which the participants have the freedom and honesty to ask questions of one another and to keep the process moving smoothly.

- A *direct* question is aimed at seeking specific information, challenging, or probing for understanding: "What makes that important?" "When did that become evident?"

- An *open-ended* question is aimed at stimulating discussion, gaining more information, or generating ideas: "What would be helpful?" "Why do you believe that?"

- A *clarifying* question is aimed at mirroring, rephrasing, or playing back a speaker's words or actions to confirm understanding by the listener: "Let me see if I understand your point . . . <rephrase>." "Did I hear you saying . . . ?"

- A *leading* question is aimed at aligning others to a particular point of view or answer, or to propose a new action: "What about . . . ?" "What other ideas are there in the area of . . . ?"

- A *refocusing* question is aimed at redirecting the group: "That sounds like a good thought to capture on our parking lot. What other ideas are there for <original topic>?" "That's an issue/action/idea for our <x> activity. Would you be willing to hold on to that until we get to that?"

- A *process* question is aimed at reflecting on the group process and ways to improve it: "Is this a good way to discover the business rules?" "When did you feel most productive?"

- A *meta* question is a question about a question; it's aimed at raising unknown issues or discovering information that might have been implied rather than stated (see Gause and Weinberg, 1989): "Are these questions helpful to us?" "What other questions should I be asking?"

Using an image helps to prepare people for the focus question and gives them energy and motivation to answer.

QA As You Go

Doneness Tests

Once you've elicited a set of user requirements, you should check its quality before adding more detail or seeking closure. Pausing to conduct quality assurance (QA) activities accelerates your workshop delivery cycle by reducing the amount of rework needed to correct errors. You can test a model's quality characteristics, such as correctness, completeness, testability, clarity, and consistency, by using your doneness tests: checklists, matrices, metaphors, and so on (see Chapter 7). You can also have participants devise their own quality checks. Note that the Divide, Conquer, Correct, Collect pattern (see the Appendix) integrates QA checking.

USING CHECKLISTS It's a good idea to integrate steps in your modeling activities whereby participants use QA checklists to find errors, missing elements, and inconsistencies in their own or another subgroup's requirements (for examples, see "QA Checklist" in Chapter 7 and the book's Web site). This process should take 10 to 20 minutes, depending on the number of requirements to be checked.

Participants can use sticky notes or colored dots to indicate which models have flaws. If you conduct the checking in subgroups, allow time for participants to point out the defects in the plenary; then allow either the producer of the model or its reviewers to correct them.

Be sure to conduct this QA checking on a set of related models before adding more detail to those models. You may need different checklists for different levels of detail. For example, high-level requirements—as expressed in forms such as use case descriptions, an event table, and the glossary—might have one checklist, whereas detailed requirements, represented by, say, attributes and business rules, might have another.

WALKTHROUGHS A *walkthrough* is a form of review in which the producers of a product—for example, the subgroup that created the steps for a given use case—describe the product and ask for comments, questions, and corrections. During a workshop, you can structure a walkthrough by using one model to walk through another; for example, participants can use scenarios to walk through their use cases.

You can also walk through related models at once. In one of my workshops, we walked through five models—use cases, business rules, prototypes, and scenarios—and discovered numerous defects. (For a story about another workshop, see the next section.) It's useful to assign one person per model to keep track of where you are in the walkthrough and to capture all the necessary changes. You can also ask participants to do role playing, pretending to be the users.

A WORKSHOP WALKTHROUGH In one of my workshops, participants delivered detailed use cases and business rules using their pre-work models:

Reviews of Software

In the context of software, a *review* is the process of examining a work product, such as a model, a document, or a piece of code, so that people other than the ones who produced it can detect flaws. Reviews, which vary in formality (walkthroughs are less formal than other kinds of reviews), are some of the most effective ways to increase the quality of software. Peer reviews can catch more than half of all defects in a piece of software, shorten development cycles, and reduce requirements creep by a healthy factor. See the references section at the end of this chapter for more about reviews.

Generally, the earlier the review, the greater the net schedule savings, so using reviews during requirements workshops—before the requirements are finalized—can help you to avoid the extra costs associated with correcting requirements later.

scenarios, the glossary, and prototype screens. The revised versions of these draft models were to be the workshop deliverables.

As the participants specified the use case steps, our recorder documented them using a laptop. The steps also appeared on the wall in sequence, left to right, on big blue sticky notes. Beneath each use case was a list of associated business rules. The team then used the scenarios to walk through each use case along with its associated business rules and the prototype screens.

Sarah, a business expert, played the role of a user. She selected a scenario and then walked through a use case posted on the wall, step by step. At the same time, Dave, the GUI designer, was poised at the overhead projector with a pile of prototype screens on acetates. Using an erasable colored pen, he wrote data from the scenarios on the acetate as Sarah walked through the steps. He not only modified the data on the screen shots but also rearranged and redrew rough screen shots to give Sarah the interface she expected to see at each point in the scenario.

We first worked through the "normal" flow of a use case. As we tested the use case with the data provided from each scenario, I asked questions such as, "How do you decide which . . . ?" or "How does the system select . . . ?" or "What does the system have to know to . . . ?" (These questions were designed to test the business rules.) When the group realized that a business rule was incomplete or unclear, the recorder noted the revisions under the use case steps for everyone to see.

After working through three or four normal scenarios, we attacked the *exceptions*: those scenarios that would occur less often or that would cause errors. We'd posted the use case steps that had exceptions using different-colored sticky notes. Exceptions appeared as branches off of the normal use case steps. Walking through these scenarios revealed numerous missing business rules; and as we walked through an exception scenario, sometimes the participants realized that they needed to add another exception. These, in turn, yielded more use case steps, test data, and changes to the flow of the prototype screens. We kept track of the corrections on the actual models. (You can also use a form to track all defects in one place.)

As we finished the walkthrough of each use case, I asked for proposals to determine its disposition. Our scribe projected our Use Case Completion form on the wall, and then I polled the group for input. Using our decision rule, the workshop sponsor made the final decision for each use case. As we discussed specifics, the scribe captured notes and the final decision on the form.

MATRICES You can also test requirements using matrices (see "Matrices" in Chapter 7) by providing each subgroup with a blank matrix. You then assign each subgroup a distinct set of requirements to analyze, followed by a review of errors and questions in a plenary session. To cross-fertilize participants' exposure to other models, you can swap models among the subgroups for completion of the matrices.

PARTICIPANT-DEVISED QUALITY CHECKS Participants can also define their own quality checks. In one of my workshops, we used participant-devised database queries and sales reports for testing quality. After defining the data model, business rules, and scenarios, the participants went through these queries and reports to ensure that all the requirements needed to create them were represented. They identified gaps, most of which turned out to be differences in business terms written on the worksheet. They defined glossary terms more precisely and added data attributes to the data model. As a result, they were able to reach closure on their requirements.

PERFORM QA ON YOUR PROCESS In addition to checking the quality of your workshop products, you should periodically stop and check the quality of the workshop process. The Self-Reflect collaboration pattern (see the Appendix) prescribes this as a regular practice. Groups rarely make the time to stop their activities, evaluate what's going on, openly discuss their behavior and interactions, and then decide what and how they can improve their work together. Healthy, productive groups regularly critique (and praise) themselves.

Frequent
Debriefs

One way to check your process involves using a circle divided into the categories Start, Stop, Continue, More Of, and Less Of. The reactions from one requirements workshop appear in Figure 9-6.

It's a good idea to facilitate a self-reflecting activity periodically (for example, twice a day for a one-day session). If the group is gathering for the first in a series of sessions, begin each session with a review of the preceding day's self-reflection, and also tell the participants how you've adjusted the process to make use of those observations.

You can also conduct a one-minute, nonverbal *thumb check*. Ask participants to put their thumbs up, down, or sideways.

- Thumbs up means the pace is fine.
- Thumbs down means it's too fast or too slow.
- Thumbs sideways indicates neutrality.

Briefly discuss thumbs down reactions.

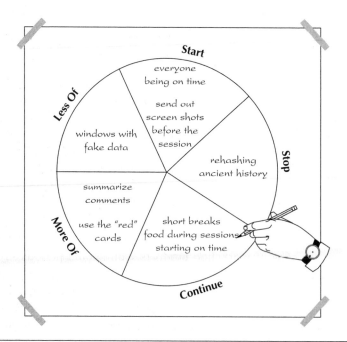

FIGURE 9-6 RESULTS OF A SELF-REFLECTING ACTIVITY

COLLABORATIVE MODES

Groups can collaborate in a workshop using different modes: sequential, reciprocal, parallel, or a combination of these.

In *sequential* collaboration, participants decompose a deliverable into parts, and then one subgroup creates one output and passes it to the next subgroup. For example:

- One subgroup writes a brief paragraph description of a use case.
- The next subgroup defines detailed steps for the use case.
- A third subgroup defines the use case for these steps.

Sequential collaboration is asynchronous: Work is completed and then handed off from subgroup to subgroup. Thus, each group is guided by what has been done before and must wait for the preceding work to be completed. Without discussion and review of the outputs, defects aren't detected until later. For this reason, you should avoid sequential collaboration in requirements workshops.

In *reciprocal* collaboration, participants work together to create common deliverables, mutually adjusting their activities in real time to take one another's edits into account. For example, the whole group works on defining a context diagram, an event table, or business rules, synchronizing on a deliverable. The early stage of the Wall of Wonder collaboration pattern provides a mechanism for reciprocal collaboration.

In *parallel* collaboration, you divide a single deliverable or set of related deliverables at about the same level of detail, and subgroups work synchronously on the deliverables. To reconcile the differences, the deliverables are then reassembled in the plenary session. For example, if your workshop has a set of detailed use cases as an input, three subgroups can work in parallel: One subgroup drafts prototype screens, another creates a high-level data model or class model, and the third draws a use case map.

Parallel collaboration is complex because multiple subgroups are working on different models. By periodically switching to reciprocal collaboration, participants can integrate their models, cross-fertilize learning points, and make corrections before going too far.

Collaboration patterns span multiple workshop activities and use a variety of collaborative modes. For example, the pattern Divide, Conquer, Correct, Collect combines parallel and reciprocal collaboration. The next section describes how you can integrate collaboration patterns into your workshop process.

COLLABORATION PATTERNS

The following subsections provide overviews of various collaboration patterns. See the Appendix for more information about these patterns.

WALL OF WONDER

The Wall of Wonder collaboration pattern is a storyboarding process in which groups use a shared wall space to build a model by successively using individual, then subgroup, and then plenary activities to generate items (see Figure 9-7). It is based on the Technology of Participation (ToP) workshop method, a story-

1. **Present** focus question. Participants answer by listing items. Form subgroups, listing one item per post.

2. **Place** posts randomly on whiteboard.

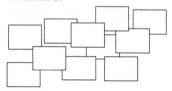

3. **Group** in related groups.

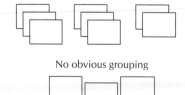

4. **Summarize** the theme that ties each group together and give it a header.

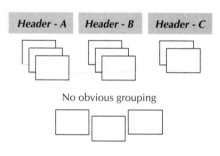

5. **Analyze** grouping for further groupings.

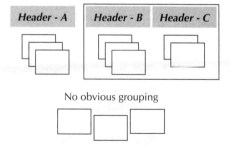

FIGURE 9-7 WALL OF WONDER STEPS

boarding technique originated by the Institute of Cultural Affairs (see Spencer's book at the end of the chapter for more information). The Institute of Culture affairs uses the phrase "wall of wonder" to refer to generating a plan's timeline. Here I use the Wall of Wonder as a pattern for a storyboarding technique of clustering cards on a wall to produce a variety of deliverables, including requirements models. Focus questions help participants to generate items for the wall. The wonderful work of the whole group is displayed on a single large wall.

Storyboarding provides groups with *shared team space*. The contents on the wall evolve over time as sequences and details are added and changed. Traditional storyboards are graphical, but in the context of a requirements workshop, the wall can contain text cards or sticky notes arranged bottom-up, top-down, or middle-out.

- In a *bottom-up* approach, participants begin specifying detailed items (for example, business rules or use case steps) and work their way up to higher-level, more abstract categories. (The categories at the highest level on the wall are designated on *header cards*.) Examples include project iterations, use case names, sets of business rules, named data entities or business classes, and data or class states. Along the way, participants sort and eliminate items.

- In a *top-down* approach, participants prepare header cards before the workshop or in a previous activity during the workshop. Then they work their way down to the lower-level details. This approach is useful when the categories are well known and accepted ahead of time.

- In a *middle-out* approach, participants generate items randomly without regard to category. Team members then sort the items, specify more detailed items, and converge on the categories. For example, you can ask participants to list use cases without a specific starting point (except the definitions of the use cases). Together, the participants sort, combine, add, and clarify all the cards or posts on the wall. Once the group has worked with a card originally listed as a use case, it may turn out to be a use case step, a set of use cases, or a use case that's out of scope.

DIVIDE, CONQUER, CORRECT, COLLECT

The Divide, Conquer, Correct, Collect (DCCC) pattern combines multiple modeling with QA activities while also using a combination of parallel and reciprocal collaboration. You decompose the deliverables (divide); assign them to subgroups to work on in parallel (conquer); reconvene to share findings and perform a quality check on the models (correct); and synchronize all the deliverables (collect).

Storyboarding

A *storyboard* is a hanging panel or wall that contains panels, sketches, or scenes depicting a plot or a sequence of actions. The idea isn't new; ancient cave drawings and hieroglyphics were early forms of storyboards.

The modern use of storyboards is widely attributed to artists at Disney, who began to use them in the late 1920s to map out the stories for cartoon films of Mickey Mouse, Donald Duck, and other characters. By pinning drawings to the wall in sequence, the artists were able to see how far along a project was and to edit it as they went.

In business, the use of storyboards has been popular for solving problems and creating collaborative plans. The same idea can be applied to any model. You can use a wall as a classic storyboard and show things in groups (alike things), in sequence (order), or in detail (decomposition). As discussed in Chapter 8 (see "Creating Sticky Walls"), I like to use sticky walls for storyboarding.

For example, if your deliverable is use cases, you first *divide* the use case into its component parts, such as its name, header information, a brief description, a stepwise description, and exceptions. To *conquer*, the participants form subgroups, which work in parallel on that use case. One group may work on the header while another writes a brief paragraph description and yet another lists the use case steps. Or each subgroup can conquer one component within different use cases (for example, the brief paragraph description) at the same time, and then the group reconvenes to share findings before moving to the next step.

Correcting involves the participants improving the quality of their interim deliverables by looking for defects. Because subgroups were working in parallel before this phase, it's often useful to ask the subgroups to share their interim products before beginning the correction activity. They can then use walkthroughs or a QA checklist to find errors. The participants can use other models; for example, they can use an event table or an actor map to find missing use cases. You can also ask subgroups to swap models and correct one another's models using a checklist. (For tips on facilitating walkthroughs in your requirements workshop, see "QA As You Go" earlier in this chapter.)

In the final phase, the group *collects* all the model elements, checks them as a whole, and then seeks closure on them. In one of my workshops, a scenario-driven walkthrough of use cases helped participants to detect missing use case steps. In another, walkthroughs driven by scenarios and business rules helped participants to discover missing use cases steps, exceptions, and missing business rules.

MULTI-MODEL

You can use the Multi-Model pattern by adapting the DCCC pattern. First, divide each model into parts; then partition parts of the same model with parts of a related model. Make sure that each group is working at about the same level of detail.

For example, if your workshop is producing a data model, statechart diagrams (for core entities), and business rules, you'd break these models into their parts:

- Entities, attributes, and relationships for the data model
- State names, triggers, and associated data attributes for the statechart diagrams
- The components to your business rule templates, such as conditions, actions, factors, and values, for the business rules

Then you'd group these parts at the same level of detail (such as data entities, entity states, and business rule conditions).

The steps for using the DCCC pattern, including how to incorporate multiple modeling, are as follows:

1. Define the deliverables.
2. Determine the parts (or components) of each deliverable.
3. Arrange all the parts into a logical sequence, and then group them by level of detail.
4. If you're using multiple models, group related model elements.
5. Select focus questions to lead the group in creating the parts.
6. Lead the group through the pattern, continually checking for quality, common level of detail, and the view of the whole.
7. Combine all parts and test the whole.
8. Check for closure using your decision rule and decision rule process.

EXPAND THEN CONTRACT

Expand Then Contract is a pattern of divergent, then convergent, thinking that enables groups to elicit diverse ideas and then narrow and focus the list.

- The *expand* phase encourages creative, open-ended, imaginative thinking, which results in large, undifferentiated lists. Because participants defer judgment, important possibilities are considered.

Multi-Modeling Using the DCCC Pattern

In one workshop I facilitated, 16 participants tackled a complex data model by delivering statechart diagrams and business rules associated with the data model. They began by agreeing on a simplified statechart of products. Subgroups came together based on business expertise in the various states, such as Purchasing, Assembling, and Packaging. Each subgroup listed data attributes and business rules for its assigned product entity state. The participants used sticky notes for the data attributes and wrote business rules on separate posters.

When the group reconvened, I asked the participants to review one another's models by pretending they were at an art gallery. They were to walk around the room and spend 15 minutes silently reading the various models and writing notes with questions. This *gallery* technique allowed the participants to review the other models at their own pace. Then they shared questions. Some subgroups discovered new substates; others found the same data attribute associated with multiple states. They also questioned numerous business rules. Then the subgroups returned to their models to adjust them based on the discussion.

Next, the group reconvened to report changes. The group used scenarios to walk through all the models: statechart diagrams (with states and substates), business rules, and the data model. The scenarios allowed them to find a few more defects. They proposed that the corrected models be accepted; using their decision rule process, the group reached closure in a matter of minutes.

- During the *contract* phase, the group removes, narrows, and trims the expanded elements by using evaluative, analytical thinking. This phase incorporates another pattern, The Sieve (see the next section), to narrow the items using criteria either created by the group in the workshop or determined before the workshop.

Web Site

You can use Expand Then Contract to, for example, define the scope of a project using an event table and a context diagram, or to decide on user requirements for the next iteration by agreeing on a list of use cases. The Web site for the book has an example of using this pattern to arrive at a list of use cases in scope.

You can expand several requirements models before entering the contract phase. For example, you might generate a list of use cases, their descriptions, associated business rules, and initiating actors. Until this point, the group hasn't reduced the number of use cases or actors because you don't want the group to remove requirements this early that they didn't know enough about. After the participants gain a high-level understanding of these requirements, they apply the criteria—

either their own, criteria devised in the workshop, or predefined criteria—and reduce the list to a realistic one.

Predefined criteria for the contract phase can come from standard schemes or from participants as pre-work. For example, the planning team might draft a set of proposed criteria such as, "The scope of the use cases will be small," "Each use case will align with more than one objective in the project charter," and "Business expertise is available for requirements and testing." In that case, the group wouldn't need to generate criteria, and it would proceed from step 1 to step 3 (see "Multi-Model" earlier in this chapter) using the predefined criteria.

THE SIEVE

Projects operate under time and resource constraints. To plan releases, begin design work, and focus project energies on the most essential requirements, a group must make defensible choices about which user requirements will be implemented and what their relative priorities are. Participants may need to select which requirements are in scope, delineate which subset of use cases will be delivered in the next release, or determine which data requirements are most important for that release.

The collaboration pattern The Sieve uses *smart filtering* in a workshop so that participants make defensible choices. First, you clearly define your criteria before enumerating the things that you need to narrow. Then you integrate this pattern into the Expand Then Contract pattern to narrow your expanded elements. The Sieve also stands alone as a workshop pattern; it works especially well if you begin the workshop with predefined user requirements that you need to prioritize.

Smart filtering with The Sieve relies on these factors:

- Knowing whether you need to arrive at one selection or multiple selections
- Knowing whether the choices are fixed or you can create or extend them during the workshop
- Defining the criteria before applying them to the choices
- Deciding, before the workshop, how to delineate the choices using a filtering tool
- Following up the filtering process with your decision rule process

Collaborative Closure

The Sieve is a tool for helping the group to reach closure; it's *not* a substitute for your decision-making ground rule. After you apply the filtering tool, you use your decision rule and decision rule process to reach closure on the choices.

MAKING ONE CHOICE OR MULTIPLE CHOICES To select the best filtering tool, you need to know whether you must narrow to one or more choices. For example, you may have a set of scope-level user requirements for your "dream" scope, but you must reduce the dream to reality. In that case, you'll select multiple scope elements. At other times, you must select one thing, as happened in one of my workshops: Participants selected one of three possible software packages to satisfy requirements elicited during other workshops.

USING FIXED CHOICES OR EXTENDING CHOICES Suppose you have decided before the workshop that the group can extend the list of choices. For example, you have a draft set of use cases as an input to the workshop, but you know that when the group begins to model the use cases, the members may discover others. In that case, they can extend the choices.

Or you might begin the workshop with a predefined set of choices. For example, a group might be choosing among several software packages that have been analyzed and selected before the workshop. You might split up workshops so that participants define requirements in one session and return to prioritize them, along with architectural dependencies and project risks, in the next workshop. In that case, the requirements are also fixed.

DEFINING CRITERIA BEFORE MAKING CHOICES Agree on the criteria before the group begins its modeling activities. When people know how they'll make choices about their requirements before they begin to model them, they're more likely to consider these while modeling and begin to intuitively prune items. This activity helps to reduce the time needed to model requirements.

In one of my workshops, the criteria came in the form of a scheme devised before the workshop to rank how strongly each use case mapped to the business goals and objectives. After I reviewed these criteria, the participants defined actors and their goals. It wasn't long before several participants challenged a particular actor/use case pairing as irrelevant to the project goals. The whole group agreed, and it eliminated the actor and the use case.

Defining criteria before the requirements workshop also yields more rigorous selection criteria. If you wait until after you define requirements to define how you'll cut them back, people tend to go easy on the requirements they have just invested time and effort to create.

FILTERING TOOLS FOR THE SIEVE   The following list describes tools that can help you filter user requirements. After you apply any of these tools in a workshop, you need to use your decision-making process to reach closure.

- *Predefined prioritization and ranking scales* are scales or schemes for evaluating options defined by a standards body. Examples include the IEEE's Essential, Conditional, Optional, and MoSCoW (Must, Should, Could, Won't) scale. You use one of these scales or schemes to prioritize and rank the scope of high-level requirements as expressed in models such as an event table, use cases, and business policies.
- *Voice of the customer* is a technique that categorizes customer needs as *expectors* (the customer takes these needs for granted and would be disappointed if they weren't addressed), *unspokens* (the customer doesn't state these needs but would be upset if the needs weren't addressed), *spokens* (the needs that customers tell you about), or *delighters* (the needs that are exciting to customers but whose absence would result in few adverse effects). This tool is particularly useful in generating and analyzing requirements expressed within use cases.
- The *$100 test* allows customers and users to metaphorically spend money—$100, naturally—on requirements. Each of them distributes the money by weighting the different requirements, after which you compute the average weightings.
- The *criteria grid* is a matrix you can use for rating options against a list of three to five agreed-upon criteria, such as impact on organizational objectives and benefits to customer service goals. You can design the matrix to reflect numerical rankings, or you can simply use an X to indicate a pairing of an option and a criterion it meets.
- You use the *portfolio matrix* to map items to phases in the context of a lifecycle metaphor: sow, grow, harvest, and plow. This mapping will help you decide where to allocate resources. This tool is especially handy when you're reallocating user requirements to match strategies or prioritize projects.

- *Ask why five times* is a *directed thinking* technique designed to increase understanding of the root cause of a goal, need, or want. For each item— for example, a use case and the requirements it addresses—you ask, "Why do you need this?" Then you respond to each answer with the same question until you've asked "Why?" five times.

You can combine tools; for example, asking why five times can be useful for getting to the purpose of a requirement because it allows you to use a predefined prioritization scale.

Web Site

The Web site for this book offers information about these and other filtering tools for The Sieve.

COMBINING COLLABORATION PATTERNS

You'll often combine collaboration patterns. For example, you might do one or more of the following:

- Incorporate The Sieve into the Expand Then Contract to narrow choices.
- Use the Wall of Wonder during Expand Then Contract.
- Use Decide How to Decide continuously, no matter which other patterns you're using, to reach closure on the requirements.

Another option is to use Expand Then Contract as an overarching pattern and then incorporate DCCC during the expand phase in order to define the scope of a project. After creating a single "wish list" context diagram, you assign logical partitions of the diagram to subgroups and then assign each subgroup tasks for further analysis.

In one of my workshops (described in "SalesTrak" in Chapter 11), subgroups did the following:

- Defined the data needed for each of the flows on the context diagram (events and event responses)
- Described each external agent (actor) on the diagram
- Estimated the frequency and volume information associated with the events
- Associated events with business goals stated in the project charter
- Rated each event with regard to its importance to the project, along a predefined scale

Then the group reviewed all the analysis in a plenary session. The contract phase began when the participants redrew the context diagram to reflect the real scope; this narrowed the original scope by more than half.

COLLABORATIVE TECHNIQUES

There are a variety of group process techniques that you can inject into a workshop to introduce variety, promote creativity, and enhance participation. Some of these techniques help groups with expanding—generating, specifying, elaborating—and others assist with contracting—clustering, evaluating, comparing. These techniques include the following:

- *Method 6-3-5,* which helps with expanding, involves generating items in response to a focus question, issue, or problem. Workshop participants list stakeholders, events, data attributes, use cases, business rules, and scenarios, and then they identify the associated risks to the project and relevant post-workshop actions.
- *Forcefield analysis,* which also helps with expanding, involves examining two opposing forces in a given situation and then assessing the risks associated with implementing requirements and enforcing the relevant business rules.
- *Lateral thinking,* which helps with contracting, is a directed thinking technique for evaluating, comparing, and assessing a set of items. You can use this approach to define the risks and opportunities associated with use cases or business rules, narrow the scope of a project, or assess a project release strategy.
- The *SWOT matrix,* which also helps with contracting, is a tool for identifying strengths, weaknesses, opportunities, and threats (thus, SWOT). This tool is handy for evaluating project scope after you create scope-level requirements models.

Note that three other collaborative techniques are discussed elsewhere in this book: the mind map (see "Output Products" in Chapter 7), role playing (see "Walkthroughs" earlier in this chapter), and the gallery (see "Multi-Modeling Using the DCCC Pattern" earlier in this chapter).

You can integrate any of these techniques into your activities to generate different ways to use collaboration patterns. For example, you can use the gallery during the *correct* phase of DCCC, or role play during the *expand* stage of Expand Then Contract.

TECHNIQUES FOR GUIDING THE FLOW

Off-target discussions are part of every group gathering. You need an arsenal of techniques for guiding the flow of group discussion, the energy of the group, and the attention paid to time constraints. Available techniques include the following:

- Use a parking lot (see the next subsection).
- Set a time limit on discussions.
- If an activity stretches across several hours, periodically summarize results.
- Read participants' faces and body language for clues.
- Use the *red card* technique to allow everyone to monitor the flow. (Give everyone a red index card at the beginning of the workshop. Tell the participants that anyone can hold her red card in the air whenever she thinks that the discussion needs to stop or move.)

THE PARKING LOT

The *parking lot* is a device for dealing with topics that are relevant to the project but not to the current activities. The parking lot is a metaphor for "parking" issues—topics that you plan to address later and don't want to forget.

You should place a poster labeled "Parking Lot" in view of all the participants. You can also use separate posters, with labels such as "Issues," "Decisions," "Actions," "Parking Lot," or a combination of these. Early in the workshop, the group might not know where a topic fits when it first arises, so start with just a parking lot poster.

The parking lot prevents the group from getting stuck on a topic and spinning its wheels. Use a five-minute rule: If the group is discussing a topic for more than five minutes, ask whether the topic is relevant to the task at hand or whether it could be parked. If you sense that the topic is important or that the group is nearing closure, allow discussion to go on. If you're not sure, say so and then let the group decide whether to move on or continue the discussion.

To post an item to the parking lot, ask someone to *headline* the topic by writing a few words or a phrase that summarizes the issue. Be sure that everyone understands the headline wording so that they'll remember it later. The parking lot belongs to the group, so nothing goes there until the whole group has been consulted. At the end of each day of a multiday workshop, or at the end of the workshop, dispose of each item (see "Addressing Parking Lot Items" later in this chapter).

"For fast-acting relief, try slowing down."
—Jane Wagner for Lily Tomlin's act

GROUP DYNAMICS

Group interactions follow a life cycle. The various phases are called by various names, such as orientation, conflict, consensus, and closure (Tubbs, 1995) and orientation, conflict, emergence, and reinforcement (Fisher, 1970). The most widely recognized cycle is forming, storming, norming, and performing (see Chapter 6). A related stage, adjourning, involves how a group ends its work (Tuckman and Jensen, 1977).

In a productive workshop, the group will move through all these stages. Awareness of them helps you to proactively assist a group to move along. The characteristics of each of these stages include the following:

- Forming: Participants are searching for understanding of the workshop situation and expectations of themselves. Anxiety and anticipation may be high.
- Storming: Participants openly express disagreement. Some may feel anger, annoyance, uncertainty, or disappointment.
- Norming: Participants find ways to resolve issues raised in the storming phase, and they begin to build trust and respect and to support one another in tasks.
- Performing: The group is productive, collaborative, and confident. The participants are willing to give and get feedback and are visibly enjoying the workshop.
- Adjourning: The group is ending its work and seeking closure.

As the group makes the transition into the next stage, you can help to facilitate the transition in these ways:

- Forming: Have the workshop sponsor or project sponsor kick off the workshop; start with simple tasks that will help the group to deliver quick results; use an opener.
- Storming: Be prepared by discovering hidden agendas before the workshop; remind the group about its ground rules; openly acknowledge and address conflicts and differences.

- Norming: Back off on structure and explicit directions; give participants more complex tasks; invite input and feedback on the workshop process.
- Performing: Reinforce positive behavior; inject frequent celebrations and brief energizers; suggest that the group begin to map out its post-workshop actions.
- Adjourning: Review and resolve issues on the parking lot; conduct a final workshop debrief; have sponsors return for a show-and-tell.

CONFLICT

Conflict is a normal part of a group's development. It takes many forms: disagreements, arguments, raised voices, unwillingness to participate, cutting people off during conversations. There are numerous reasons people may exhibit conflict, including these:

- Not hearing the reasons behind a position
- Not understanding the other person's point of view because of differing values and experiences
- Personality differences or prior negative history
- Inadequate preparation
- Insufficient or misleading communication before the workshop
- Personal values, biases, prejudices
- Competition over resources
- Semantic misunderstanding, in which participants are using words differently
- Insufficient direction or leadership about the purpose for attending the workshop or for the project as a whole
- Personal problems, including substance abuse, depression, and anxiety

Although dealing with participants' personal problems is outside the scope of this book, you often must manage the other sources of conflict in your requirements workshops. To manage conflict, you must understand its value and have tools for handling it.

THE VALUE OF CONFLICT

Conflict can be valuable to healthy group development. When you address it openly and directly, it can bring honesty to real issues. This is particularly im-

IT'S BEST TO DEAL WITH THE TOUGH STUFF HEAD-ON.

portant when you have limited resources, as is the case in most projects. Tough decisions must be made about competing priorities. Honest discussion can emerge about lack of communication and sharing of relevant information. This is healthy because it permits people not only to vent their frustrations but also to make commitments to change behavior to the benefit of the project, the group, and individual relationships.

Trust

Conflict also can be healthy as a means of surfacing real issues, providing more ideas, building trust, and avoiding dysfunctional behavior such as groupthink.

GROUP DYSFUNCTION

Groupthink is the situation in which participants' desire to be "as one" is viewed as more important than their individual points of view (Janis, 1982). Groupthink stifles the exploration of alternatives and the discovery of beneficial or dangerous possibilities, and it can lead to suboptimal decisions. In *groupshift*, a variation of groupthink, individuals move to a more extreme position in the direction they were leaning, taking on either more cautious or riskier decisions (Robbins, 2000). To avoid groupthink and groupshift in your workshop, use these techniques:

- Ensure that participants represent diverse points of view.
- Mix membership in subgroups.
- Use lateral thinking tools (see "Collaborative Techniques" earlier in this chapter).

- Reward people for surfacing difficult issues.
- Use multiple perspectives.
- Use the degree of agreement scale before taking decisions (see "Reaching Closure" in Chapter 6).
- Encourage members to speak out.
- Appoint a devil's advocate.

Another problem with groups, the *Abilene paradox,* occurs when a group makes a decision that contradicts what individuals privately want to do (Harvey, 1988). This failure to manage disagreement results from not questioning and not challenging assumptions and decisions because of the fear of taking risks or becoming alienated or distrusted. Here are ways to avoid the risks associated with this problem in a requirements workshop:

- Establish and consistently use a decision-making process and decision rule.
- Use anonymous polling during decision making.
- Conduct a structured discussion of options before polling the group.
- Rotate membership in subgroups.
- Ensure that the ground rules promote and even reward the sharing of legitimate disagreement.
- Ask questions before the workshop to find out whether there are problems such as fear of speaking the truth and distrust among stakeholders.

When you find a great deal of distrust among participants, consider not conducting a requirements workshop until these deeper issues have been addressed openly and honestly.

HOW TO DEAL WITH DIFFICULT PARTICIPANTS

When a family has a "problem child," that child is merely the "identified patient." The family is really a system, one that supports, enables, and contributes to a deeper problem. When one or more participants act in a difficult way in a workshop, it's the whole group's problem.

Frequent Debriefs

At times, the difficult behavior diverts the group from attending to the heart of the issue. A difficult participant may be raising issues that the group needs to deal with, but his manner of doing so is likely to be distracting and negative. At other times, the difficult behavior is isolated and reflects an individual's personal issues.

The worst thing you can do in a workshop is to ignore difficult behavior. You must allow the persons to vent and help them and the group to name the specific issue. The group can help to solve the problem by asking the difficult participant for suggestions about how to overcome the issue being raised. The key for the facilitator is to acknowledge the difficult behavior, remain neutral, practice active listening, and summarize and paraphrase the discussion.

Addressing difficult behavior can result in an issue for the parking lot. At other times, it requires spending a few minutes sharing information because participants may have been given insufficient or conflicting information.

There are common patterns of difficult participant behavior that challenges even the most experienced facilitators. Here are some difficult styles and tactics for handling them:

- *The Complainer* hangs on to a point or stands on particular ground to the point that it drains the group's forward movement. Ask whether the complaint must be dealt with immediately in order to get the next deliverable done; set a time limit for the person to talk.

- *The Latecomer* consistently comes in late and may ask questions or whisper to others to try to catch up. Hand out toys, rewards, or points for being on time, and ask each participant to find a "buddy" who will fill them in during the next break.

- *The Dominator* consistently interrupts and holds up the group process. Look directly at her and say, "Thank you. Now let's hear from some others." Also, establish a ritual for talking in which participants must ask for a physical tool, such as a Koosh ball, to gain the floor.

- *The Silent One* participates to a minimal extent or perhaps not at all. Use a discussion in which each person chooses when to speak. Make nonverbal contact with the person and encourage him to participate.

- *The Preoccupied One* may start doing unrelated work, check her beeper, fidget, or scribble. Ask all the participants to clear their work spaces. Also, move closer to the offender.

FUN AND GAMES

Serious Play

People are more productive when they're having fun. Fun is not only "ha ha" belly laughing but also an experience referred to as *flow*, which is a teetering between anxiety and boredom (Csikszentmihalyi 1991).

A successful workshop combines play with the work. Toys, for example, can be used to prompt conversation, to diffuse tension, and to promote creativity.

I often bring a colorful bag loaded with small inexpensive toys, such as gliders, sticky bugs, bubbles, putty, bendable aliens or dinosaurs, and other silly items. When a participant makes a useful comment, suggestion, or reinforcing remark, I let him choose a toy. After he finds something he likes and shows it to the rest of the group, I tell the group that the bag is now its to use. I suggest that the participants offer it to those who make useful or fun contributions. Being offered "a pick from the bag" becomes an enjoyable ritual for many groups; it also gives participants toys they can share during the workshop and keep as mementos. (Be sure to choose toys that don't make noise.)

Read your group to decide which of these techniques will work. Ask your planning team's advice, and even query participants during your workshop information gathering to determine how acceptable or useful fun and games will be for your group.

Both Sides of the Brain

Here are some ways to have serious fun:

- Incorporate energizer activities.
- Provide meeting-worthy toys and tactile tools such as Silly Putty, Koosh balls, soft foam balls, and squishy bags.
- Play music (baroque and classical) during subgroup work and dance or energizing music during breaks.
- Use creative thinking techniques.
- For energizers or the workshop closer, try simulations or improvisational games.
- Pass out or display brain teasers for use during breaks.
- Use whistles, chimes, bells, or poppers to get people's attention after breaks or in finishing an activity.

Web Site

See the Web site for the book for online resources about energizers and openers, meeting-worthy tools, and activities that fit various kinds of learning styles.

"Every exit is an entry somewhere."
—Tom Stoppard

Serious Fun at the Dentist

For about a year, I paid periodic visits to an orthodontist. I looked forward to these appointments. The practice is large, about 15 chairs. It's constantly busy. The two dentists have numerous energetic support staff. The office is well run—they're on time most of the time—but that's only part of the reason I liked being there. It's a friendly place, with people smiling and joking. In fact, when I arrived for one visit, the dentist was teasing his assistant in front of me about forgetting "the thing." It turned out that they had a cupcake for me to celebrate my birthday that week.

One day, I walked in five minutes early for a 7:30 A.M. appointment. The automated sign-in was operating, and fresh coffee was brewing, but the place was deserted, silent. Suddenly, at 7:30 on the nose, a gaggle of people emerged from one of the rooms, buzzing—laughing, talking, moving around. When I asked about this, I was told that each morning the staff has a 15-minute, all-hands meeting.

During this meeting, they go over the day's work and then do an "affirmation." It isn't religious; rather, it's a few minutes during which someone from the office (a different person each day) brings in something positive or fun: a quick game, some popcorn to make right then, a (clean) joke, a true story of appreciation. They take this responsibility seriously. They have serious fun.

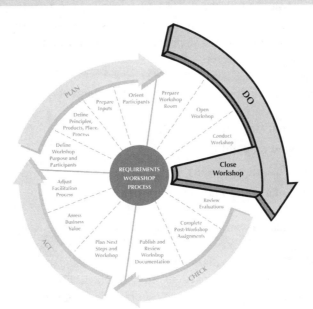

CLOSING THE WORKSHOP

The workshop closing wraps up loose ends, defines post-workshop commitments, and enables the participants to make the transition back to the outside world. This is also the time for reflecting on the workshop process and group experience in order to learn about and identify things to change and celebrate. By doing this, participants experience self-reflection, a behavior you want them to carry back to their respective teams.

Adapt the order and specifics for your workshop closing to include these tasks:

- Prepare for the show-and-tell.
- Conduct the show-and-tell.
- Review and make decisions about the parking lot or issues list.
- Review actions and decisions.
- Conduct a final workshop debrief.

Because sponsors sometimes raise points that must be converted into actions or issues, I recommend making the show-and-tell the first step in closing.

THE SHOW-AND-TELL

The show-and-tell begins the closing process. In addition to educating and informing sponsors and stakeholders, the show-and-tell requires that participants review and reflect on their work. Budget no more than 45 minutes to prepare, and 30 minutes to present.

Participants tell their show-and-tell audience

- What they created
- How they did it
- What they learned
- What issues and concerns they have

They also answer questions as necessary.

To prepare for the show-and-tell, form small groups to work on each topic, and make sure that each participant is involved. Encourage participants to take turns presenting or to elect a spokesperson for each topic. By this point in your session, everyone should be self-sufficient and should need little help from you to get ready.

During the show-and-tell, retreat to the back of the room and let the participants run the show.

ADDRESSING PARKING LOT ITEMS

The end of the workshop should include disposing of each item on the parking lot or issues poster. Taking one item at a time, ask whether it still needs to be addressed. In longer workshops (a day or more), at least half of the items are no longer applicable because the group will have addressed them in the course of the workshop. For multiday workshops, review and dispose of the parking lot items daily.

Any remaining items should be assigned to a participant for follow-up, in terms of *who* (will follow up), *what* (she will do to address it), *when* (she will get back to the group), and *how* (she will contact the group: e-mail, the next workshop, a follow-up meeting). If multiple people volunteer to work on an issue, ask which one will be the coordinator.

FINAL DEBRIEF

Frequent
Debriefs

A final workshop *debrief* or *retrospective* is a closing ritual that permits participants to adjourn from their work together and discover ways to work better together in this or another group. This idea, embodied in the collaboration pattern Self-Reflect (see the Appendix), is practiced on an ongoing basis, not just during the workshop closing. For a definitive discussion of the value of debriefs and for techniques that you can adapt for requirements workshops, see Norm Kerth's *Project Retrospectives* (Kerth, 2000).

Allow about half an hour for the debrief activity. Budget more time if this is the last in a series of workshops or if the workshop lasted multiple days. Start by passing out a paper workshop evaluation form (see "Happy Sheets" in Chapter 12); this allows participants to quietly and individually reflect on the workshop. Next, facilitate a group debrief. You can use a poster or a wall prepared with items from a debrief template such as "Things That Worked" and "Things We Didn't Do Well." Find out not only what could be improved but also what worked well; the latter should be repeated in other workshops. You can also facilitate a workshop debrief using a structured discussion method or a technique designed specifically for debriefing.

TIPS

- Plan an appropriate opener to get the group comfortable and engaged.
- Design activities for groups of related requirements.
- Build in quality checking of workshop deliverables.
- Continually check on the effectiveness of the workshop process.

- Use mini-tutorials and focus questions to jump-start modeling tasks.
- Iterate using parallel and reciprocal group activities.
- Limit off-track discussions
- Address conflict directly and openly.
- Make the workshop fun.
- Allow time to prepare and present the show-and-tell.
- Always debrief after the workshop.
- End with the next beginning in mind.

TOOLS FOR THE WORKSHOP PROCESS

The Web site for this book provides tools that will help you to plan and manage the workshop process, including the following:

- Workshop design template
- Workshop agenda template
- Useful focus questions to guide the flow of discussion
- Focus questions for requirements modeling tasks
- QA checklists for requirements models
- Briefings on filtering items for The Sieve
- An example of using Expand Then Contract for listing use cases
- Sample workshop evaluations (Happy Sheets)
- Resources for workshop energizers and openers
- Suggested meeting-worthy toys

FOR MORE INFORMATION

Bens (2000) provides essential information about the facilitation process, including facilitation stages, ways to deal with conflict, decision making, and meeting management.

de Bono (1994) provides explanations of tools for changing thinking patterns via lateral thinking. You can use many of these thinking tools as workshop activities to help participants evaluate their ideas, models, and decisions.

de Bono (1999) describes simple and useful role-playing techniques that use six modes of thinking. You can use these methods during workshops to facilitate evaluation and analysis of topics and deliverables.

Justice and Jamieson (1999) is a large collection of useful resources, tools, templates, and guidelines that is likely to be of value for any group facilitator.

Kayser (1990) is a useful guidebook for making meetings and workshops productive. It offers specifics about many useful techniques for new facilitators along with reminders and refreshers for experienced meeting leaders.

Ritter and Brassard (1998) is a mini-book (3.5 inches by 5.5 inches) that offers a concise collection of methods and steps, as well as short examples, for creative thinking. These include mind mapping, a brainwriting pool, the idea cards method, the purpose hierarchy, and more.

Spencer (1989) presents the "technology of participation" (ToP) facilitation technique for strategic planning. This book includes highly useful methods for workshops of all kinds, including the focused conversation method, the workshop method, the card technique, and the action planning method. This methodology is based on the author's many years of practical experience worldwide involving both commercial and nonprofit entities.

Stanfield (1997) expands on the conversation method from the technology of participation methodology (see Spencer, 1989) with a four-phase structure for asking questions that can be useful in many kinds of workshops and in a variety of business settings. The book is full of sample questions for each phase: objective/data, reflective/feeling, interpretive/meaning, and decisional/action.

Strachan (2001) contains great questions to ask in a variety of workshop situations, including workshop opening and closing, thinking critically, and enabling action.

VanGundy (1988) is an extensive reference book that describes more than 100 techniques for redefining and analyzing problems, generating ideas, and evaluating and selecting ideas. It also provides fundamentals that you can tailor for your workshops for techniques such as the gallery method, method 6-3-5, rolestorming, and a brainwriting pool.

Wiegers (1999) is a comprehensive book on software requirements. Chapter 13 describes a detailed way to prioritize requirements based on value, cost, and risk.

Wiegers (2001) is a concise, practical guide to reviews, walkthroughs, and inspections—some of the most effective techniques for increasing the quality of software.

PART THREE

REQUIREMENTS WORKSHOP
DESIGN STRATEGIES

Chapters 10, 11, and 12 describe strategies for navigating through your requirements workshop, case studies to illustrate these strategies and ways to exploit workshop success ingredients, and suggestions on how to move forward with implementing requirements workshops in your organization.

10

WORKSHOP NAVIGATION STRATEGIES

"The means prepare the end and the end is what the means have made it."
—John Morley

You can design your requirements workshops using three kinds of strategies: horizontal, vertical, or zigzag.

You can use the same strategy throughout a workshop or over a series of workshops, or you can start with one strategy and shift to another within a workshop or during a follow-up workshop. Regardless of how you implement the navigation strategy, using it requires that you select a subset of models, plan how you'll connect them during the workshop, know how well the requirements scope is agreed upon by the participants, and identify input models and workshop aids to expedite the workshop process.

THE HORIZONTAL STRATEGY

With the *horizontal*, or *wide and shallow*, strategy, your workshop activities lead participants to create a variety of models along one level of detail (scope, high, or detailed) using multiple requirements focuses (who, what, when, why, where, and how). Like snorkelers, participants stay at roughly the same level of model detail in order to get a broad understanding of the requirements. From there, you design activities to move up or down the level of detail, either in the same workshop or in different workshops.

There are three options with regard to level:

- *Top-down:* scope-level, then down to high and detailed levels
- *Middle-out*: high-level, then up to scope level or down to detailed level
- *Bottom-up*: detailed-level, then up to high and scope levels

PICKING YOUR HORIZONTAL STRATEGY

Table 10-1 shows heuristics for choosing which level to start with in the context of a horizontal workshop strategy. You can use these in considering which level, or combination of levels, makes sense as a starting level in your situation.

A top-down strategy is imperative if your project scope is unclear or it keeps shifting. Either of these conditions indicates that deeper issues are in play. Perhaps the business problem isn't well understood, or the business is continually changing. Often, business stakeholders don't have a shared understanding of the business problem they're trying to solve, or they have competing priorities and needs. In this case, a well-planned workshop can be highly effective in saving time and money. Participants will need to explore the scope of the project and not delve into details. For example, once you've defined a context diagram and events, you might list use case names. Doing this means that you're moving

TABLE 10-1 PICKING YOUR HORIZONTAL STRATEGY

Strategy	Conditions
Top-down	■ Scope isn't well understand. ■ Team hasn't used workshops before. ■ Sponsor is at high level and will be in workshop. ■ Application is new type for organization.
Middle-out	■ Scope is fairly well agreed upon. ■ Some models at high level already exist, such as data model or list of use cases.
Bottom-up	■ Subject matter experts are present. ■ Project involves replacing existing system. ■ No high-level participants are present in workshops. ■ Project is not yet chartered or sponsored. ■ Scope is very narrow. ■ There is little risk that scope will change after design and development commence.

down to the next tier, so be careful not to allow participants to get into too much detail, such as listing use case steps.

TAKE SHORT DIVES   If you've ever snorkeled, you know that you float at the surface of the water wearing a mask and breathing through a tube that sticks out of the water. If something interesting appears, you can take a deep breath and dive down to investigate. Your dive is short and, hopefully, sweet. If you dive too often, though, you use up your energy and limit the surface area you can cover. And if you dive too deep or stay down too long, you can run out of air.

In a scope workshop, you must make sure that participants stay at the surface and take short dives only when something unusually interesting appears. To conserve the group's energy, you should also limit the number of dives. It's a common mistake to allow groups to get off-track with detailed discussions that should be saved for another time or investigated as a follow-up activity.

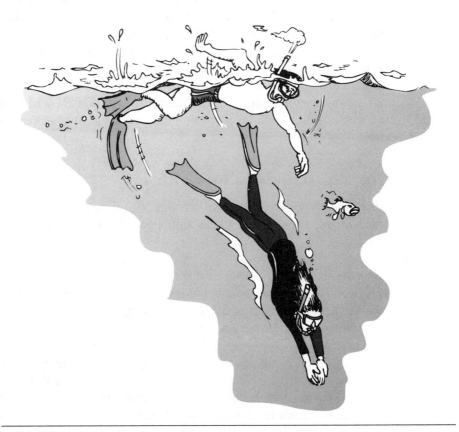

WHEN YOU'RE SNORKELING, IT'S BEST TO TAKE SHORT DIVES.

Listen carefully for discussions about the steps, procedures, and rules of the proposed system. You'll hear people talk about a business process and say things such as, "And then . . . ," "But if . . . ," and "After that . . . ." These are tip-offs that people are talking about what happens inside the system.

You must manage such discussions carefully. If participants take too many dives, examine your process. Perhaps you're not controlling the discussion, or the participants may be unable to think at a higher level, or they're spending too much time teaching others about details. Capturing these details might be useful, but you must weigh that benefit against your immediate goal, which is to define the project's scope. You don't want to spend time on details that turn out to be out of scope or postponed to a later release.

I facilitated a one-day workshop for a project in which the software team was asked to install a package. The sponsors gave the software manager only a vague scope. The manager said that he and his team couldn't define requirements without knowing which of the many package modules were needed. They needed to clarify scope before defining which requirements to implement and how they might need to be adjusted in the package. I chose a horizontal top-down strategy. In the one-day session, participants defined a context diagram, stakeholder classes, and an event list. In the afternoon, they scaled back their "dream" scope from the one they had outlined that morning, and that allowed them to plan a next step: defining high level requirements with the involvement of the direct users.

THE TOP-DOWN APPROACH

Figure 10-1 shows the horizontal strategy with the elements of a top-down approach circled. The diagram shows all the possible models to select from at that level.

Remember to choose a subset of these models, not all of them. Conduct subsequent workshops, or at least activities within a given workshop, to navigate down and across the focuses and levels, with the goal of gaining a more complete understanding of the requirements.

For example, you might start your workshop with a horizontal top-down strategy that uses the who, what, and when focuses. Participants would define stakeholder classes, a context diagram, and an event table and also agree on some basic glossary terms. If the business stakeholders wish to rethink business policies, include these as workshop deliverables. Lay out a sequence of activities to

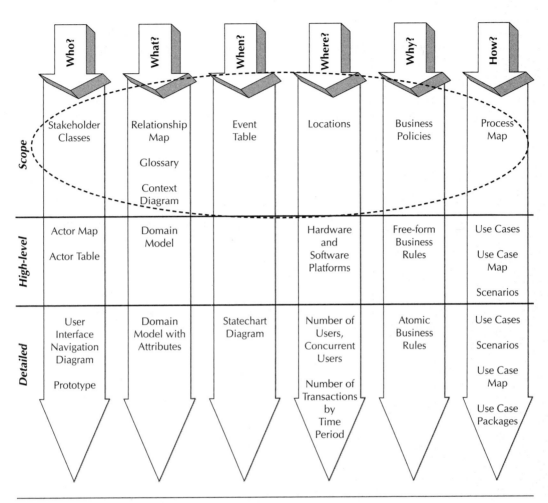

FIGURE 10-1   HORIZONTAL TOP-DOWN STRATEGY

deliver them, as described in "Sequencing Activities" in Chapter 9. Determine what input products participants can use as input to each activity (see "Input Products" in Chapter 7) and develop focus questions that will help them do their modeling tasks (see "Using Focus Questions" in Chapter 9).

Before the workshop, you might assign the participants pre-work, such as reviewing the project charter or reviewing and commenting on the draft project glossary. In addition, you and your workshop planning team should also create a QA checklist to use in the workshop for performing doneness testing of your models, and you should also use templates to help participants to understand the desired end state of their requirements (see "Templates" in Chapter 7).

Depending on the complexity and size of the software you're building, the number of participants, their familiarity with one another, and the quality of the charter, you might need one-half to two days to define deliverables in a horizontal, top-down workshop.

THE MIDDLE-OUT APPROACH

A middle-out strategy assumes that the team understands the scope of the project, or at least that some requirements are well understood at a high level. Participants work on the high-level requirements and then shift up or down to a different level of detail.

Figure 10-2 shows an example of how to navigate models using a horizontal middle-out strategy. Assume that the team has a list of use cases before the workshop. You can start the workshop by having them further define each use case by writing a brief, one-paragraph description and completing the header portion of your use case template. Next, participants list the data attributes and actors needed by each use case. Then they create a use case map to see how the use cases depend on one another. From there, participants move up a level to capture scope-level models (a context diagram, stakeholder classes, and events). Finally, in the same workshop or a different workshop, they can move down to detailed use cases, scenarios, business rules, and screen flow sketches or a user interface navigation diagram.

The example in Figure 10-2 shows participants moving from the high-level tier up to the scope tier. By the time this happens in the workshop, the participants will have a good understanding of their requirements and will be familiar with the workshop process, and this means that they will likely create the scope-level models very quickly—within an hour or so.

Moving up a level before going down a level helps everyone understand the scope of the requirements. For many projects, this is an important step; it ensures that everyone agrees to the big picture before getting into detail. It's not uncommon for issues—such as restructuring the business workflow or changing job responsibilities—to emerge at this point. You may also need to confirm the scope with your sponsor and other stakeholders before spending time on requirements details. But if the scope is fairly well agreed upon when you began the workshop, you can move down to detailed models.

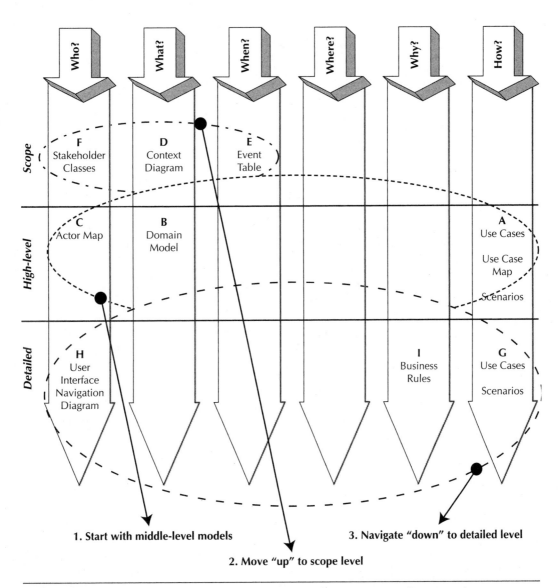

FIGURE 10-2 A HORIZONTAL MIDDLE-OUT STRATEGY IN ACTION (LETTERS INDICATE THE SEQUENCE OF STEPS)

One project wanted to use a workshop to finalize and reach closure on the detailed requirements. They had use cases, business rules, and a class model. However, when I talked with the business sponsor to plan the workshop, she told me she was uncertain about the requirements in this format and wasn't comfortable signing off on them as complete.

The Five-Minute Scope Test

I'd rather know what I don't know early in the software development game than later. Creating a context diagram in a scope workshop is a quick and meaningful way to expose important issues associated with scope.

Recently, I had coffee with a colleague who was just starting a new project that involved adding functionality to a Web site. She wanted to hash out some ideas on how to conduct her first requirements workshop with people from the company's marketing and product development departments.

"The scope is pretty small," she said. "I was thinking of starting with a workshop focusing on use cases. What do you think?" I asked her my favorite scope questions: "Who needs to get things from the system? What do they get? What other people or things must give or get information?" As she supplied the answers, I began drawing a context diagram on a coffee napkin.

In less than five minutes, it became clear that this project had numerous actors of various types. For example, one class of actors she mentioned was health care workers. Further questioning revealed that this category included nurses, doctors, social workers, and physician assistants, each with different needs. To make matters worse, my friend wasn't clear on what the real-world inputs and outputs might include. Finally she threw up her hands. Smiling wryly at me, she said, "I guess I'd better not define use cases yet."

The drawing, along with her inability to answer the questions precisely, had told her that the scope was larger than she had thought, as well as unclear. Now she knew where she needed to start.

I chose a middle-out strategy for working with the existing models, but I also asked the team to prepare more models as inputs to the workshop, based on what, how, and who focuses. I wanted these inputs to elaborate on the points of view expressed by the current requirements. Subsequently, the data analyst drafted a logical data model and a glossary; the business subject matter experts created scenarios for testing each use case; and the user interface designer created prototype screens for each use case.

We defined a list of QA checklist questions, settled on a use case completion form, and defined the decision rule for reaching closure on each of the dozen use cases. As the workshop progressed, we moved horizontally across the high-level models, and then down to the detailed models. The team reached closure on 9 of the 12 use cases, defined many more business rules that needed more detail by the business owner, and revised the screens and their flows appropriately.

THE BOTTOM-UP APPROACH

Another option is to start your requirements with a bottom-up horizontal approach. This involves creating user interface prototypes, detailed scenarios, lists of data elements, and detailed business rules. Then you work your way up, abstracting use cases, policies, and domain elements. Abstraction works by taking specifics and making them more general. For example, you list scenarios, group those that are alike, and then generalize similar sets of scenarios into use cases. Next, the participants abstract those into the scope models.

Generally, a bottom-up strategy makes sense when the team has already agreed on the project's scope, the project sponsorship is strong, the team has defined scope-level requirements using other requirements methods (such as interviews), and the group wants to use collaborative techniques to bring team players together. On the other hand, the bottom-up strategy is the riskiest one to start with when your scope isn't clear or you don't have strong project sponsorship. Perhaps you're waiting for formal sponsorship to be engaged and you anticipate that it's only a matter of time. If you can't get a sponsor to attend the workshop, you might do well to start with a bottom-up approach.

THE VERTICAL STRATEGY

To follow the *vertical*, or *narrow and deep*, strategy, you navigate down to detailed models in a single focus. You use one model just as a starting point, and then, as if you were scuba diving, you delve into the details of that model and perhaps one or two related models at the same level.

In Figure 10-3, the vertical path goes through the *how* focus of the various models. Beginning with the process map, participants would continue navigating down to models at successively lower levels. When each model is well understood and satisfies your doneness tests, you continue to move down into further detail.

PICK A STARTING MODEL

You use the starting model to trigger participants' thinking along the primary focus. This model acts as a thread that begins the process of weaving together a set of related models.

Figure 10-3 shows two possible starting models: the process map and the event table. (The latter appears with dotted lines; this notation indicates that you can vary the model that starts your navigation.) The key is to use a model that will

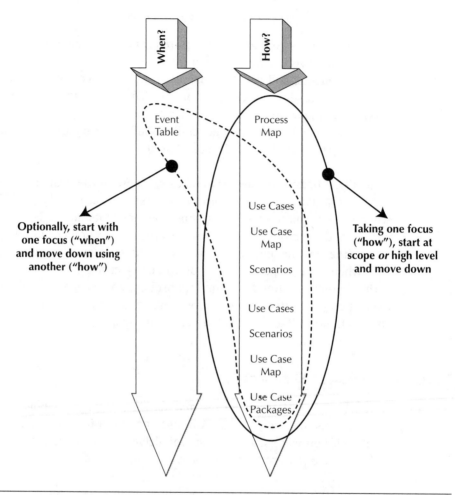

When?

How?

Event
Table

Process
Map

Use Cases

Use Case
Map

Scenarios

Use Cases

Scenarios

Use Case
Map

Use Case
Packages

**Optionally, start with
one focus ("when")
and move down using
another ("how")**

**Taking one focus
("how"), start at
scope *or* high level
and move down**

FIGURE 10-3 A VERTICAL STRATEGY

allow participants to make connections to the vertical path they'll follow during the workshop.

For example, for a downward path that starts with events, you might have a starting list of unfiltered events, as gathered in a pre-workshop assignment. During the workshop, participants decide which events are really in scope. These events drive the next activity: listing use cases that handle the responses to the events. Then the participants write a one-paragraph description of each event; perhaps they perform this activity in subgroups working in parallel. Next, the group gets back together, and the participants list scenarios for each other's use cases; then they test the use case descriptions using those scenarios.

You might insert a task here in which the participants identify nonfunctional requirements for their use cases, such as projected volume and frequency. When they finish this task, they can lay out cards for each use case on the wall to form a use case map and test the flow with their scenarios. At some point, they can follow a similar process for the detailed-level models.

PICK A PRIMARY FOCUS

The vertical requirements workshop strategy uses one of four primary focuses:

- *Who-first*: stakeholders, actor table, actor map, user interface, or prototype
- *What-first*: relationship map, glossary, context diagram, or domain model
- *When-first*: event table
- *How-first:* process map, use cases, use case map, or scenarios

It's difficult to begin with where- or why-focused models because they provide less operational context for subject matter experts and analysts. Asking, "What do you need to do in these different locations?" (a where question) or "What decision or rules do you need to follow?" (a why question) yields less modeling information than does a question about information, people, events, or behavior.

START AT THE SCOPE LEVEL OR THE HIGH LEVEL

If you're using a vertical strategy, you should begin your navigation with either scope-level models or high-level models. For example, to start with a who-first strategy at the high level, you'd begin with a list of actors.

Starting at the high level versus the scope level makes sense when you're certain about the scope. For example, perhaps you're into the second or third release of the system and in a prior workshop you have already prioritized remaining use cases to arrive at a release strategy.

Nevertheless, you should be prepared to address potential scope issues. Participants may need to be reminded of the big picture. Have at hand your scope models and text statement about project scope. You can even post them in the room as reminders. Be sure that questions and issues are adequately addressed. You don't want participants to plow down through requirements that may be unimportant, out of scope, or irrelevant.

In one workshop, I found that a scope document, created in a previous workshop, helped to prevent what was starting to become an off-track discussion. As participants began to question why they weren't addressing a different use case, I asked them to open their workshop binders and go to the tab marked "Background Information." In that section was a page that listed use cases by release. I asked them whether these releases still made sense. They all agreed that they did, and they moved on with their modeling work.

MOVE OVER

The vertical strategy involves staying primarily in one focus, but you can move horizontally to address one or two related models. For example, if you're following a vertical how-first path, you can shift to the who focus by having participants create an actor map. This might take an hour or so, but it's likely to be well worth it. Before moving down into a detailed use case with steps and exceptions, be sure that all your use cases are actually necessary. After they create the actor map, ask participants to associate use cases with actors on the actor map. This short task usually yields important information—such as unnecessary or poorly named use cases, extraneous actors, or the need to combine roles—that will help you to save time later.

THE VERTICAL STRATEGY WITH MULTIPLE WORKSHOPS

As with the horizontal strategy, you can use several workshop and post-workshop assignments to define requirements while you're operating vertically. Here's an example.

WORKSHOP 1   Activities (how-first, starting at high level):

1. List use cases (using good naming conventions).
2. For each use case, name the scenarios.
3. For each use case, create a brief paragraph description.
4. For each use case, define the use case header.
5. For each use case, define the initiating actor and location(s) of that actor.
6. Create an actor map that shows all actors.
7. Revise the use cases as necessary.

Note: Participants have now moved over to add *who* and *what* requirements.

Post-workshop activities:

1. Create a context diagram.
2. Create an event table.
3. Draft a glossary that contains all relevant business terms.

WORKSHOP 2   Activities (how-first, detailed level):

1. Review and agree on glossary terms.
2. Review and agree on the scope models (context diagram and event table).
3. Revise use case headers with the trigger (event) and outcome (event response).
4. For each use case, list use case steps.
5. For each use case, name the data elements.
6. For each use case step, write the business rules.
7. For each use case, write exceptions.
8. For each use case exception, write the business rules.

Note: Participants have now moved over to add *what* and *why* requirements.

Post-workshop activities:

1. For each use case, list the scenarios.
2. For each use case, create a prototype.
3. Using the scenarios, conduct a team review of each prototype; make adjustments as necessary.
4. Using the scenarios, prototypes, and use cases, conduct user and customer reviews; make adjustments as necessary.

Using this approach, you harvest your requirements top-down, but for a narrow scope. You'd continue to do this for all the events, diving down to the lowest level before going back up and capturing other events. In this way, you're defining the requirements vertically. Although you might not ignore requirements that are wider in scope, you do put them aside. You don't dwell on scope; rather, you return to it iteratively.

The risk of taking the vertical approach is that you may spend time diving into requirements that end up being out of scope or not part of the release you're trying to focus. The best way to offset this risk is to begin the requirements process with a workshop that takes a horizontal slice of the requirements and achieves agreement for participants and the sponsor, and then proceed with a workshop using either the vertical strategy or the zigzag strategy.

THE ZIGZAG STRATEGY

The zigzag strategy involves navigating through different focuses, moving around like a skateboarder: down, over, and then down again or perhaps up. This strategy provides wider overall coverage of models and results in less precise deliverables.

The example in Figure 10-4 shows events as the starting model. Participants then create an actor map that contains roles that handle each event, and they follow that by modeling all the use cases needed to satisfy the actors' goals, as triggered by the events. Participants then return to the actor map, associating use cases with actors. Next, they capture domain information needed by each use case. They end the workshop by drafting user interface navigation sketches.

The zigzag approach is useful when you want a mix of breadth and depth. It's also useful when you need only a few models that, taken together, can express your user requirements.

I used the zigzag strategy illustrated in Figure 10-5 for a series of workshops that primarily defined business rules (see "BestClaims" in Chapter 11). We began by drafting a statechart diagram that showed states only for a single domain class. We moved up one level to list more data domains, and then we listed events that triggered transitions from state to state. This activity gave subject matter experts insight into their domains—they began to see subtypes. This, in turn, prompted them to revise their statechart diagrams.

For each state, participants created business rules following a structured template we designed before the workshop. They posted the business rules on the walls using color-coded cards, and they tested the rules using scenarios that they elaborated between sessions. (Note that this is an example of how you can navigate up or down using the zigzag strategy, not just top-down.)

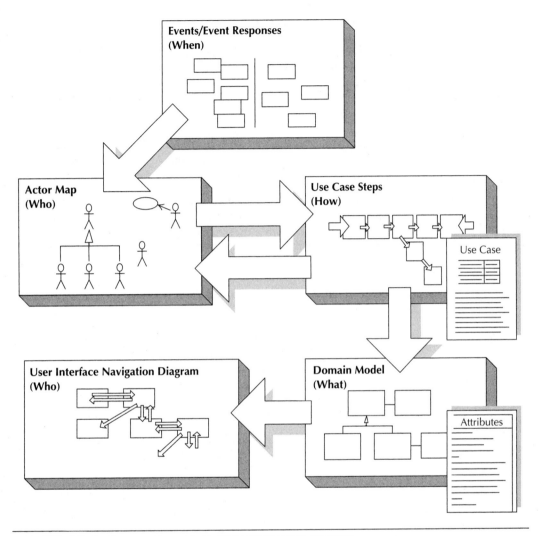

FIGURE 10-4 ZIGZAG STRATEGY, STARTING WITH EVENTS

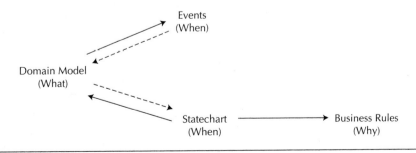

FIGURE 10-5 ZIGZAG STRATEGY, WITH FOCUS ON BUSINESS RULES

Comparing the Strategies

Table 10-2 summarizes the key characteristics of each navigation strategy. The key is planning: If one strategy doesn't work, be prepared to shift strategies. This requires that you prepare to be spontaneous.

TABLE 10-2 Comparing Navigation Strategies

Strategy	Strength	Starting Point (Level of Detail)	Number of Focuses Covered
Horizontal	Breadth	Scope, high, or detailed	3 or more
Vertical	Depth	Scope or high	1 (primarily)
Zigzag	Mix of breadth and depth	Scope, high, or detailed	3 or more

Chapter 11 provides examples of these strategies in action.

11

WORKSHOP
CASE STUDIES

"Plans get you into things, but you got to work your way out."
—Will Rogers

This chapter describes four case studies based on workshops I've facilitated over the years. To protect confidentiality, I've disguised the names and certain details not relevant to our purposes.

SALESTRAK

The workshop I did for a company named SalesTrak followed a horizontal, top-down strategy in the course of one six-hour session.

We defined the scope for a contact and customer relationship management (CRM) system for commissioned brokers who contacted independent insurance agents in their territories to make and close sales. Under the status quo, contact and customer information was inconsistent, and the data was of low quality. Broker managers had a hard time predicting sales and supporting their territory of brokers; the home office wanted more accurate information to facilitate cross-selling and to promote the use of competitive analysis on sales calls. They also wanted to be able to project sales and commissions and clean up "dirty" data.

Two marketing vice presidents wanted to buy and install an existing commercial package offering a wide array of modules. They had asked the software organization to learn and install the package but hadn't involved the software people in the selection process. The package was complex, with numerous modules that had to interface with a variety of legacy applications.

Other key issues included the following:

- There were conflicting needs and desires among the customers (home office senior management) and the users (brokers, broker managers, and sales support staff).
- The company wanted to implement a system within nine months.
- Brokers generally were not involved in any home office decisions.
- The marketing VPs didn't believe that the involvement of brokers in the project was necessary.
- There was no formal business case. It was typical at this firm for marketing to get financial sponsorship for its projects with little challenge.
- At Marketing's request, the software organization had already invested time in training two of its staff on the favored package.

We agreed to focus on these deliverables during the workshop:

- Stakeholder classes
- User classes (actors and indirect users)
- Context diagram
- Prioritized list of project constraints
- Prioritized list of problems and opportunities
- Issues
- Follow-up action items
- Projected next steps

Figure 11-1 shows the flow of activities we followed during the workshop.

We used three collaboration patterns along the way.

- Expand Then Contract framed the day's work. Participants created a "dream" scope using a context diagram that depicted every possible thing that any stakeholder wanted from the system. Using self-defined criteria during their final workshop activity, the group reduced the diagram to reflect a more realistic, focused scope.
- Divide, Conquer, Correct, Collect helped the group to work with logical chunks of the context diagram. Subgroups were formed to define the details of each external actor and each flow on the context diagram. I gave each subgroup a template to fill out to capture its detailed elements in a

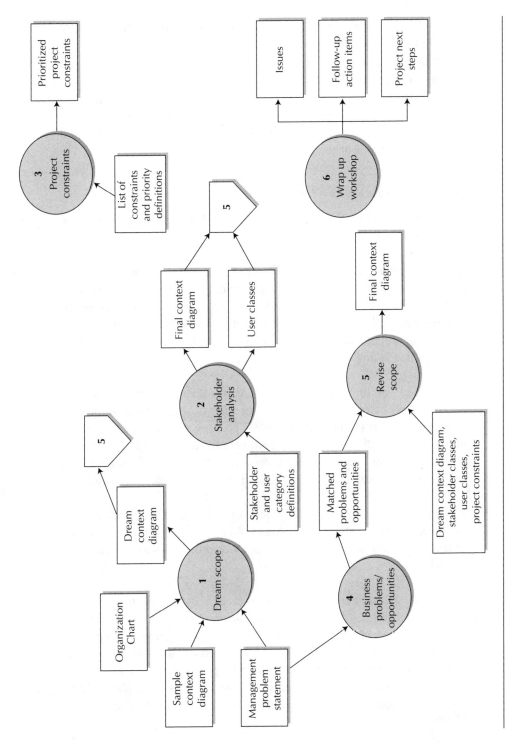

FIGURE 11-1 Salestrak Workshop Activity Flow

standard format. During a plenary activity, the participants reviewed one another's work and made corrections.

- The Sieve helped the group to define, and then apply, criteria for reducing the scope from dream to reality. The primary criterion was a prioritized list of business opportunities that the system should exploit. Subgroups evaluated whether or not a portion of the dream context would meet the high-priority business opportunities. As a result, the entire group eliminated more than half of the original actors.

WHAT WORKED WELL

The following subsections describe what worked well in the SalesTrak requirements workshop.

SELF-DEFINED CRITERIA The criteria were business opportunities that the system should exploit. They were defined by the group as ways to overcome current problems. The participants matched each element of their dream context diagram to business opportunities to determine how strongly it addressed the opportunity. This gave them a direct and visible correlation between business needs and functional scope.

As it turned out, the highest-priority need for SalesTrak was to enable brokers to improve their sales potential by having easy access to valid information. To do that, they needed product scripts, agent profiles, and the capabilities to check on underwriting status, to obtain competitive information, and to generate marketing letters. The dream scope included those capabilities along with a number of others, such as support for ordering supplies, projecting sales, and tracking expenses.

When the focus shifted from the home office needs to the needs of the brokers—the direct users—the software product requirements came into focus. This shift in focus also provided incentive for the vice presidents to engage brokers in the project.

ASKING FOR HIDDEN AGENDAS By asking the software manager for hidden agendas during my information gathering, I learned that the VPs wanted to avoid brokers' involvement in the entire project except during implementation. The software manager had argued against this to no avail, and he hoped that the workshop process would help the vice presidents understand the importance of the direct involvement of the brokers. To address this problem, I included an activity to list stakeholders, classify them, and then further classify all direct users.

During our closing activity, listing actions, one of the VPs said, "We need to get the detailed requirements from the brokers and broker managers." She offered to help create a list of brokers who would be good to do that job.

HAVING THE SESSION OFFSITE   The marketing VPs were known to get easily distracted. During each break, they checked messages and chatted with one another about things happening at the office. Breaks were brief. Before each break, I announced when we would reconvene, and I always started on time, whether or not the vice presidents were off the phone. They got the message right away to keep their calls brief.

USING A NEUTRAL FACILITATOR   SalesTrak benefited from having an outside facilitator because it helped preserve the goodwill between the software and the business groups.

PITFALLS AND LEARNING POINTS

The following subsections describe the pitfalls and learning points of the SalesTrak workshop.

ALLOW TIME FOR SELF-REFLECTION   During the debrief, there was no time for me to ask additional questions about how the group members might take the learning points from their interactions back to their day-to-day work on the project. It would have been useful to have budgeted time for doing so.

BETTER REPRESENT THE DIRECT USERS   Only one representative broker was present, and he was a home office broker manager—a surrogate broker. As the facilitator, I could have pushed the vice presidents more on this point before the workshop.

CREATE A DRAFT GLOSSARY   We didn't have a draft glossary before this workshop. If we had, we would have saved time during the plenary activity when subgroups corrected one another's portions of the context diagram. Having a glossary also would have saved pre-work time for the subsequent detailed-level workshops that I conducted with the brokers.

RegTrak

The purpose of the RegTrak workshop was to define detailed requirements for a product registration system to be used by analysts in ten countries to register medical equipment. During the workshop, we followed a horizontal, bottom-up strategy in two contiguous six-hour sessions.

The scope for each of a series of releases had been clearly defined before the workshop. A knowledgeable and highly motivated group of three subject matter experts acted as surrogate users, representing the global analysts. The software development team had drafted use cases using a template that described user interface details (such as buttons to press) and results, along with loosely written business rules. The surrogate group wasn't satisfied; the members didn't believe that they represented the users' requirements. Other key issues included the following:

- The business rules were complex, and the set was missing a number of country-specific regulations. The rules were also inconsistently and incompletely specified across use cases.
- The data modeler wasn't communicating with the object modelers.
- There was no glossary.
- The software team's analyst believed that the use cases were in good shape and didn't understand why the customers (the surrogate group) wouldn't sign off on them.
- The use cases described user interface actions, rather than the essential user tasks that accomplished the relevant goals. In addition, the use case text was very fine-grained.
- Scenarios were expressed at a high level, whereas the use cases were at a very low level. There were no error or exception scenarios.
- Software as well as business participants were skeptical of doing a workshop. Several weeks before, they had attended a two-day workshop in which the facilitator, an external object orientation expert, ran a CRC (class responsibility collaboration) session using the high-level scenarios. The participants had protested that they were confused, but the facilitator was unwilling to use another group process. "Why did we do class modeling when we really didn't yet understand the user requirements?" they asked.

We agreed to focus on these deliverables during the workshop:

- Detailed use cases
- Free-form business rules
- Prototype screens
- Additional scenarios
- Glossary

- Issues
- Follow-up action items
- Projected next steps

Figure 11-2 shows the flow of activities we followed during the workshop.

We used two collaboration patterns along the way.

- Multi-Model helped the group to gain a more complete understanding of the requirements. This required much pre-work, including separating the who (user interface) and the why (business rules) from the use case text, adding more detailed scenarios, drafting a conceptual data model, and creating nonworking prototype screens for each use case. The foundation of the work was the glossary, which also needed to be drafted before the workshop.

  During the workshop, the participants worked on one use case at a time. One subject matter expert role-played a scenario while the others listed steps on posts and placed them in sequence on the wall. At the same time, the participants wrote associated business rules below the steps. Next, the group walked through the screen prototypes using the same scenarios, and they revised the use case steps and glossary terms along the way. After the group cleaned up these items and wrote more business rules, they followed the same process for exception scenarios.

- Decide How to Decide helped the group to reach closure on each use case and the related elements of the other models. The rule was that Pamela, the manager of the user group, would decide after discussion. We closed 9 of 12 use cases during the session, with revisions noted in our use case completion log. Pamela and her staff knew how correct the requirements were; the software team participated in the polling process for each use case, and this gave Pamela a better understanding of how complete the requirements were from the software viewpoint. Using the predefined decision-making process accelerated the flow of the session.

WHAT WORKED WELL

The following subsections describe what worked well in the RegTrak requirements workshop.

PRE-WORK AND DRAFT MODELS Having all the draft models prepared before the workshop gave us an excellent starting point. We also prioritized

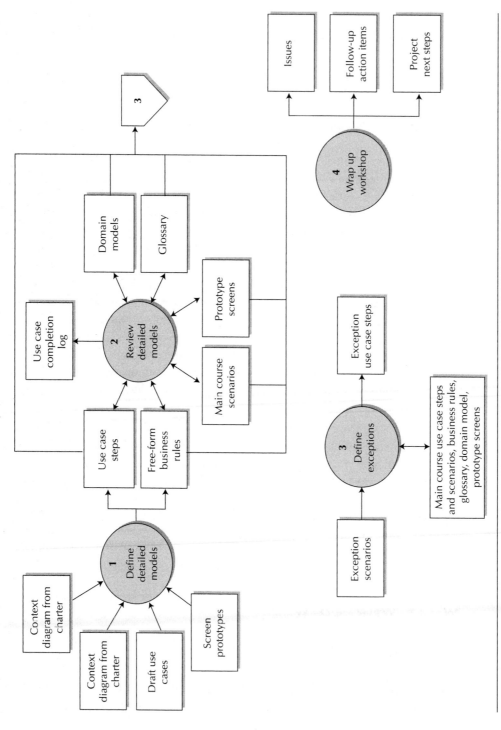

FIGURE 11-2   REGTRAK WORKSHOP ACTIVITY FLOW

the use cases before the session, so we knew which ones to focus on during our time together.

ROLE PLAYING AND HANDS-ON APPROACH TO USE CASES The text of the use cases didn't appeal to the business experts as a way to express and verify their requirements. Several months after the session, Pamela told me two things that she would always remember about the session: the acts of physically laying out use case steps on the wall and role-playing the scenarios. She commented that these techniques had been extremely useful to the group's ability to define the requirements.

DEFINING ROLES DURING MODELING ACTIVITIES Rotating among the models allowed the participants to see many related parts at the same time. It was mentally draining but fun. Occasionally we'd lose our place, but we recovered by having one person take responsibility for each individual model. Our glossary guardian (see "Draft Models" in Chapter 7) kept terms up-to-date, and our technographer captured details to be fixed in our use case completion log.

DEVELOPERS AS OBSERVERS The developers, a mix of consultants and company team members, were onboard and eager to "just code." I suggested that they draft a conceptual class model and statechart diagrams and then make notes on them as they observed the workshop. This technique helped prepare the developers to think about making the transition from requirements to design. They later commented on how critical it was for them to hear the requirements directly from users and how useful being at the session was for their later interactions with users.

THE GLOSSARY Before the workshop, the team members had received several lists of data attributes and entities, with names but no definitions, from the data modeler. Formalizing terms by defining them in a glossary enabled better mutual understanding between business and software team members. Participants were told to inspect each glossary item as part of their pre-work. As it turned out, we devoted time to resolving some contentious terms during the first morning of the workshop. This activity served to build shared meaning around several key business concepts.

The business domain was very behavior-oriented, so use cases were a natural requirements model to employ. Having agreed-upon terms allowed us to deemphasize the structural models (data and class models) while still giving them their due.

PITFALLS AND LEARNING POINTS

The following subsections describe the pitfalls and learning points of the RegTrak workshop.

CREATE A BUSINESS RULES TEMPLATE   The rules on the wall were written as free-form text, as opposed to using a structured template. We could have designed a precise business rules template before the workshop and had the data analyst start fitting the free-form rules into the template. This would have saved us time in specifying business rules more precisely after the workshop.

USE THE STATECHART DIAGRAM   There was no time to review the one statechart diagram that was drafted before the workshop. I suspect that if we'd done so before we began the use case modeling activities, we would have clarified more glossary terms and unearthed some very important business rules that cropped up later.

ARRANGE FOR PLENTY OF WALL SPACE   The setting was the living room of a guest house owned by the company. My challenge was to create enough wall space. Fortunately, I'd gone to the site and discovered this problem in time. We ordered three movable walls for the session. Still, we could have used more wall space. As it was, we had to remove the use cases we'd already posted; those use cases would have given us fast visual clues during the multi-modeling activities.

HaveFunds

The purpose of the HaveFunds workshop was to define the detailed requirements for a system that would establish financial accounts for employee funds. The accounts had to comply with complex state and federal rules. They were also tailored according to a configuration of allowable fund plans provided by numerous groups, including account management, legal, and funds management. The account managers were the direct users. The workshop followed a vertical, how-first strategy in the course of seven consecutive four-hour sessions. There were post-workshop assignments between each pair of workshops.

The software team members already had lists of actors and potential use cases, along with a template they wanted to use for capturing use cases. They wanted to start at a high level because the project charter already defined the scope of the project. A full-time account manager was assigned to the project for requirements and testing. Other key issues included the following:

- The project team had a mixed history of success. There had been two unsuccessful releases to this point, only one of which had been installed. The project was currently stalled because of problems with gathering requirements, team and customer relationship issues, and team and management changes. Relationships between the software group and the business group were strained. However, a recent project retrospective had given everyone new hope of reaching a better understanding of the project's problems and had heightened the desire to meet customer needs.

- By now, the account managers were turned off by prior broken promises. Nevertheless, a former account manager with solid expertise had been assigned to work on the project full-time and represent his colleagues' needs.

- The team was working in a process-heavy organization and was being asked to use new tools while at the same time deliver on budget, on time—or face the consequences.

We agreed to focus on these deliverables during the workshop:

- Detailed use cases
- Detailed business rules
- Prototype screens
- Scenarios
- Glossary
- Use case map
- Issues
- Follow-up action items
- Projected next steps
- Data model
- Class model

Figure 11-3 shows the flow of activities we followed during the workshop.

We used three collaboration patterns along the way.

- Divide, Conquer, Correct, Collect helped us to specify and test use cases. We began by dividing our use cases into their component parts (name, header information, brief description, stepwise description, and exceptions); then we "conquered" several use cases a day. We defined the end state for each workshop and tested for doneness before going down to the next level of detail.

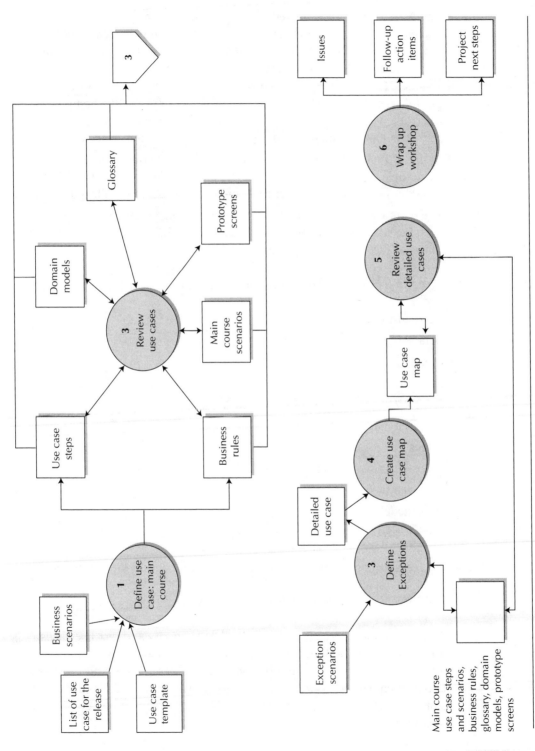

FIGURE 11-3 HAVEFUNDS WORKSHOP ACTIVITY FLOW

To "conquer" the stepwise version of each use case, we role-played user interactions using the conversational style introduced by Rebecca Wirfs-Brock. In this style, the use case is described as a dialog having two columns: one for user actions and the other for system responses. Using a Koosh ball to control the flow of control during the session, the account manager acted out a scenario, playing the direct user, while the technical lead acted out the system responsibilities.

Our technographer wrote the text, which was projected on a screen, in the appropriate column. The other participants made notes and asked relevant questions about the models for which they had responsibility. As you might expect, the user action side of the conversation revealed user interface prototype screen requirements, and the system response side revealed business rules and data requirements.

The "correct" part of the pattern involved testing the use cases with other requirements such as scenarios, business rules, and our QA checklist. Next, we "collected" all the use cases and tested them using related models and scenarios. We also tested the full set using a use case map and the process map that had been created along with the project charter.

■ Multi-Model helped us to add details to use cases, the data model, business rules, and user interface navigation diagrams, all at the same time. We worked reciprocally on the models, with use cases as the driving model. Each person was responsible for recording details about one model or element of a model.

■ Decide How to Decide helped us to reach closure on each use case and its related requirements models. The account manager was the final decision maker. We took proposals for closure only after we'd tested each use case, including the main course and exceptions, using scenarios. The number of use cases changed over the six days. Some were collapsed as "included" use cases (use cases within use cases), whereas others that had been steps in one use case warranted being converted into distinct use cases. Using the decision rule helped everyone to be clear on where we stood. We used the same process in reviews with the customers. In those sessions, unanimous agreement among the customers was the decision rule.

WHAT WORKED WELL

The following subsections describe what worked well in the HaveFunds requirements workshop.

BREAKING UP SESSIONS We devoted four hours in the morning to several use cases, working our way through the details. In the afternoon, everyone (including the subject matter expert) had follow-up assignments from the morning, including the following:

- Add attributes to the data model and class model.
- Specify business rules using our business rule template.
- Draft prototype screen sketches using a low-end tool.
- Print screen shots to add to the prototype model the next day.
- Specify more scenarios for the next day's use cases.

Each morning, we began our session by reviewing and cleaning up the prior afternoon's models. We iterated in three stages: We started with "normal" cases, then added exceptions and variations, and then did a final iteration to revise the requirements after two customer review meetings.

FOLLOWING UP WITH CUSTOMER REVIEWS We followed our series of workshops with two reviews: one with the larger user group and a second with the customer group. In the first session, we used scenarios to walk through printouts of screens to detect further defects. During an additional review meeting, we used our decision rule process to reach final closure on the requirements.

PITFALLS AND LEARNING POINTS

The following subsections describe the pitfalls and learning points of the HaveFunds workshop.

USE A BUSINESS RULE TEMPLATE Initially, we captured business rules as free-form text during the morning sessions; then in the afternoon we asked the subject matter expert to delineate the business rules using our template. This proved overwhelming for him. He was also responsible for answering software team members' questions and for his own pre-workshop assignments to write scenarios for the next day's workshop. We revised our strategy and had him work on the free-form rules each afternoon with the data analyst. She later transformed the rules into the form of the business rule template.

DISTRIBUTE THE GLOSSARY TO CUSTOMERS We spent time during customer reviews clarifying some of the business terms, which by that time were consistent and of high quality. We would have saved time during those reviews if we had distributed the glossary ahead of time and then held a brief glossary review meeting with the customers.

BestClaims

The BestClaims workshop delivered detailed requirements for ordering research and investigation information to help benefit analysts adjudicate insurance claims. The rules were complex, and it took years to train benefits analysts. Senior management initiated BestClaims to standardize and streamline the processes of claim recording, viewing, reviewing, decision making, and case management. The primary users of the BestClaims system would be the benefit analysts. Management launched two parallel projects: one to establish the technical environment, and a second one to define the user requirements to be implemented. We followed a zigzag strategy in the course of three five-hour sessions spread out over five weeks.

Other key issues included the following:

- The current system had a complete, up-to-date data model.
- The project had strong and active sponsors.
- The benefits analysts were overworked, busy training junior benefits analysts while carrying heavy case loads. The director of claims was very concerned about the need for analysts to take time away from their jobs to participate in the workshop.
- There were concerns about conducting a workshop involving "group writing," in which people listed business rules in a Dilbert-like, boring manner. (We needed to design a process that was interesting and fun.)
- There were no requirements management tools, nor was there any automated facility for capturing and storing business rules.

We agreed to focus on these deliverables during the workshop:

- Detailed business rules
- Scenarios
- Statechart diagrams
- User interface navigation diagrams
- Glossary

Figure 11-4 shows the flow of activities we followed during the workshop.

We used three collaboration patterns along the way.

- Multi-Model helped us to reveal business rules using a statechart diagram. As this diagram grew in complexity during the sessions with the addition of substates and more events, we revised it 11 times. The benefit analysts created this diagram by themselves while they created the business rules.

- Divide, Conquer, Correct, Collect helped us to partition the business rules into groups of rules associated with a claim state. This allowed two groups to work in parallel on opposite walls and then switch sides and test each other's rules with scenarios. During the correct phase, we used scenarios to test the business rules. Although the benefits analysts didn't refer to the data model, the software participants constantly used the model to verify business rules and clarify glossary terms.

- Decide How to Decide helped us to reach closure on sets of business rules. We'd pause to review the rules that we'd just tested and use the decision rule: unanimous agreement of the three benefits analysts. After a few days, one participant brought in plastic fingers that we used to indicate degrees of agreement; this made a game of the process while still honoring it.

WHAT WORKED WELL

The following subsections describe what worked well in the BestClaims requirements workshop.

HOLDING THE CHARTER WORKSHOP FIRST We conducted a six-hour project charter workshop before starting the business rules workshops. We did this in order to define the scope of claims to be covered, the stakeholders in the project, and ways to handle project risks, especially the risk associated with the lack of availability of the benefits analysts. Subsequently, we had no scope creep issues in the workshops. The business sponsors managed to define creative ways to free up the time of the experts so that they could participate in the workshops.

EXPLOITING A COGNITIVE PATTERN The business rules for this domain are knowledge-intensive. To design a workshop process that simulated this, I drew on a set of *cognitive patterns* (also called *problem-solving templates, thinking patterns,* or *template knowledge models*) that define a sequence of simple, abstract steps that humans often use instantly at a subconscious level to arrive at a conclusion.

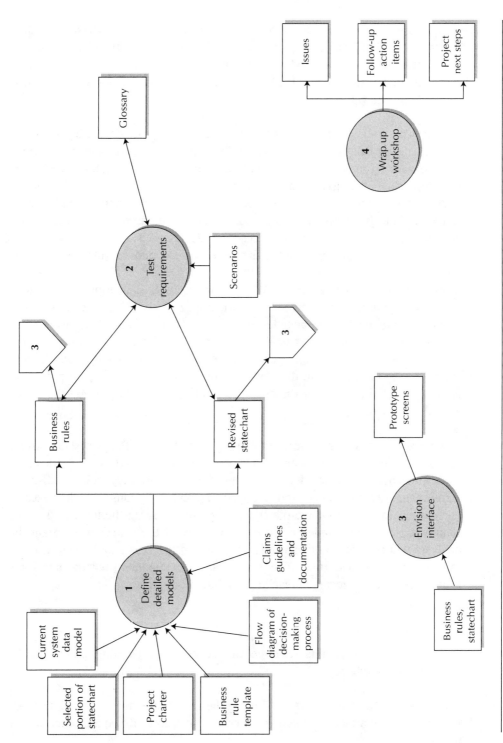

FIGURE 11-4 BESTCLAIMS WORKSHOP ACTIVITY FLOW

One pattern, Assessment (or Suitability Assessment), involves decision making. The thinker compares an expected value with a data value; the result is a decision that he can modify based on compensating factors. Using that pattern as a base, I created a simple diagram of the flow of steps we would use to build a business rule on the wall.

TESTING THE BUSINESS RULE TEMPLATE   Designing and testing a business rule template was essential. The template was made of divided parts, or factors, most of which we had defined before the workshop. The factors included policy provision, claim stage, and product type. We also defined a set of known possible values or sets of values for each factor, and then we loaded these values into our business rule capture tool (a database based on a business rules metamodel we adapted for this project). We also created colored cards for each factor and value, which we used in the workshop to build the rules on the wall.

ORIENTATION MEETING   We held an orientation meeting, which lasted an hour and a half, a week before the workshops started. The sponsor, key management stakeholders, the benefits analysts, and the software team were present. We reviewed the project goals, the facilitation process, the business rule template, the decision rules, the cognitive template, the workshop logistics, and the schedule. To my delight, the benefits analysts appeared with pom-poms and food! This set the stage for the energy and fun that would pervade the whole workshop series.

KICK-AND-CLOSE   The workshop sponsor kicked off the session, and a group of highly positioned stakeholders came to the show-and-tell. Participants made presentations describing what they did and how they did it, "ah-has," learning points, and short- and long-term recommendations. One key recommendation was to reorganize the claims department along the lines of the way claim decisions were made, which roughly followed the statechart diagram the analysts had created. In other words, the business process should be structured to follow the business rules. The group also recommended revising the claims training program to focus on teaching the business rules.

PITFALLS AND LEARNING POINTS

The following subsections describe the pitfalls and learning points of the BestClaims workshop.

ALLOW TIME TO LEARN   During the first day of the workshop, the participants created a mere three business rules—far below our expectations. By the end of the next day, they had 33. The volume of rules increased slightly during the next session and then leveled off. This result reinforces the idea that workshops are living, learning labs.

DO SCENARIOS BETWEEN WORKSHOPS Initially, we spent workshop time creating scenarios. After one session, we realized that we could create templates to help us define scenarios and then allow the participants to create scenarios between workshops. This saved precious workshop time.

MANAGE THE PARKING LOT The ongoing list of parking lot items grew quite large over the days and had to be carefully managed. We numbered each item and noted the day it was listed. We had to be sure to review issues at the end of each session, assign each issue to one person, add a due date, and give the issue a status. I'd recommend using a simple tracking database in the future. Or we could have simplified the long list by classifying each issue into "long-term parking" or "short-term parking."

12

MOVING FORWARD

"Action removes the doubt that theory cannot solve."
—Tsiu Hsich

"Do not try; there is no try, only do!"
—Yoda

Requirements workshops are a best practice. Any practice must be done regularly and refined continually in order to become, and remain, a best practice. It requires the support of software and business management. This support

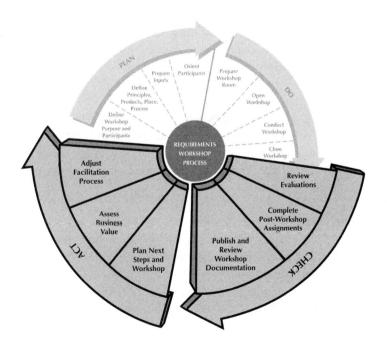

is especially important because planning a workshop can reveal weaknesses in software practices and become a starting point for positive transformation.

To make workshops a best practice in your organization, actively seek feedback on your workshop immediately afterward and again a month or so later. Collect and review data from your workshop products, process, and participants. Determine how to integrate workshops into your requirements process. Use metrics to continually improve your workshop practices.

Work to improve the skills and knowledge of the internal staffers who will facilitate or plan requirements workshops. Focus on creating a culture of continual learning through reading, training, education, mentoring, and study groups. This is a serious undertaking for the requirements facilitator. Fortunately, for both the facilitator and the organization, these skills are highly transferable to your work on any team.

MAKING THE CASE TO MANAGEMENT

Some managers sponsor requirements workshops because they're in the habit of improving their software processes. Others are willing to consider workshops because of pain they're currently experiencing, such as inadequate customer involvement, poor-quality requirements, or an inability to elicit requirements clearly. They may have tried other elicitation methods with less than stellar success, or they may come from project environments that are unstructured and under constant schedule pressure.

Some sponsors and managers intuitively understand the value of workshops. They tend to be managers who support active user interaction in the requirements process or members of project communities wanting to improve their requirements elicitation. They may be people who are using agile methods and who recognize that good requirements workshops are well-planned, high-quality agile modeling sessions.

Others, however, are a harder sell. These managers aren't considering changing their requirements processes because they believe no changes are needed. They need real data about the results of requirements *churn*, or the inability to reach closure on requirements—results such as excessive requirements defects, elongated requirements closure, and missed delivery cycles. The following subsection provides such data.

THE BUSINESS VALUE OF REQUIREMENTS WORKSHOPS

Not getting requirements right for your software will lead to big problems. The formal requirements phase takes about 5 percent of your software effort, but the accumulated time spent on requirements—formal requirements plus creeping requirements—takes as much as 30 percent of your time (Boehm, 1981; Jones, 2000).

Software products are notoriously error-prone. Many defects originate in the requirements phase (Boehm, 1987; Jones, 1996c), and they cost a lot in rework. As a whole, the area of requirements, if not done well, is the aspect of a software development effort that can cost you the most in time, money, and customer dissatisfaction.

Here are some data:

- Problems with requirements—specifically, frequent changes, missing requirements, insufficient user communication, poor specifications, and insufficient analysis—account for the five top causes of poor software cost estimation (Davis, 1995).
- Requirements are the major source of severe problems that generate expensive downstream changes (Leffingwell, 1997; Jones, 2000).
- Requirements errors contribute to one-third of total delivered defects (Leffingwell and Widrig, 1999).
- Requirements processes are the source of most (50 percent or more) serious quality problems (Weinberg, 1997).
- Fixing requirements errors consumes 70 percent to 80 percent of a project's rework costs (Leffingwell, 1997). Overall, rework costs 40 percent to 50 percent of the total software development budget (Jones, 1986; Boehm, 1987). The result is that *requirements errors consume 28 percent to 42.5 percent of total software development costs.*
- Finding and fixing requirements defects after system delivery is often 100 times as expensive as finding and fixing them during the requirements and design phases (Bochm and Basili, 2001).
- The development team can spend as much as 30 percent to 80 percent of their project effort reworking mistakes they made earlier (Fagan, 1976).
- Reworking a requirements problem costs 50 to 200 times what it would take to fix it during the requirements phase (Boehm and Papaccio, 1988).

- The cost of rework is 10 to 100 times less if it's done earlier in the software life cycle (McConnell, 1996).
- Scope creep is one of the most common, and sometimes the most common, source of cost and schedule overruns, and it is a major factor in project cancellations (Jones, 1994; Lederer and Prasad, 1992; Vosburgh et al., 1984).

Well-designed and well-executed workshops are the most effective and stable way to define user requirements (Jones, 2000). Data supports the assertion that the use of requirements workshops increases quality and reduces costs. Requirements workshops can

- Reduce the risk of scope creep from 80 percent to 10 percent, and to 5 percent when combined with prototyping (Jones, 1996a)
- Cut requirements creep in half (Jones, 2000)
- Cut the elapsed time of requirements specification by 20 percent to 60 percent, and total project effort by 20 percent to 60 percent (August, 1991)
- Provide a 5 percent to 15 percent overall savings in time and effort for the project as a whole (Jones, 1996a)
- Reduce defects delivered in software by 20 percent (Jones, 1996a)
- Reduce project failure and cancellation rates by about 50 percent (Jones, 1996a)
- As a customer-oriented requirements gathering practice, increase productivity by 10 to 50 percent (Vosburgh et al, 1984)
- Provide a 10-to-1 return on investment ($10 for every $1 invested; Jones, 1996a)

CRITICAL SUCCESS FACTORS

To help ensure that your early attempts to integrate requirements workshops into your project will be successful, use requirements workshops under appropriate project conditions. This includes having a sponsor and the right players attend, taking time to plan, and having a neutral facilitator. If any of these factors is missing, you're likely to have a less than successful requirements workshop.

SURFACING PROBLEMS

Your early attempts to use requirements workshops might surface project and team problems. Table 12-1 shows some common ones.

TABLE 12-1 TEAM AND PROJECT PROBLEMS THAT IMPACT WORKSHOP SUCCESS

Problem	Indicators
Inability to identify project goals	Can't identify a statement of project purpose
Lack of project or workshop sponsorship	Sponsor or stakeholders unwilling to kick off workshop or come to show-and-tell; sponsor or stakeholders can't be identified.
Inability to get customers and users involved	Customers and users not named as participants in work shop; customers and users not encouraged to participate in workshop.
Weakness in requirements processes	Inability to identify or agree upon which requirements models to use; inability to know how or when to conduct workshop; lack of resources or knowledge for establishing doneness tests for requirements
Inexperienced or partial facilitator	Facilitator has difficulty guiding workshop planning process; facilitator unable to handle conflict and disagreement during workshop; participants perceive that facilitator is biased.
Decision-making dysfunction	Can't identify decision leader; unwillingness to make collaborative decision.
Project or company politics have poisoned players' ability to collaborate	Participants can't agree on ground rules for conducting the workshop.

These problems aren't insurmountable. The willingness to plan and conduct a workshop can help a team to get back on track early in the project life cycle. One project's business–software team relationship was transformed by sharing the workshop experience. In another project, success with workshops helped the larger organization to become more rigorous in its requirements management practices. Yet another team realized that some project requirements can be defined more loosely early on by integrating prototyping, customer and user reviews, and early beta testing into project processes.

How to Evaluate Workshops

You can use data, survey results, and ongoing workshop debriefs to help you to continually improve your requirements workshop practices.

WHAT TO REPORT

Prepare a brief summary of each workshop as a means of sharing results and tracking outcomes. Include a mix of data that reports on workshop products, process, work effort, and participant satisfaction.

Pre-workshop data can include the following:

- The number of elapsed days between planning and workshop
- The effort expended to prepare (total time spent by everyone involved in planning and providing information for the workshop, pre-work, and orientation meeting time)
- The number of pre-workshop interviews conducted
- Participant satisfaction with pre-workshop involvement

Data from the workshop itself can include the following:

- The number of participants
- The number of workshop hours
- The effort expended
- The number of deliverables (see "Deliverable Data to Capture" next)
- The number of issues raised
- The number of issues needing post-workshop follow-up
- Decisions made
- What worked well
- What needs improvement
- Short-term satisfaction with the workshop process

Post-workshop data can include the following:

- The elapsed time between workshops
- The elapsed time for follow-up actions to be completed
- Customer, user, and software organization suggestions for improvement
- Long-term satisfaction with the workshop
- Assessment of whether to use the process again
- Estimated savings

DELIVERABLE DATA TO CAPTURE

You should capture information related to the deliverables in terms of how much and in what period of time. Here are some sample metrics from workshops I've facilitated:

- In a business rule workshop, participants delivered 35 business rules at the end of the third workshop day (an average of 12 per day), and they were able to add an additional 20 by the end of day 4 and an additional 35 business rules by the end of day 5.

- In a use case modeling workshop, participants tested their data model and structural business rules using 55 scenarios in less than 1.5 hours.

- A workshop delivering business events generated 119 business events, classified them, and then removed those not in scope over a 2-hour period.

- In 3 hours, a team validated a data model of medium complexity and made decisions about the scope of the data on which business performance metrics would be based.

- In 3.5 hours, participants built a complete set of relationship maps. These maps enabled them to identify, in detail, current business processes and problem areas.

Track your data over time as you adjust your requirements workshop practices. Use this data to make the case to management about the benefits of requirements workshops. As you gain more experience, establish goals for requirements elicitation and select metrics from those goals (see "Improvement Data" later in this chapter).

COST-BENEFIT DATA TO CAPTURE

A cost-benefit case for requirements workshops shows the savings gained, ranging from fewer person-hours needed to capture and reach closure on requirements to less overall elapsed time to complete requirements. Estimate costs using your conventional elicitation methods such as interviews and surveys. Compare those estimates with the costs of planning, conducting, and following up on requirements workshops. One colleague, who performs facilitation services in-house, makes an agreement with his workshop customers to complete a cost-benefit form after the workshop. An example of such a worksheet appears on the Web site for the book.

HAPPY SHEETS

During your closing (see "Closing the Workshop" in Chapter 9), ask participants to complete a workshop evaluation. This form is also called a *happy sheet* because it gauges participants' immediate gut responses to the workshop. (The Web site provides examples.) These paper evaluations should be supplemented by a real-time discussion among participants about the workshops. An honest discussion also gives people the chance to make commitments about how to specifically change and improve their behavior and interactions in project activities outside the workshop setting.

THE POST-WORKSHOP SURVEY

Poll key participants or the planning team four to six weeks after the workshop. This time gap gives people a better perspective on the workshop's usefulness in the context of the project's life cycle. The results of this survey can provide important workshop improvement information. For example, one organization reviewed results of several workshops and detected a pattern of difficulty in selling the idea to their business sponsors after requirements work started. To mitigate this problem, they implemented a practice of selling requirements workshops to business sponsors earlier, during their project startup and chartering activities.

IMPROVEMENT DATA

Metrics can provide information that helps you to understand how to improve your workshop practices. The data you collect also makes visible the results of your workshops, provides a focus for improvement efforts, and helps you to set realistic expectations for workshops in your organization. Any metrics you capture should be noninvasive and shouldn't create a bureaucracy.

The best way to determine what to measure is to use the goal-question-metrics technique (Basili and Weiss, 1984). Begin by asking what goals you want to achieve by using requirements workshops. You may, for example, want to increase customer satisfaction or reduce the number of defects originating in requirements. Next, determine the questions you need to ask in order to know whether you've met your goals. For example, you might ask, "How did customers rate our delivered products?" or "How many defects did we deliver?" Then establish the needed metrics based on the answers. For example, you might collect data on customer satisfaction, defects delivered by project phase, level of defect severity, and cost to correct defects by phase.

Here are some sample goals for requirements workshops:

- Reduce the number of changes to requirements after they're baselined.
- Increase customer involvement in the requirements process.
- Increase customer satisfaction with project outcomes.
- Reduce the rate of canceled or postponed projects due to requirements problems.
- Increase the quality of requirements.
- Reduce the time it takes to capture requirements.

REGULAR WORKSHOP DEBRIEFS

Capturing metrics data is a waste of time and effort unless you use it to learn. You should establish a practice of regular debriefs of the data in which workshop stakeholders review the data, determine improvement areas, and make specific action plans for process improvement. If you conduct debriefs or retrospectives at the completion of major phases or deliverables, make this process part of those debriefs in which your requirements process is assessed.

INTEGRATING WORKSHOPS INTO THE REQUIREMENTS PHASE

To begin determining how workshops can be integrated into your requirements process, plan a set of three or four requirements iterations, each of which will result in a set of requirements in a predefined state of completeness or detail. Then, within each iteration, intersperse workshops.

In addition to incorporating walkthroughs into your requirements workshop (see Chapter 9), you should conduct reviews or walkthroughs *outside* your workshops to verify requirements that were modified as a result of post-workshop work.

If only a few subject matter experts can participate in workshops, reviews are also useful for checking the resulting work products with a larger user constituency. As your requirements products begin to reach the level of precision and quality you expect, conduct inspections, another type of review.

Figure 12-1 illustrates how to combine workshops with reviews.

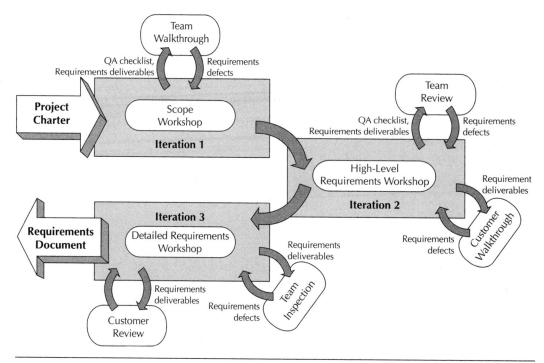

FIGURE 12-1 INTEGRATING WORKSHOPS AND REVIEWS INTO THE REQUIREMENTS PROCESS

The steps are as follows:

1. Define which models (text and diagrammatic) you'll use to represent the requirements, and determine how the models will be linked.

2. Design an iterative process for the whole requirements phase, using three or four iterations.

3. For each iteration, define the specific end state of each requirement.

4. Integrate workshops into the iterations.

5. Integrate software prototypes where feasible.

6. Define workshop deliverables based on the iteration, the required end state, attributes such as priority or volume, and links among the requirements deliverables for each requirement.

7. Before the first workshop, establish a requirements traceability environment (process, tools, and procedures) and repository in which to store all your workshop assets.

8. Employ more rigorous facilitation techniques in initial workshops; loosen up as the team builds trust.

9. Inject walkthroughs and QA checklists to help the group reach closure on each workshop deliverable.

10. Ensure that some subject matter experts are active workshop participants.

11. Ensure that some test and quality analysts are workshop observers or participants.

12. Use reviews to verify and reach closure on requirements post-workshop tasks.

BECOMING A SKILLED REQUIREMENTS WORKSHOP FACILITATOR

A requirements facilitator needs a set of core competencies in the art and science of group facilitation as well as methods and techniques associated with software requirements.

The facilitator should also have a body of *knowledge*, which means, in this context, familiarity with and awareness of relevant topics. A requirements facilitator's knowledge should include familiarity with the following:

- Requirements models and requirements management
- Software engineering
- System development methodologies, processes, and techniques
- Systems thinking
- Group dynamics
- Personality styles and human communication modes
- Decision-making models and techniques
- Cultural differences of groups

Skills are demonstrable behaviors. A requirements facilitator should be able to do the following:

- Gather information from project team members and stakeholders and help them to articulate their immediate needs.
- Create a requirements workshop agenda and delineate essential deliverables along with a logical sequence of group activities for delivering them.

- Observe and understand the group process and decide when and how to intervene.
- Ask the right kinds of questions at the right times.
- Summarize, clarify, redirect, and actively listen.
- Encourage and guide group participation.
- Have a toolkit of group processes, and know when to use which tool.
- Dynamically change the flow of the group process.
- Ask for, take, and give feedback.
- Handle conflict when it arises.
- Be able to stay calm, poised, and neutral.
- Ethically address conflict and controversy.
- Display compassion and empathy.

"To handle yourself, use your head. To handle others, use your heart."
—Eleanor Roosevelt

Your work as a facilitator is considerably more than making sure the group produces its deliverables. It is also work of the heart, enabling people to connect in new ways. This requires a growing awareness of yourself. You are the best tool you have.

There are a variety of ways you can grow and develop your skills. You should use a combination of approaches, including formal training, reading, attending software and facilitation conferences, observing other facilitators, beginning a mentoring program, and starting a learning circle. It's also a good idea to pursue certification by the International Association of Facilitators (IAF).

THE IAF

The IAF is a worldwide organization of facilitators whose mission is to promote, support, and advance "the art and practice of professional facilitation through: methods exchange, professional growth, practical research, collegial networking and support services" (IAF, 1999). Members work in a wide variety of businesses and not-for-profit concerns.

The IAF is the certifying body for a professional certification program that addresses facilitator competencies in the areas of managing the facilitation event, managing the process, managing groups and individuals, managing your learning, and managing yourself. Competencies in the area of managing the process, for example, include evoking participation and creativity, showing flexibility in the process, and using a facilitative style to match the changing needs of the group.

These competencies are a framework for facilitation skills. As a certified professional facilitator (CPF), I can attest to the quality of the certification process and professionalism that it symbolizes. The Web site for this book has a link to the list of competencies and information on the certification program.

How Much Must the Facilitator Know?

The ideal requirements facilitator is an expert in group dynamics and requirements models. She gives participants the techniques that enable them to generate, combine, differentiate, evaluate, prioritize, and make decisions about requirements. The facilitator understands the possible models from which to choose and helps the team to decide, given the business problem and the project methodology, which models are most appropriate.

She also uses her knowledge of the requirements models to test the quality of the workshop deliverables. At a moment's notice, the facilitator may have to intervene when the quality of the models is falling below expectations, as established before the workshop with the planning team.

In one of my sessions, I asked subgroups to write brief summaries of each use case they'd identified earlier in the session. Then I asked them to read and listen, without comment, to each other's use cases. I listened as well, not for the content so much as the quality of the use cases. What I heard was this:

- Some use cases sounded like descriptions of the business rules.
- Others sounded like a series of definitions of terms.
- Others were written from the point of view of the system (not that of the direct users).
- Still others sounded like descriptions of user-system interactions (what use cases *should* be).

In response, I asked participants to review the characteristics of a high-quality use case description, using a checklist we'd prepared ahead of time. Next, I asked them to return to their subgroups and rework their use case descriptions, this time writing them according to the characteristics of a good use case. In this way, the quality of the use cases improved markedly over the duration of the workshop.

WHAT DO BUSINESS USERS NEED TO KNOW?

Business users participating in a requirements workshop don't need to learn modeling techniques before the workshop. Requirements analysts, the facilitator, and the workshop planning team are responsible for providing guidance on which models to use and how to connect them. They're the ones who need to know the syntax and format of the models and the strategies and reasons for finding gaps, errors, and inconsistencies in and among the models.

Business users *do* have to fill gaps, correct errors in the models, and resolve inconsistencies. This clear delineation of their responsibility liberates them from having to know the forms of the models, but it requires them to be expert in their function. You can convey sufficient training and education for business people by conducting short tutorials before each modeling activity, showing examples, providing guidelines for modeling activities in the workshop, and explaining the workshop process at the opening of the session or during a workshop orientation meeting.

GROUND RULES FOR THE FACILITATOR

"A leader is best when people barely know he exists.
Not so good when people obey and acclaim him.
Worst when they despise him.
But of a good leader, who talks little,
When his work is done, his aim fulfilled,
They will say, 'We did this ourselves!'"

—Lao Tzu

A facilitator is a special kind of leader. As facilitator, you use your own personal ground rules to help you to manage not only the group but also yourself. These ground rules, a few of which I describe here, help to remind you about your values as a facilitator.

One important ground rule is to *pay attention to what important words mean.* This involves listening for terms that might not be clear or understood by some of the participants. You can spot this development if there's disagreement among participants from different functional groups or at different organizational levels, or when someone uses a business term that's not in the glossary. The best way to handle this problem is to comment on the disagreement and ask, "What do you mean by <term>?" Request that someone write a definition for the term, and ask the group to review it, before further discussion on the topic continues.

Remember this ground rule, too: *The whole group is your client.* We have a natural tendency to ally ourselves with the more powerful members of a group, anyone we already know, and whoever initially asked us to facilitate the workshop. When you are the facilitator, your client is the entire group. If you find that you're concerned about the opinions of only one or two people, stop yourself. To handle this situation, conduct regular debriefs with the group to get everyone's input on how the process is working, and ask the participants for feedback on your performance as facilitator.

Another useful ground rule is to *ask the group for help with the process* when it's ready to provide that help. Groups are much wiser than any one person, including the facilitator. Once the group members have passed the forming and storming stages, you'll notice that they're productive—they're in a working flow. Participants often have ideas for saving time and increasing the quality of their work. If your planned agenda hasn't been adjusted, if ground rules are unchanged, or if there have been multiple ground rules violations, pay attention. Any of these may indicate that you haven't tapped the group's wisdom. The best way to handle this situation is to surface process suggestions using process checks.

Another critical ground rule is to *pay attention to the passions and energies of the group.* When energy is high, you're close to the core of the current issue or near closure on a deliverable. Shifting focus away from this passion and energy, even if it appears to be negative, can result in enabling dysfunctional behavior or destroying the group's sense of accomplishment. Examples of negative energy include the beginnings of moaning or grumbling as you explain an activity, suggestions to pursue some other task, and looks of annoyance and anger when you attempt to refocus the group. The best way to handle this to point out the specific behaviors that indicate that the topic is "hot" or that energy seems high, and then ask the group to discuss the reasons for the energy and what to do about it.

An important ground rule is to *tell the truth without blame or judgment.* Be specific about your observations, both positive and negative. Often, people are not aware of their behavior or its impact on the group. Hearing a neutral person make observations in a nonblaming or unthreatening way allows us to be more aware of our behavior. You can spot the need to offer truthful observations when you're feeling uncomfortable about what's happening in the group. (For me, it's a strange sensation in my stomach.) You might also begin to feel defensive, vulnerable, or angry with a participant or the group itself. These feelings are telling you that something important is happening!

Deal with it head-on. First, decide whether it's purely your own issue, or whether there are observable behaviors triggering these responses. If the latter is true, share your *specific* observations with the group, without any interpretation on your part. Ask the group whether you heard and saw things accurately. Wait and let the group decide what to do about the behaviors.

The Fourfold Way

Research by anthropologist and corporate consultant Angeles Arrien into the shamanic traditions of indigenous peoples reveals practical wisdom that is applicable to groups in corporate settings. Her work on the four archetypal principles of the Native American medicine wheel provides a set of useful ground rules (Arrien, 1993):

- Show up and choose to be present ("The Way of the Warrior").
- Pay attention to what has heart and meaning ("The Way of the Healer").
- Tell the truth without blame or judgment ("The Way of the Visionary").
- Be open to outcome, not attached to outcome ("The Way of the Teacher").

A ground rule related to the one just described is to *make generous interpretations* before intervening or jumping to conclusions. This wisdom comes from family therapist Virginia Satir. When a person is acting in a "difficult" manner, we're apt to interpret the behavior in a negative way. You can detect this when you start blaming participants for problems in the workshop (explicit or in your head). You might also start feeling angry or worried. To best handle this, try to form three generous interpretations for the difficult person's behavior. This will help you to stay calm, open-minded, and more fully present with the group process.

A very important ground rule is to *maintain confidences*. During your information gathering, you'll build trust by actively listening to stakeholders. You'll also be seen as a helper because you're neutral. It's not uncommon for people to reveal confidences to you. Be careful when you start thinking wishful thoughts such as, "If everyone knew this, they'd get it together." You may be tempted to share the information with the larger group, in the hope that its members will trust and like you. However, maintaining confidences is the only ethical thing to do, and when you violate confidences you lose not only credibility but also self-worth.

If you believe the information is relevant to the group and its work, ask permission to share it with the group, or ask the confider to share it. If this doesn't work and if you truly believe that not having the information will be a barrier to the group's success, share your discomfort with the confider and try to arrive at a mutually satisfactory way to handle the situation.

Draw on multiple sources, such as values from the skilled facilitator approach (see "Values-Based Ground Rules" in Chapter 6), the IAF, and wisdom drawn from the archetypal principles of the Native American medicine wheel, on an ongoing basis. For an effective facilitator, the learning never stops.

EPILOGUE

The payoffs for using requirements workshops can be dramatic. Even though gathering your requirements may seem to be a small part of the effort you devote to a project, getting your requirements as right as they can be the first time, through the use of collaborative workshops, can have a big impact on your quality of work—and your work community's health.

Further Readings

FOR MORE INFORMATION

Arrien (1993) offers wisdom on being more fully human, gleaned from the author-anthropologist's study of native spirituality and shamanism.

Basili and Weiss (1994) is a landmark article that describes an elegant and simple technique for finding the right metrics.

Bohm (1996) is a superb book that describes *dialogue* as deep communication that transcends opinion and positions. This book is intense reading about the collective exploration of our thought processes. It's a book you can revisit throughout your life and understand more of, in different ways, each time you read it.

Weinberg (1994) presents an in-depth look at congruent behavior and what can prevent or block congruence. His careful treatment of acting congruently in stressful situations is highly relevant to every workshop facilitator (and any other human).

Weinberg (1997) shares wisdom on change and explains how you can become a change artist. Weinberg is the guru of the human side of software engineering, and this book provides useful guidance to anyone who wants to change, learn to change, or facilitate change.

APPENDIX

COLLABORATION PATTERNS

Name	Decide How to Decide
Context	A group needs closure on a specific issue. People must know when and whether a decision is made.
Problem	Often, the "rule" for how a group will reach decisions is not explicit. Topics are discussed without a specific process for reaching closure, leaving individuals uncertain as to whether a decision was reached. How do you know something is "decided" or "finished" if the rule for knowing that something is closed is not made explicit?
Solution	Establish a decision rule: deciding how to decide.

- Use an explicit process to handle decision making.
- Educate the decision leader (the person in charge) about decision rules and guide her to choose one.
- Review the pros and cons of various decision rules.
- Employ various decision rules for various decisions.

Consequences	Closure on decisions; if a participatory decision rule is used, more integrative data on the decision topic is generated, and people have greater commitment to making the decision stick.
Entry Criteria	

- Need for a decision that has nontrivial stakes for the people affected by the decision
- An identified decision leader
- Explanation of decision rule choices
- Explanation of the decision rule process

Exit Criteria	A decision has been made on the item or topic needing closure.
Uses	Deciding on a project's scope, deciding whether to accept user requirements, deciding on the priority of user requirements, selecting a software package, designing an organizational structure, choosing technologies, making strategic business decisions

Name	Divide, Conquer, Correct, Collect
Context	A complex product needs to be created quickly by people with differing expertise. Individuals need to be familiar with the content to reduce the learning curve later in the project.
Problem	How do you make sure that all participants have input and verify the product? How do you permit participants to work on aspects of a product with which they are familiar and those with which they are unfamiliar?
Solution	<ul><li>*Divide:* (1) Partition each product into component parts and categorize them.</li><li>*Divide:* (2) Map out the relationships between the parts in logical order, ensuring that concurrencies as well as dependencies are shown.</li><li>*Conquer:* Allocate partitions to subgroups with expertise in that category of the product.</li><li>*Correct:* Conduct whole-group QA activities.</li><li>*Collect:* Synchronize the product's elements.</li></ul>
Consequences	Closure on decisions; because participants have created the end product by partitioning it, working in parallel, and sharing details of each element, they obtain greater in-depth knowledge of the product.
Entry Criteria	<ul><li>Shared time and space with knowledgeable participants</li><li>The ability to subdivide participants by deliverable or by experience</li><li>The ability to logically partition the deliverable</li><li>A list of quality criteria for each deliverable</li><li>The active involvement of knowledgeable users</li></ul>
Exit Criteria	An end product has been created that is agreed upon by all participants and for which all participants have had input in both creation and quality checking.
Uses	Writing a statement of business goals and objectives, creating use cases, business rules, statechart diagram, project plan, migration strategy, communication plan, actor map

Name	Expand Then Contract
Context	A group of stakeholders with diverse experiences and points of view needs to create a common deliverable quickly. Deliverable can be product elements, options, ideas, or choices.
Problem	Different stakeholders hold legitimate but sometimes divergent perspectives, knowledge, and experience. How do you use these differences to strengthen the quality of the end deliverable?
Solution	▪ Ensure that the right participants are present during both the expand and the contract phases. ▪ *Expand:* Allow individuals to describe their perspectives and knowledge; promote free thinking and use of imagination; encourage mutual understanding. ▪ *Contract:* Apply techniques to narrow the elements, including criteria as in The Sieve, and apply Decide How to Decide to reach closure.
Consequences	Deliverable is achieved more quickly and includes broader items; it is smaller, but it includes more choices or elements. Participants gain increased understanding of alternative ideas and perspectives.
Entry Criteria	▪ A need for more comprehensive elements, options, ideas, or choices ▪ Identified people who have the capacity or knowledge to provide broader elements
Exit Criteria	Participants have created a list of smaller and more focused elements or choices.
Uses	Providing a list of requirements for a release, generating release criteria, defining possible software designs, defining candidates for software vendors

Name	Is There a Norm in the Room?
Context	A group needs to interact to create deliverables, make decisions, or exchange information. This group, like any other, will follow a natural cycle in which members search for norms of group behavior.
Problem	Groups will implicitly establish guidelines for interaction, some of which might not be helpful to their process and products. Without explicit guidelines, group interactions can become dysfunctional. Individuals make assumptions and interpretations of one another's words and behavior, resulting in miscommunication, a poor group process, and a low-quality group product.

Solution	<ul><li>Establish guidelines for participation that are congruent with both individual and group needs.</li><li>*Before:* Name guidelines individually; take the time to transform them into guidelines owned by the group; make them visible to all participants.</li><li>*During:* Anyone can check on adherence to the guidelines at any point; updates can be made as needed.</li><li>*After:* Analyze the effectiveness of the guidelines on group interactions.</li></ul>
Consequences	The group is able to establish guidelines for behavior more quickly. Deliverables can be produced faster. Sometimes, difficult conversations can be held in an open, safe setting without fear of reprisal. Trust is built among the members of the group.
Entry Criteria	<ul><li>The need for a group to gather to create a product or products</li><li>A shared understanding of the purpose of the gathering and a stake by the participants in the outcome of the session</li><li>A neutral party who can solicit individual guidelines and then feed it back to the group</li><li>Willingness by attendees to participate in setting the guidelines</li><li>The ability to challenge or question adherence to the guidelines at any point in the group process</li></ul>
Exit Criteria	An agreed-upon list of guidelines for participants has been developed collaboratively and is adhered to in the group session.
Uses	Any group gathering in which deliverables need to created, decisions need to be made, or sensitive or controversial topics need to be discussed

Name	Multi-Model
Context	Quickly create functional requirements for a software project.
Problem	No single model can fully express requirements. Each model emphasizes one or two points of view. Developing one model promotes the discovery of elements present only in the chosen model and ignores orthogonal solutions.
Solution	<ul><li>Select two or more models for the problem domain and model them concurrently.</li><li>Involve customers in discovery and verification of the models.</li><li>Repeatedly refine and synchronize the models.</li><li>Weave verification of the models into the discovery process.</li><li>Exploit the power of groups by using collaborative events during the multi-model process.</li></ul>

- Use in conjunction with Divide, Conquer, Correct, Collect.
- Use Decide How to Decide to reach closure.

Consequences The group delivers more complete and correct requirements; delivery of functional requirements is streamlined.

Entry Criteria
- Knowledge of requirements models and their points of view
- Understanding of which points of view fit the problem at hand
- Selection of two or more appropriate models
- Active involvement of knowledgeable users
- Time and place to conduct the modeling activity
- Use of flexible group processes to handle the many changes and iterations needed

Exit Criteria The group has created functional requirements, expressed using two or more models (text or visual).

Uses Creating user requirements in a group setting with a variety of representation forms (text and visual), such as use case text, use case map, business rules, actor map, statechart, data model

---

Name Self-Reflect

Context A group is working together to deliver one or more products over a period of time. The members must continue to work both together and separately to produce the product.

Problem Group members often meet and work together without stopping to evaluate their own behavior—helpful and harmful—as a group. They may miss opportunities to learn what is working and what should be changed in order to improve both their product and their productivity. How do you get a group to quickly and effectively generate meaningful information that reinforces, helps people to improve, and leads to commitment for action?

Solution
- Always take time at the end of each collaborative event to assess how effective a job the group did.
- Make sure that all comments are treated as valid.
- Visibly record comments as they are presented.
- Seek commitment for new and reinforcing behaviors.

Consequences The group members know how to make the group more productive in the future, and they acknowledge accomplishments. People are able to tell the truth without blame or judgment. For groups with consistent membership, there is a higher likelihood of the team jelling.

Entry Criteria
- A group that has just spent time (one hour or more) together to deliver a result
- Freedom to tell the truth in a group setting without fear of retribution
- An agreement to take the time to self-reflect in order to learn and to save time in future collaborations

Exit Criteria   Learning points have been documented or verbally acknowledged.

Uses   Debriefing a requirements workshop, reflecting on a software technique review or inspection, debriefing after the delivery of a project phase or product

---

Name   The Sieve

Context   A group or leader needs to select from competing elements—for example, functional scope or the priority of increments to build.

Problem   Different stakeholders have different needs and therefore different priorities or choices. How do you make a "clean" choice, in which no stakeholder is a "loser" in the selection? How do you get everyone to participate in and accept the final and best choice?

Solution   Filter the choices through well-defined and agreed-upon criteria. Involve stakeholders in defining both the filters and the filtering process. Additionally,

- Know whether you need to arrive at one or multiple prioritized selections.
- Collaboratively decide how to delineate the choices (for example, by ranking, prioritizing, weighted prioritization).
- Establish whether choices are fixed or can be extended by the stakeholders.
- Define the criteria before applying them to the choices.
- Evaluate the choices against the criteria.
- Combine with the Decide How to Decide pattern.

Consequences   A defensible decision is made based on well-defined criteria. There is greater commitment to the choice as a result of the participation of multiple stakeholders in defining the filters and analyzing them against the choice. If the criteria are clear, agreed upon, and ranked, decisions are made more quickly. Participants have a "win-win" agreement on how to proceed.

Entry Criteria	■ A list of elements to be filtered
	■ Participants who are knowledgeable in or who will champion the different elements from which a selection must be made
	■ A need to choose among competing elements that present comparative advantages and disadvantages
	■ A desire to involve stakeholders in the selection process
	■ The time to gather and evaluate criteria, review and expand choices, and analyze choices against the criteria
	■ A decision rule
Exit Criteria	One or more elements have been selected according to predefined criteria.
Uses	Selecting user requirements for a release from a list of possible requirements, choosing among multiple software products to purchase, choosing which requirements models to use, selecting among several possible migration strategies, determining which user involvement strategy to use

Name	Wall of Wonder (WoW)
Context	A group of stakeholders needs to solve a problem or create a deliverable such as a model or plan. A group setting seems to be a good choice because it will speed the process.
Problem	Groups are not always the best way for participants to interact. If there are introverts, more vocal individuals, or more organizationally powerful people present, some valuable input may be lost.
Solution	■ In a group meeting, allow time for individual thinking, followed by small group work to combine individual ideas and then whole group work on the wall.
	■ Begin with a clear focus question.
	■ Have all work visible on the wall.
	■ Permit the group to logically arrange the elements on the wall
	■ Respect individual time and the need to think alone and then post the result on the wall.
	■ Establish a pattern of individual → triad → whole group → individual.
	■ For longer collaborative events, rotate membership in subgroups.
Consequences	Integrating multiple perspectives produces a higher-quality product than one produced by a subset of individuals. Greater team collaboration and

goodwill are established because the process allows participants to think both alone and together. As a result, teams create complex models, plans, or structures in a short time (one hour to one day).

Entry Criteria
- Knowledgeable participants representing all key perspectives who are sharing the same time and place
- An understanding of what deliverables are to be created and what is required to create them
- Focus questions
- Room(s) with sufficient wall space
- Low-tech tools such as sticky notes or sticky wall with large cards; or high-tech tool such as an outliner or drawing tool along with a technographer

Exit Criteria

All deliverables are visible on one or more walls; the deliverables contain both detailed and summary items, are logically cohesive, and are understood and agreed on by all participants.

Uses

Defining use cases by release, determining the scope of events or use cases, defining a data or class model, creating an actor (role) map, specifying business rules in a template format, associating business rules with use cases, defining goals and objectives, designing an organization, creating a communication plan, generating a project, phase, or iteration plan, defining selection criteria for a software package, designing a low-tech user interface prototype, specifying use case steps

GLOSSARY

Abilene paradox The situation in which a group makes a decision in contradiction to what individuals privately want to do.

abstract use cases See *use cases*.

actor catalog See *actor table*.

actor hierarchy See *actor map*.

actor map A *requirements model* that defines the relationships among the *actors* in the *actor table* in terms of how their roles are shared and disparate. The map shows both human and nonhuman actors arranged in hierarchies.

actor table A *requirements model* that defines the roles played by people and things that will interact directly with the system. The contents typically include names, brief descriptions, physical locations, and necessary job aids.

adjourning The stage of a group development process in which the group acknowledges its work, reflects on its collaboration, and says goodbye.

Arbitrary A *decision rule* that involves making decisions by some arbitrary means, such as flipping a coin.

Ask why five times A "directed thinking" technique designed to increase understanding of the root cause of a goal, need, or want. For each item—for example, the workshop purpose or a use case and the requirements it addresses—you ask, "Why do you need this?" Following the response, you then repeat the question until you have asked "Why?" five times.

atomic business rules See *business rules*.

bandwidth The ability for information to flow quickly and concurrently.

business case A document designed to answer the question, Why do this project?

business change document A document that contains information such as current and changed business processes, impacted organizations and roles, changes to documentation (such as manuals), guidelines, standard operating procedures, plans for user training and education, a communication plan, and a change management plan.

business glossary See *glossary*.

business-level scenarios See *scenarios*.

business policies The principles and regulations that influence the behavior and structure of the business being modeled. These policies provide the basis for decomposing *business rules*.

business requirements Higher-level needs that when addressed will permit the organization to do things such as increase revenue, avoid costs, improve service, and meet regulatory requirements.

business rules Specific guidelines, regulations, and standards that must be adhered to. Attributes of business rules include its owner, its source, the source category (for example, human or document), its jurisdiction, and its relative complexity.

business rule template A standard, precise syntax for writing *business rules*.

business scenarios See *scenarios*.

closure The condition in which a deliverable is considered complete.

cognitive patterns Patterns that define sequences of simple, abstract steps that humans use in an instant and at a subconscious level, in many cases, to arrive at a conclusion.

collaboration A continuous feedback loop that enhances both the quality and the speed of communication and thereby the products created in requirements workshops.

collaboration pattern A reusable collection of group behavior applied to software projects.

collaborative closure The condition in which decisions are congruent with the goals of the group and are satisfactory to the individuals who influence or implement the decisions.

collaborative decision A decision characterized by stakeholder participation in the decision-making process in a way that meets the needs of the individuals and the group, includes the diverse views of all stakeholders, and enhances the group's ability to continue to work together effectively.

collaborative technology A catchall term for computer-aided facilitation.

The Complainer A person who hangs on to a point or stands on particular ground, draining the group's forward movement.

concepts catalog See *glossary*.

conceptual class model See *domain model*.

conceptual data model See *domain model*.

concrete use cases See *scenarios*.

Consensus A *decision rule* that involves a state of mutual agreement in which all legitimate concerns of individuals have been addressed to the satisfaction of the group.

constraints See *business rules*.

content adviser A person, such as a legal or regulatory expert, who has relevant information about the *requirements*.

context diagram A diagram that shows the system as a whole in its environment.

context-level use case See *context diagram*.

creeping user requirements See *scope creep*.

criteria grid A matrix that *participants* can use for rating options against a list of three to five agreed-upon criteria, such as impact on organizational objectives and benefits to customer service goals.

cross-functional process map See *process map*.

customer A person who sponsors a development project by providing money and resources. For commercial and business systems software, the customers are the people or organizations who commission a software project. For shrink-wrap software, the customers are the end users of the software.

debrief A closing ritual that permits *participants* to adjourn from their work together and discover ways to work better together in this same group or another group.

decision diagram See *decision tree*.

decision leader A person who has the authority to implement a decision or to obtain resources to implement it, and the responsibility to ensure that the decision is supported in the organization.

Decision Leader Decides after Discussion A *decision rule* that involves the *decision leader* making a decision after consulting with the other stakeholders.

Decision Leader Decides without Discussion A *decision rule* that involves the *decision leader* making a decision without consulting any of the other stakeholders.

decision rule An agreed-upon way of making decisions during a *requirements workshop*.

decision table A table that describes the conditions associated with particular actions or decisions, and also the constraints on the associated behavior.

decision tree A diagram that describes the conditions associated with particular actions or decisions, and also the constraints on the associated behavior.

Delegation A *decision rule* that involves the appointment of one person to make decisions.

detailed-level workshop A requirements workshop in which the participants evolve high-level requirements to a fairly rich level of detail.

dialog map See *user interface navigation diagram*.

direct user See *user*.

direct users list See *actor table*.

Divide, Conquer, Correct, Collect A *collaboration pattern* that combines multiple modeling with QA activities while also using a combination of *parallel collaboration* and *reciprocal collaboration*.

documenter See *recorder*.

domain model A *requirements model* that defines groups of information that must be stored in the system and the relationships among these groups.

domain statechart diagrams See *statechart diagrams*.

The Dominator A person who consistently interrupts and holds up the group process.

doneness test A set of criteria to judge whether a particular deliverable is complete, clear, and correct enough to be acceptable.

dyad A subgroup comprising two people.

end user See *user*.

energizer A way for participants to share their backgrounds, interests, or hobbies.

entity life history diagrams See *statechart diagrams*.

essential use cases See *use cases*.

event list See *event table*.

event table A table that defines the triggers of events to which the system responds.

Expand Then Contract A collaboration pattern of divergent, then convergent, thinking that enables groups to elicit multiple, diverse ideas and then narrow and focus the list.

facilitation The art of leading people through processes toward agreed-upon objectives in a manner that encourages participation, ownership, and productivity from all involved.

facilitator The person responsible for planning and designing a *requirements workshop* and then leading the group through its activities.

feature creep See *scope creep*.

flow A teetering between anxiety and boredom.

focus questions Specific questions that a *facilitator* uses to start a workshop activity to direct the *participants'* attention to the specific topic.

forcefield analysis A technique that involves examining two opposing forces in a given situation that can help a group with the expanding phase of *Expand Then Contract*.

forming The stage of a group development process in which the group finds common goals.

free-form business rules See *business rules*.

frequent debriefs Periods during *requirements workshops* that involve the participants reviewing, playing back, and thinking retrospectively about how the group process is working (or not working),

functional requirements Requirements that specify the functionality that users expect.

glossary A *requirements model* that defines the meanings of all business terms relevant to the system being built. These terms serve as the foundation for all requirements models and business rules; the goal of the glossary is to provide a common vocabulary on which all the stakeholders can agree.

glossary guardian A person in charge of keeping the *glossary* up-to-date during a *requirements workshop*.

ground rules Guidelines for group participation in a *requirements workshop*.

groupshift The situation in which individuals move to a more extreme position in the direction they were leaning, taking on either more cautious or riskier decisions.

groupthink The situation in which *participants*' desire to be "as one" is viewed as more important than their individual points of view.

groupware See *collaborative technology*.

guidelines See *business policies*.

header cards The categories at the highest level on a *Wall of Wonder*.

hidden agenda A need, want, or motivation closely held by one or more participants in a *requirements workshop*.

high-level business rules See *business policies*.

high-level scenarios See *scenarios*.

high-level workshop A requirements workshop in which the participants evolve scope-level requirements to a somewhat more detailed level.

horizontal strategy A strategy for conducting a *requirements workshop* that involves activities that lead participants to create a variety of models along one level of detail (scope, high, or detailed) using multiple *requirements* focuses (who, what, when, why, where, and how).

huddle A fast, stand-up consultation meeting with the planning team during a *requirements workshop*.

icebreaker See *opener*.

indirect user A person who will come in contact with the system's outputs, such as files and reports, or system by-products such as decisions.

intervention The ability of the *facilitator* to decide whether to make a comment, suggestion, or recommendation to the group to shift the current process.

invariants See *business rules*.

iterative development process A process that involves delivering cohesive chunks of the end product incrementally over the course of numerous *releases*.

JAD See *Joint Application Design or Development (JAD)*.

Joint Application Design (JAD™) or Development. A workshop technique, originated at IBM in the late 1970s, whose purpose is to help groups overcome obstacles in achieving high-quality requirements and design deliverables and to promote active customer involvement.

kickoff The part of a *requirements workshop* during which the *workshop sponsor* sets the stage for the group.

The Latecomer A person who consistently comes in late and who may ask questions or whisper to others to try and catch up.

lateral thinking A directed thinking technique for evaluating, comparing, and assessing a set of items that helps a group with the contracting phase of *Expand Then Contract*.

logic table See *decision table*.

low-fidelity prototype A representation of screens or screen flows created on whiteboards or posters or with posts on a wall.

Majority Vote A *decision rule* that involves the group making decisions by counting the number of votes for two or more options.

metaphor A symbol, image, or figure of speech.

method 6-3-5 A technique that helps a group with the expanding phase of *Expand Then Contract*. It involves generating items in response to a *focus question*, issue, or problem.

mind map An unstructured diagram that shows groupings of ideas and concepts associated with a central theme or topic. A mind map starts with a central image or idea, which forms a focus for both eye and brain. It then branches out in an organic manner, with each branch representing a grouping or category.

Multi-Model A *collaboration pattern* whose use involves dividing each of a number of models into parts and then partitioning parts of the same model with parts of a related model while making sure that each group is at about the same level of detail.

Negotiation A *decision rule* that involves compromising to a middle position that incorporates the most important positions of all sides.

nonfunctional requirements Requirements that define the constraints under which the software will perform in terms of the "-ilities" (security, maintainability, and so forth) and also quality attributes such as performance criteria.

norming The stage of a group development process in which the group finds ways, both healthy and unhealthy, to interact.

norms Standards for interacting within a group.

observer An interested party who watches, listens, and learns during a *requirements workshop*.

$100 test A technique that allows *customers* and *users* to metaphorically spend money on *requirements*. Each of them distributes the money as weights on the different requirements, after which the average weightings are computed.

opener A starting activity that allows *participants* to get familiar with one another and begin the *forming* process.

organizational context diagram See *relationship map*.

parallel collaboration A form of *collaboration* that involves dividing a single deliverable or set of related deliverables at about the same level of detail; subgroups then work synchronously on the deliverable(s).

parking lot A device for dealing with topics that are relevant to the project but not to the current activities.

participants The people who play active roles in a *requirements workshop*, from inception to post-workshop follow-up.

performing The stage of a group development process in which the group is task-oriented and focuses on producing its agreed-upon work products.

plenary The whole group within a *requirements workshop*.

policies See *business policies*.

portfolio matrix A matrix that *participants* can use to map items to phases in the context of a lifecycle metaphor: sow, grow, harvest, and plow. This mapping helps the project team to decide where to allocate resources.

posters Charts, visible to the *participants* in a *requirements workshop*, that contain information about things such as *purpose*, *products*, the *workshop agenda*, and items in the *parking lot*.

principles See *ground rules*.

The Preoccupied One A person who may start doing unrelated work, check his beeper, fidget, or scribble.

pre-work Specific assignments for *participants* to complete before a *requirements workshop*. Examples include the creation of draft requirements, templates, or forms.

problem-solving templates See *cognitive patterns*.

process map A diagram that shows the organization context in terms of the flows of inputs and outputs across functions or roles for a specific work process.

products Inputs to, and outputs from, a *requirements workshop*.

project glossary See *glossary*.

project sponsor A person who has the authority and legitimacy to make a given project happen.

prototype Anything that captures the look and feel of the user interface to be built for the new system and allows users to play with it. This can take the form of a fully working, albeit bare-bones, "system," or something more low-tech such as screen shots and low-fidelity sketches (for example, Visio diagrams).

purpose The definition of the reason that a *requirements workshop* is being held.

QA checklist A series of questions, usually stated in binary format, about a *requirements model* or its elements, and also questions about how one model cross-checks another.

quality assurance checklist See *QA checklist*.

quality function deployment (QFD) A systematic methodology for deriving and evaluating product features from both customer and designer points of view.

reciprocal collaboration A form of *collaboration* that involves *participants* working together to create common deliverables, mutually adjusting their activities in real time to take one another's edits into account.

recorder The person who documents the group's work as it proceeds during a *requirements workshop*.

relationship map A *requirements model* that shows the organization context in terms of the relationships that exist among suppliers and external customers.

release A version of the system produced by an *iterative development process*.

requirements The needs or conditions to be satisfied on behalf of *users* and *suppliers*.

requirements creep See *scope creep*.

requirements model A blueprint for a software product that takes the form of a diagram, list, or table, often supplemented with text, that depicts a user's needs from a particular point of view. Examples include *event lists*, *use cases*, data models, class models, *business rules*, *actor maps*, prototypes, and *user interface navigation diagrams*.

requirements workshop A structured meeting in which a carefully selected group of stakeholders and content experts work together to define, create, refine, and reach closure on deliverables that represent *user requirements*.

retrospective See *debrief*.

review The process of examining a work product, such as a model, a document, or a piece of code, so that people other than the one(s) who produced it can detect flaws.

scenarios Descriptions of typical uses of the system as narratives or stories. Each narrative can be a few sentences or a few paragraphs.

scope A broad definition of the who, what, when, why, where, and how associated with project goals and objectives. Scope determines the context for the user requirements effort.

scope creep The condition in which the scope of the project continues to expand as development work proceeds.

scope model See *context diagram*.

scope workshop A *requirements workshop* in which the participants take a bird's-eye view of what *user requirements* should be addressed by the development project.

screen transition diagram See *user interface navigation diagram*.

scribe See *recorder*.

secondary user See *indirect user*.

self-reflection The process in which a group examines its own interactions with the purpose of learning and improving.

sequential collaboration A form of *collaboration* that involves *participants* decomposing a deliverable into parts, and then one subgroup creating one output and passing it to the next subgroup.

shared purpose A clear, concise statement of purpose that all the participants in a *requirements workshop* understand and share a stake in.

shared space The room in which the participants in a *requirements workshop* gather, plus places and tools for content to be shared.

show-and-tell. A presentation by the workshop *participants* on their deliverables: models, actions, issues, and decisions.

The Sieve A collaboration pattern that uses smart filtering to help *participants* to make defensible choices about which user *requirements* will be implemented and what their relative priorities are in order to plan releases, begin design work, and focus project energies on the most essential requirements.

The Silent One A person who's participating to a minimal extent or perhaps not at all.

software requirements Requirements specifically associated with a software solution to a business problem and a user problem.

Spontaneous Agreement A *decision rule* that involves waiting until participants quickly and spontaneously arrive at a decision without considering the decision factors.

stakeholder classes A list or table of definitions of the people who care about—and the people who *should* care about—the system being developed.

standards See *business policies*.

statechart diagrams Diagrams that define how time affects your *domain model*, in terms of the possible states that elements of that model can assume and the transitions between those states.

state diagrams See *statechart diagrams*.

state models See *statechart diagrams*.

steps Specific tasks that the group will do within an activity, along with relevant *focus questions*.

sticky wall A wall containing paper sprayed with repositionable or remountable spray, which makes a tacky surface for holding cards that enables *participants* to reposition them as they like.

storming The stage of a group development process in which the members openly disagree. Under healthy circumstances. storming strengthens the group and promotes deeper understanding and diversity.

storyboard A hanging panel or wall that contains panels, sketches, or scenes depicting a plot or a sequence of actions.

supplier A person—such as a developer, an architect, an analyst, a software engineer, a tester, or a project manager—or a group that provides software.

surrogate See *surrogate user*.

surrogate user A stand-in *user* who takes the place of an actual user.

swimlane diagram See *process map*.

SWOT matrix A matrix that helps a group with the contracting phase of *Expand Then Contract*. It is a tool for identifying strengths, weaknesses, opportunities, and threats.

system context use case See *context diagram*.

techniques Group methods such as listing, a brainwriting pool, role play, a gallery review, and walkthroughs that permit groups to generate, specify, categorize, prioritize, and select models and modeling elements.

technographer A special type of *recorder* who works in conjunction with the *facilitator* by using technology to capture group content interactively and introducing group activities and agenda items.

template A standardized format that *participants* use during workshop activities to structure the contents of an output product.

template knowledge models See *cognitive patterns*.

tertiary user See *content adviser*.

thinking patterns See *cognitive patterns*.

thinkLet A pattern of thinking similar to higher-level *collaboration patterns* and cognitive patterns studied by knowledge engineering methodologists.

triad A subgroup comprising three people.

universal model A generic business model documented in books or available for purchase from some consulting companies. A universal model uses generic business terms (*business party, transaction, event, agreement*) that *participants* can use as starting points for modeling activities.

use case activity diagram See *use case map*.

use case dependency diagram See *use case map*.

use case flow diagram See *use case map*.

use case groups See *use case packages*.

use case map A *requirements model* that illustrates the predecessor and successor relationships among *use cases*.

use case navigation diagram See *use case map*.

use case packages Cohesive groups of use cases that can form things such as a logical architecture, a test group, or a release of the system.

use cases Descriptions of the major functions that the system will perform for external actors, and also the goals that the system achieves for those actors along the way.

use case scenarios See *scenarios*.

user Anyone who affects or is affected by the product: a person or thing (devices, databases, external systems) that interacts directly with the system being modeled.

user classes See *stakeholder classes*.

user interface navigation diagram A diagram that shows the layout of the user interface (screens, windows, dialog boxes, HTML pages) and the navigation that is possible among the elements of the interface.

user interface prototype See *prototype*.

user interface storyboard See *user interface navigation diagram*.

user requirements Requirements specifically associated with the user problem to be solved.

vertical strategy A strategy for conducting a requirements workshop that involves navigating down to detailed models in a single focus, using one model only as a starting point and then delving into the details of that model and perhaps one or two related models at the same level.

voice of the customer A technique that categorizes customer needs as *expectors* (customers take these needs for granted, and they'd be disappointed if they weren't addressed), *unspokens* (customers don't state these needs, but they'd be upset if the needs weren't addressed), *spokens* (the needs that the customers tell you about), or *delighters* (the needs that are exciting to customers but whose absence would result in few adverse effects).

walkthrough A form of *review* in which the producers of a *product*—for example, the subgroup who created the steps for a given *use case*—describe the product and ask for comments, questions, and corrections.

Wall of Wonder A *collaboration pattern* that takes the form of a *storyboarding* process in which groups use a shared wall space to build a model by successively using individual, then subgroup, and then *plenary* activities to generate items.

warm-up See *opener*.

window user interface See *prototype*.

workflow map See *process map*.

workshop agenda An ordered list of activities planned for a *requirements workshop*.

workshop aids Tools—such as static *posters* for participants to reference, sample models, instructions or tips to use while working on the models, worksheets for documenting changes to models, and materials and supplies—for use in conducting activities during a *requirements workshop*.

workshop repository One or more areas where soft copies of workshop *products*, *pre-work*, and post-workshop products are stored. This might take the form of a project Web site, a requirements management tool, a network folder, or some combination of these.

workshop sponsor A person who has the authority and legitimacy to make a *requirements workshop* happen. The sponsor's responsibilities include validating the workshop's *purpose,* ensuring that the right participants are present, engaging the *facilitator* and the *scribe,* kicking the workshop off and then returning for the *show-and-tell*, and (optionally) making workshop decisions.

zigzag strategy A strategy for conducting a *requirements workshop* that involves navigating around different focuses, moving down, over, and then down again or perhaps up.

BIBLIOGRAPHY

Argyris, Chris. 1993. *Knowledge for Action*. Jossey–Bass.

Argyris, Chris, and Donald A. Schön. 1996. *Organizational Learning II: Theory, Method and Practice*. Addison-Wesley.

Arrien, Angeles. 1993. *The Four-Fold Way: Walking the Paths of the Warrior, Teacher, Healer and Visionary*. HarperSanFrancisco.

August, Judy H. 1991. *Joint Application Design: The Group Session Approach to System Design*. Yourdon Press/Prentice Hall.

Avery, Christopher. 2001. *Teamwork is an Individual Skill: Getting Your Work Done When Sharing Responsibility*. Berrett-Koehler.

Basili, Victor R. 1997. "Evolving and Packaging Reading Technologies," *Journal of Systems and Software*, vol. 38, no. 1, pp. 3–12.

Basili, Vic, and D. M. Weiss. 1984. "A Methodology for Collecting Valid Software Engineering Data," *IEEE Transactions on Software Engineering*, vol. 10, no. 6, November, pp. 728–738.

Bens, Ingrid. 2000. *Facilitating with Ease: A Step-by-Step Guidebook with Customizable Worksheets on CD-ROM*. Jossey-Bass.

Berry, Daniel K. 1995. "The Importance of Ignorance in Requirements Engineering," *Journal of Systems and Software,* vol. 28, no. 1, February, pp. 170–184.

Beyer, Hugh, and Karen Holtzblatt. 1998. *Contextual Inquiry: Defining Customer-Centered Systems*. Morgan Kaufman.

Boehm, Barry. 1981. *Software Engineering Economics*. Prentice Hall PTR.

Boehm, Barry. 1987. "Improving Software Productivity," *IEEE Computer*, September, pp. 43–57.

Boehm, Barry, Alexander Egyed, Julie Kwan, Dan Port, Archita Shah, and Ray Madachy. 1998. "Using the WinWin Spiral Model: A Case Study," *IEEE Software*, vol. 31, no. 7, July, pp. 33-44.

Boehm, Barry, and Hoh In. 1999. "Cost vs. Quality Requirements: Conflict Analysis and Negotiation Aids," *Software Quality Professional*, American Society for Quality, vol. 1, no. 2, March, pp. 38–50.

Boehm, Barry, P. Bose, Ellis Horowitz, and M. Lee. 1994. "Software Requirements as Negotiated Win Conditions," *Proceedings of the First International Conference on Requirements Engineering*, Colorado Springs.

Boehm, Barry, and Philip N. Papaccio. 1988. "Understanding and Controlling Software Costs," *IEEE Transactions on Software Engineering*, vol. 14, no. 10, October, pp. 1462–1477.

Boehm, Barry, Paul Grünbacher, and Robert O. Briggs. 2001. "Developing Groupware for Requirements Negotiation: Lessons Learned," *IEEE Software*, May/June, pp. 46–55.

Boehm, Barry, and Victor R. Basili. 2001. "Software Defect Reduction Top 10 List," *IEEE Computer*, vol. 34, no. 1, pp. 135–137.

Bohm, David. 1996. *On Dialogue*. Routledge.

Briggs, R. G., G. de Vreede, J. Nunamaker, Jr., and D. Tobey. 2001. "ThinkLets: Achieving Predictable, Repeatable Patterns of Group Interaction with Group Support Systems (GSS)," *Proceedings of the 34th Annual Hawaii International Conference on System Sciences* (HICSS-34).

Brooks, Frederick P., Jr.. 1995. *The Mythical Man-Month*. Anniversary Edition. Addison-Wesley.

Buzan, Tony. 1989. *Use Both Sides of Your Brain*. Penguin Books.

Carmel, Erran, Joey F. George, and Jay F. Nunamaker. 1992. "Supporting Joint Application Design (JAD) and Electronic Meeting System: Moving the CASE Concept into New Areas of Software Development," *Proceedings of the International Conference on Information Systems*, pp. 223–232.

Carmel, Erran, Randall D. Whitaker, and Joey F. George. 1993. "Participatory Design and Joint Application Design: A Transatlantic Comparison," *Communications of the ACM*, vol. 36, no. 4, June, pp. 40–47.

Carmel, Erran, and Ritu Agarwal. 2001. "Tactical Approaches for Alleviating Distance in Global Software Development," *IEEE Software*, vol. 18. no. 2, March/April, pp. 22–29.

Cartwright, D., and Alvin Zander. 2000. "Origins of Group Dynamics." In *Group Dynamics*, Third Edition, 1968. Reprinted in "Group Facilitation: A Research and Applications Journal," vol. 2, no. 2, Winter, pp. 38–53.

Chin, Kenneth F. 1995. "A JAD Experience," Proceedings of the 1995 ACM SIGCPR Conference on Supporting Teams, Groups, and Learning Inside and Outside the IS Function: Reinventing IS, pp. 235–236.

Cockburn, Alistair. 2000. *Writing Effective Use Cases*. Addison-Wesley.

Cockburn, Alistair. 2001. *Agile Software Development*. Addison-Wesley.

Cohen, Lou. 1995. *Quality Function Deployment: How to Make QFD Work for You*. Addison-Wesley.

Constantine, Larry, and Lucy Lockwood. 1999. *Software for Use: A Practical Guide to the Models and Methods of Usage-Centered Design*. Addison-Wesley.

Crawford, Anthony. 1994. *Advancing Business Concepts in a JAD Workshop Setting: Business Reengineering and Process Redesign*. Yourdon Press/Prentice Hall.

Csikszentmihalyi, Mihaly. 1991. *Flow: The Psychology of Optimal Experience*. HarperCollins.

Damelio, Robert. 1996. *The Basics of Process Mapping*. Productivity Inc.

Date, C. J. 2000. *What Not How: The Business Rules Approach to Application Development*. Addison-Wesley.

Davis, Alan M. 1993. *Software Requirements: Objects, Functions, and States*. Prentice Hall.

Davis, Alan M. 1995. *201 Principles of Software Development*. McGraw-Hill.

de Bono, Edward. 1994. *de Bono's Thinking Course, Revised Edition*. Facts on File.

de Bono, Edward. 1999. *Six Thinking Hats: The Power of Focused Thinking*. MICA Management Resources.

DeGrace, Peter, and Leslie Hulet Stahl. 1990. *Wicked Problems, Righteous Solutions: A Catalog of Modern Software Engineering Paradigms.* Yourdon Press Computing Series.

DeKoven, Bernie. 1999a. "The Technologies of Play and the True Origins of Technography," MightyWords, Inc.

DeKoven, Bernie. 1999b. "Using the Dynamic Outline to Facilitate Collaborative Meetings: An Introduction to the Art of Technography," MightyWords, Inc.

DeMarco, Tom, and Timothy Lister. 1999. *Peopleware: Productive Projects and Teams,* 2nd Edition. Dorset House.

Dion, Raymond. 1993. "Process Improvement and Corporate Balance Sheet," *IEEE Software*, vol. 10, no. 4, July/August, pp. 28–35.

Doyle, Michael, and David Strauss. 1976. *How to Make Meetings Work.* Berkley Books.

Fagan, Michael E. 1976. "Design and Code Inspections to Reduce Errors in Program Development," *IBM Systems Journal*, vol. 15, no. 3.

Fisher, Aubrey. 1970. "Decision emergence: Phases in group decision making," *Speech Monographs,* 37.

Fisher, Roger, and William Ury. 1991. *Getting to Yes: Negotiating Agreement Without Giving In.* Penguin Books.

Foss, Burry W. 1993. "Fast, Faster, Fasterest Development," *Computerworld*, May 31, pp. 81–83.

Fowler, Martin, with Kendall Scott. 1999. *UML Distilled: A Brief Guide to the Standard Object Modeling Language, Second Edition.* Addison-Wesley.

Freedman, Daniel P., and Gerald M. Weinberg. 1990. *Handbook of Walkthroughs, Inspections and Technical Reviews,* Third Edition. Dorset House.

Gardner, Karen M., Alexander Rush, Michael K. Crist, Robert Konitzer, and Bobbin Teegarden. 1998. *Cognitive Patterns: Problem-Solving Frameworks for Object Technology.* Cambridge University Press.

Gause, Donald G., and Brian Lawrence. 1999. "User-Driven Design: Incorporating Users into the Requirements and Design Phase," *Software Testing and Quality Engineering*, vol. 1, no. 1, January/February.

Gause, Donald C., and Gerald M. Weinberg. 1989. *Exploring Requirements: Quality Before Design.* Dorset House.

Geier, Jim, 1996. "Don't Get Mad, Get JAD," *Software Development,* vol. 4, no. 3, March. Reprinted in Larry Constantine (editor), *The Unified Process Inception Phase: Best Practices in Implementing the UP*, 2000, CMP Books.

Gilb, Tom, and Dorothy Graham. 1993. *Software Inspection.* Addison-Wesley.

Gottesdiener, Ellen. 1994. "Building a Team and a Project with JAD: A Case Study," *System Development Management*, December. Reprinted in *Handbook of Application Development.* Warren, Gorham and Lamont.

Gottesdiener, Ellen. 1997. "Facilitated Business Rule Workshops: 12 Guidelines for Success," *Database Newsletter*, vol. 25, no. 1, January/February.

Gottesdiener, Ellen. 1999. "Capturing Business Rules," *Software Development*, vol. 7, no. 12, December. Reprinted in Larry Constantine (editor), *Beyond Chaos: The Expert Edge in Managing Software Development,* 2001, Addison-Wesley.

Gottesdiener, Ellen. 1999. "Decode Business Needs Now," *Software Development*, vol. 7, no. 12, December. Reprinted in Larry Constantine (editor), *The Unified Process Inception Phase: Best Practices in Implementing the UP*, 2000, CMP Books.

Gottesdiener, Ellen. 1999. "Harvesting Business Rules in Workshops," *Data To Knowledge Newsletter*, vol. 27, no. 2, March/April.

Gottesdiener, Ellen. 1999. "Turning Rules into Requirements," *Application Development Trends*, vol. 6, no. 4, July.

Gottesdiener, Ellen. 2001. "Collaborate for Quality: Using Collaborative Workshops to Determine Requirements," *Software Testing and Quality Engineering*, vol. 3, no. 2, March/April.

Gottesdiener, Ellen. 2001. "Decide How to Decide," *Software Development*, vol. 9, no. 1, January.

Gottesdiener, Ellen. 2001. *Facilitation Essentials: Practical Techniques for the JAD Practitioner* (course materials, EBG Consulting, Inc.).

Gottesdiener, Ellen. 2001. *Requirements Modeling with Use Cases and Business Rules* (course materials, EBG Consulting, Inc.).

Gottesdiener, Ellen. 2001. "Specifying Requirements with a Wall of Wonder," *Rational Edge*, November.

Grove Consultants International, The. 1994. *Effective Facilitation: Achieving Results with Groups.* The Grove Consultants International.

Grove Consultants International, The. 1997. *Investment Portfolio Leader's Guide.* The Grove Consultants International.

Guinta, Lawrence R., and Nancy C. Praizler. 1993. *The QFD Book: The Team Approach to Solving Problems and Satisfying Customers Through Quality Function Deployment.* Amacom.

Hackett, Donald, and Charles L. Martin. 1993. *Facilitation Skills for Team Leaders.* Crisp Publications.

Hammond, John S., III, Ralph L. Keeney, and Howard Raiffa. 1998. *Smart Choices: A Practical Guide to Making Better Decisions.* Harvard Business School.

Hanson, Mirja P. 1996. *Golden Groundrules: Leaders Guide.* Meeting Needs.

Harvey, Jerry B. 1988. *The Abilene Paradox and Other Meditations on Management.* New Lexington Press.

Highsmith, James A., III. 2000. *Adaptive Software Development: A Collaborative Approach to Managing Complex Systems.* Dorset House.

Hirokawa, Randy, Dennis Gouran, and Amy Martz. 1988. "Understanding the Sources of Faulty Group Decision Making: A Lesson from the Challenger Disaster," *Small Group Behavior,* vol. 19, no. 4, November, pp. 411–433.

Hooks, Ivy F., and Kristin A. Farry. 2001. *Customer-Centered Products: Creating Successful Products through Requirements Management.* Amacom.

Howell, Johnna L. 1995. *Tools for Facilitating Team Meetings.* Integrity Publishing.

Hubbard, Dr. Rick, Charles N. Schroeder, and Nancy R. Mead. 2000. "An Assessment of the Relative Efficiency of a Facilitator-Driven Requirements Collection Process with Respect to the Conventional Interview Method," *Proceedings of the 4th International Conference on Requirements Engineering,* June.

Hunter, Dale, Anne Bailey, and Bill Taylor. 1995. *The Art of Facilitation: How to Create Group Synergy.* Fisher Books.

Hunter, Dale, Anne Bailey, and Bill Taylor. 1995. *The Zen of Groups: The Handbook for People Meeting with a Purpose.* Fisher Books.

Institute of Cultural Affairs. 1994. *Technology of Participation: Group Facilitation Methods* (course guide).

Institute of Electrical and Electronic Engineers. 1998. IEEE Std 830-1998: "IEEE Recommended Practice for Software Specifications," IEEE Computer Society Press.

International Association of Facilitators (IAF). 1999. *Group Facilitation: A Research & Applications Journal,* vol. 1, no. 1, Winter.

Janis, Irving. 1982. *Groupthink: Psychological Studies of Policy Decisions and Fiascoes.* Houghton Mifflin College.

Johnson, Jim. 1996. "Achieving a Clear Statement of I/IS Project Requirements," *Application Development Trends*, vol. 6, no. 3, June, pp. 28–29.

Jones, Capers. 1986. *Tutorial Programming Productivity: Issues for the Eighties*, 2nd Edition. IEEE Computer Society Press.

Jones, Capers. 1994. *Assessment and Control of Software Risks.* Prentice Hall.

Jones, Capers. 1996a. *Patterns of Software Systems Failure and Success.* Thomson Computer Press.

Jones, Capers. 1996b. "Software Change Management," *IEEE Computer*, vol. 29, no. 2, February, pp. 80–82.

Jones, Capers. 1996c. "Strategies for Managing Requirements Creep," *IEEE Computer*, vol. 29, no. 6, June, pp. 92–94.

Jones, Capers. 1997. "Becoming Best in Class: Taking the Path to Software Excellence" (paper presented at Software Development Conference, August).

Jones, Capers. 2000. *Software Assessments, Benchmarks and Best Practices.* Addison-Wesley.

Jones, Capers. 2001. "Conflict and Litigation Between Software Clients and Developers, Version 10" (technical report, Software Productivity Research), April.

Justice, Tom, and David W. Jamieson. 1999. *The Facilitator's Fieldbook*. HRD Press.

Kaner, Sam, with Lenny Lind, Catherine Toldi, Sarah Fisk, and Duane Berger. 1996. *Facilitator's Guide to Participatory Decision-Making*. New Society Publishers.

Katzenbach, Jon R., and Douglas K. Smith. 2001. *The Discipline of Teams: A Mindbook-Workbook for Delivering Small Group Performance.* John Wiley & Sons.

Kayser, Thomas A. 1990. *Mining Group Gold: How to Cash In on the Collaborative Brain Power of a Group.* Serif Publishing.

Kearny, Lynn. 1995. *The Facilitator's Toolkit: Tools and Techniques for Generating Ideas and Making Decisions in Groups.* HRD Press.

Keil, Mark, and Erran Carmel. 1995. "Customer-Developer Links in Software Development," *Communications of the ACM*, vol. 38, no. 5, May, pp. 33–44.

Kelsey, Dee, and Pam Plumb. 1997. *Great Meetings! How to Facilitate Like a Pro.* Hanson Park Press.

Kerth, Norman L. 2001. *Project Retrospectives: A Handbook for Team Reviews.* Dorset House.

Keuffel, Warren. 1992. "Is Graphical Always Better?" *Computer Language,* vol. 9, no. 9, September.

Kipling, Rudyard. 1996. *Just So Stories.* William Morrow & Company.

Kovitz, Benjamin. 1999. *Practical Software Requirements: A Manual of Content and Style.* Manning Publications.

Kulak, Daryl, and Eamonn Guiney. 2000. *Use Cases: Requirements in Context.* Addison-Wesley.

Lawrence, Brian. 1996. "Unresolved Ambiguity: The Silent Source of Risk in Your Project," *American Programmer*, vol. 9, no. 4, April.

Lawrence, Brian. 1997. "Requirements Happen," *American Programmer*, April, pp. 6–7.

Lederer, Albert L., and Jayesh Prasad. 1992. "Nine Management Guidelines for Better Cost Estimating," *Communications of the ACM*, vol. 35, no. 2, February.

Leffingwell, Dean. 1997. "Calculating the Return on Investment from More Effective Requirements Management," *American Programmer*, vol. 1, no. 4, April, pp. 13–16.

Leffingwell, Dean, and Don Widrig. 1999. *Managing Software Requirements: A Unified Approach.* Addison-Wesley.

Lilly, Susan. 2000. "Use Case Pitfalls: Top 10 Problems from Real Projects Using Use Cases," *Software Development*, vol. 8, no. 1, January, pp. 40–45.

Lucas, Mark. 1993. "The Way of JAD," *Database Programming & Design*, July, pp. 42–46.

Mallens, Paul. 2000. "The Alignment Between Business and IT: Business Modeling as the Basis for Defining Business Rules," proceedings, Business Rules Forum 2000 conference.

McConnell, Steve. 1996. *Rapid Development: Taming Wild Software Schedules*. Microsoft Press.

McGraw, Karen L., and Karan Harbison. 1997. *User-Centered Requirements: The Scenario-Based Engineering Process Approach*. Lawrence Erlbaum Associates.

McMenamin, Stephen M., and John F. Palmer. 1994. *Essential Systems Analysis*. Yourdon.

Mittleman, D. D., R. O. Briggs, and Jay F. Nunmaker, Jr. 2000. "Best Practices in Facilitating Virtual Meetings: Some Notes from Initial Experience," *Group Facilitation: A Research and Applications Journal*, vol. 2, no. 2, Winter, pp. 5–14.

Muller, M., and S. Kuhn. 1993. "Participatory Design," *Communications of the ACM*, vol. 35, no. 3, June, pp. 24–28.

Nunamaker, J. F. 1999. "Collaborative Computing: The Next Millennium," *IEEE Computer*, vol. 32, no. 9, September, pp. 66–71.

Nutt, Paul C. 1998. "Leverage, Resistance and Success of Implementation Approaches," *Journal of Management Studies*, vol. 35, no. 2, March, pp. 213–240.

Pardee, William J. 1996. *To Satisfy & Delight Your Customer*. Dorset House.

Pedler, Mike, John Burgoyne, and Tom Boydell. 1991. *The Learning Company: A Strategy for Sustainable Development*. McGraw-Hill.

Ritter, Diane, and Michael Brassard. 1994. *The Memory Jogger II: A Pocket Guide of Tools for Continuous Improvement & Effective Planning*. GOAL/QPC.

Ritter, Diane, and Michael Brassard. 1998. *The Creative Tools Memory Jogger: A Pocket Guide for Creative Thinking*. GOAL/QPC.

Robbins, Stephen F. 2000. *Essentials of Organizational Behavior*, Sixth Edition. Prentice Hall.

Robertson, Suzanne, and James Robertson. 1999. *Mastering the Requirements Process*. Addison-Wesley.

Ross, Ronald G. 1998. *Business Rule Concepts*. Database Research Group.

Rummler, Geary A., and Alan P. Brache. 1995. *Improving Performance: How to Manage the White Space on the Organizational Chart,* Second Edition. Jossey-Bass.

Rush, Gary. 1985. "A Fast Way to Define System Requirements," *Computerworld*, October 7, pp. 11–12.

Saint, Steven, and James R. Lawson. 1994. *Rules for Reaching Consensus: A Modern Approach to Decision Making.* Jossey-Bass.

Schrage, Michael. 1995. *No More Teams: Mastering the Dynamics of Creative Collaboration.* Currency Doubleday.

Schrage, Michael. 2000. *Serious Play: How the World's Best Companies Simulate to Innovate.* Harvard Business School.

Schreiber, Guss, J. M. Akkemans, A. A. Anjewierden, R. de Hoog, N. R. Shadbolt, W. Van de Velde, and B. J. Wielinga. 2000. *Knowledge Engineering and Management: The CommonKADS Methodology*. MIT Press.

Schuman, Sandor P. 1996. "Do You Need an Outside Facilitator?" Adapted from Sandor P. Schuman, "The Role of Facilitation in Collaborative Groups," in C. Huxham (editor), *The Search for Collaborative Advantage*, Sage Publications.

Schwarz, Roger M. 1994. *The Skilled Facilitator.* Jossey–Bass.

Senge, Peter, Charlotte Roberts, Richard Ross, Bryan Smith, and Art Kleiner. 1994. *The Fifth Discipline Fieldbook: Strategies and Tools for Building a Learning Organization*. Doubleday.

Simsion, Graeme C. 2001. *Data Modeling Essentials: Analysis, Design and Innovation,* Second Edition. The Coriolis Group.

Smith, Larry W. 2000. "Project Clarity through Stakeholder Analysis," *Crosstalks*, vol. 13, no. 12, December, pp. 4–9.

Spencer, Laura J. 1989. *Winning Through Participation: Meeting the Challenge of Corporate Change With the Technology of Participation.* Kendall/Hunt.

Stanfield, Brian. 1997. *The Art of Focused Conversation: 100 Ways to Access Group Wisdom in the Workplace.* The Canadian Institute of Culture Affairs.

Stapleton, Jennifer. 1997. *DSDM Dynamic Systems Development Method: The Method in Practice.* Addison-Wesley.

Stevens, Richard, Peter Brook, Ken Jackson, and Stuart Arnold. 1998. *Systems Engineering: Coping with Complexity*. Prentice Hall Europe.

Strachan, Dorothy. 2001. *Questions that Work: A Resource for Facilitators.* ST Press.

Straker, David. 1997. *Rapid Problem-Solving with Post-it Notes.* Fisher Books.

Tubbs, Stewart. 1995. *A Systems Approach to Small Group Interaction.* McGraw-Hill.

Tuckman, Bruce W. 2001. "Developmental Sequence in Small Groups," *Psychological Bulletin*, vol. 63, no. 6, pp. 384–399, 1965. Reprinted in *Group Facilitation: A Research and Applications Journal*, Spring, issue 3.

Tuckman, Bruce W., and Mary Ann Jensen. 1977. "Stages of Small Group Development Revisited," *Group and Organizational Studies,* vol. 2, no. 4, pp. 419–427.

VanGundy, Arthur B. 1988. *Techniques of Structured Problem Solving*, Second Edition. Van Nostrand Reinhold.

Vosburgh, J. B., et al. 1984. "Productivity Factors and Programming Environments." In *Proceedings of the 7th International Conference on Software Engineering*, IEEE Computer Society, pp. 143–152.

Wiegers, Karl E. 1996. *Creating a Software Engineering Culture.* Dorset House.

Wiegers, Karl E. 1999. *Software Requirements.* Microsoft Press.

Wiegers, Karl. 2001. *Peer Reviews in Software: A Practical Guide.* Addison-Wesley.

Weinberg, Gerald M. 1994. *Quality Software Management, Volume 3: Congruent Action.* Dorset House.

Weinberg, Gerald M. 1997. *Quality Software Management, Volume 4: Anticipating Change.* Dorset House.

Wood, Jane, and Denise Silver. 1995. *Joint Application Development,* Second Edition. John Wiley & Sons.

Zahniser, Rick A. 1990. "How to Speed Development with Group Sessions," *IEEE Software*, vol. 7, no. 3, May/June, pp. 109–110.

Zahniser, Richard A. 1993. "Design by Walking Around," *Communications of the ACM*, vol. 36, no. 10, October, pp. 114–123.

Zachman, John. 1987. "A Framework for Information System Architecture," *IBM Systems Journal*, vol. 26, no. 3, IBM Publication G321-5298.

Index

A

Abilene paradox, 214
Abstract use cases. *See* Use cases
Act phase, requirements workshop
    processes, 65–66
Activities during workshops
  basics, 182–183
  elements of each activity, 186–188
  estimating time, 191, 192
  example, 188–191
  focus questions, 191–193, 194
  framing, 185
  imaging, 193–194
  mini-tutorials, 185–186
  QA (quality assurance), 194–198
  sequencing, 183–185
  templates, 190
Actor catalog. *See* Actor tables
Actor hierarchy. *See* Actor maps
Actor maps
  basics, 37
  behavioral view, 30
  focus of models, 33
  focus questions, 32
  high-level requirements, 34, 35
Actor tables
  basics, 37–38
  behavioral view, 30
  focus of models, 33

  focus questions, 32
  high-level requirements, 34, 35
Actors, harvesting business rules, 140
Adjourning, group development process,
    110–111, 211–212
Affinity groups, visual products, 135
Agendas, requirements workshops, 152
Arbitrary decision rule, 124, 125
As-is requirements models, 36
Ask why five times technique, 69–70,
    208
Asynchronous time, workshops, 170
Atomic business rules. *See* Business rules

B

Behavioral view, requirements models,
    28–30
  aligning with business problems,
    136–138
Best practices, requirements workshops,
    261–262
Body language of participants, 210
Both sides of brain usage, requirements
    workshop success factor, 61–62
Bottom-up approach
  horizontal workshop navigation strategy,
    226, 233
  storyboards, 201
  workshop purpose, 77

BPR (business process reengineering),
    similarity to as-is requirements
    models, 36–37
Business cases. *See* Charter documents
Business changes
    documents, 27
    effects on user requirements, 25–27
Business glossaries. *See* Glossaries
Business managers, as workshop
    sponsors, 86
Business policies
    basics, 38
    control view, 30
    focus of models, 33
    focus questions, 32
    harvesting business rules, 140
    scope-level requirements, 34, 35
Business problems, aligning with
    requirements models, 136–138
Business process reengineering (BPR),
    similarity to as-is requirements
    models, 36–37
Business project managers, 87
Business requirements
    basics, 24–25
    charter documents, 24–25
    constant changes, 8
    documentation methods, 6–7
    evolution of requirements, 22–24
Business rules
    basics, 38
    control view, 30
    detailed-level requirements, 34, 35
    focus of models, 33
    focus questions, 32
    generating, 140
    templates, 156
    zigzag navigation strategy, 239
Business scenarios. *See* Scenarios
Business users, 274
Business value, 17, 263–264

C
Case studies, requirements workshops
    BestClaims, 255–259
    HaveFunds, 250–255
    RegTrak, 245–250
    SalesTrak, 241–245
Certified Professional Facilitator (CPF),
    273
Charter, project, 6, 14–16, 20, 38
Charter documents, business requirements,
    24–25
Charter workshops, deliverables, 14–16
Check phase, requirements workshops,
    65–66
Checklists, QA (quality assurance), 195
Clarifying focus questions, 194
Closure
    basics, 217–218
    collaborative, types of decision rules,
        59–60
    collaborative, workshop success factor,
        59–60
    debriefing, 219–220
    decision-making rules, 119–120
    parking lot items, addressing, 219
    show-and-tell, 218
Clusters, visual products, 135
Co-located space, workshops, 170
Collaboration
    decision making, 121–122
    decision rules, 122–126
    modes, 199–200
    reaching closure, 126–128
    reaching closure, example, 128–129
    reaching closure, success factor,
        59–60
    requirements workshop role, 10
    techniques, 209–210
Collaboration patterns
    combining, 208–209
    Decide How to Decide, 279–280

Divide, Conquer, Correct, Collect (DCCC), 143, 188, 199–200, 200–201, 204, 280
Expand Then Contract, 203–205, 281
Is There a Norm in the Room?, 111, 281–282
Multi-Model, 37, 203, 204, 282–283
Self-Reflect, 117, 197, 283–284
The Sieve, 205–208, 284–285
Wall of Wonder (WoW), 187-188, 200–201, 285–286
Collaborative technology
advantages/disadvantages, 173–174
basics, 172–173
electronic polling, 174
thinklets, 172
warnings, 175
Complainer, type of participant, 215
Computer supported collaborative work (CSCW), 172
Computer-aided facilitation. *See* Collaborative technology
Concensus, type of decision rule, 124, 125, 126
Concepts catalogs. *See* Glossaries
Conceptual class or data models. *See* Domain models
Concrete use cases. *See* Scenarios
Conflicts during workshops, 212–215
Constraints. *See* Business rules
Content advisers, participant roles, 90
Content balance, facilitators, 13
Content participants, 85, 89–91
Context diagrams
basics, 39
behavioral view, 30
five-minute tests, 232
focus of models, 33
focus questions, 32
scope-level requirements, 34, 35

Context-level use cases. *See* Context diagrams
Control-oriented view, requirements models, 28–30
aligning with business problems, 136–138
Courtesy, ground rules, 112
Creeping user requirements. *See* Scope creep
Criteria grid matrix, 207
Cross-functional process maps. *See* Process maps
CSCW (computer supported collaborative work), 172
Culturally aware ground rules, 115–116
Customers, defined, 5
"Cutting to the chase," 113

D
Data flow diagram, 37
DCCC (Divide, Conquer, Correct, Collect)
collaboration pattern, 1188, 199–201, 280
iterative requirements deliveries, 143
with Multi-Model pattern, 204
Debriefing sessions, 219–220
evaluation process, 269
frequency as workshop success factor, 63–64
Decide How to Decide collaboration pattern, 279–280
Decision diagrams. *See* Decision trees
Decision Leader Decides Without/After Discussion rule, 125
Decision rules, 122–128
closure, 126–128
decision leaders, 122–126
decision leaders, role in closure, 126–128
examples, 128–129
Sieve collaboration pattern, 206–207
types, 123–125

Decision tables
  basics, 39
  control view, 30
  focus of models, 33
  focus questions, 32
Decision trees
  basics, 39
  control view, 30
  focus of models, 33
  focus questions, 32
Decision-making rules (closure),
  119–120
Delegation decision rule, 123, 124
Delighters, 207
Deliverables
  data for workshop evaluation, 267
  defined, 9
  requirements workshops, 14–16
Detailed-level workshops, 141–142
  deliverables, 15–16
  horizontal navigation strategy, 226,
    240
  vertical navigation strategy, 237, 240
  zigzag navigation strategy, 240
Dialog maps. See User interface navigation
  diagrams
Direct focus questions, 194
Direct users. See Users
Direct users list. See Actor tables
Distributed space, workshops, 170
Distributed teams, participant roles, 92
Divide, Conquer, Correct, Collect (DCCC)
  collaboration pattern, 188, 199–201,
    280
  iterative requirements deliveries, 143
  with Multi-Model pattern, 204
Do phase, workshops, 65–66
Documentation methods, requirements,
  6–7
  system and user documentation, 154
Documentators. See Recorders

Domain experts, 5
Domain models
  basics, 39–40
  focus of models, 33
  focus questions, 32
  harvesting business rules, 140
  high-level requirements, 34, 35
  structural view, 30
Domain statechart diagrams. See Statechart
  diagrams
Dominator, type of participant, 215
Doneness tests
  combining with pre-work, 150
  decision-making process, 120, 149,
    150
  defining, 145–149
  requirements workshop success factor,
    57–59
Draft models, 152–153
Dynamic view, requirements models,
  28–30
  aligning with business problems,
    136–138

E
Electronic meetings (EMs), 172
Electronic polling, 174
End users. See Users
Energizers, group process development,
  117–118
Entity life history diagrams. See Statechart
  diagrams
Essential use cases. See Use cases
Event lists. See Event tables
Event tables
  basics, 40
  dynamic view, 30
  focus of models, 33
  focus questions, 32
  scope-level requirements, 34, 35
Executive sponsors, 87

Expand Then Contract collaboration
    pattern, 203–205, 281
Expectors (customers), 207

F
Facilitators, 271–272
    and requirements workshops, 11
    as planners and designers, 97–98
    as process leaders, 97, 98–100
    basic responsibilities, 96–97
    decision making, 98
    defined, 9
    hiring outside personnel, 101–103
    intervention skills, 100–101
    observation skills, 100–101
    participant roles, 85, 96–103
    responsibilities, 13–14
    skills/knowlege needed, 273–274
Feature creep. *See* Scope creep
Filtering with The Sieve collaboration
    pattern, 205–208
Five-minute scope tests, 232
Flexible structure, workshop success
    factor, 60–61
Focus questions
    horizontal middle-out navigation
        strategies, 231
    mixing with view models, 140–141
    requirements models, 30–32
    requirements workshop success factor,
        53–54
    vertical navigation strategies, primary
        focus, 235
    workshop processes, 191–193, 194
Forcefield analysis collaborative technique,
    209
Forming, group development process,
    110–111, 211–212
Fourfold way, ground rules, 276
Free-form business rules. *See* Business
    rules

Fun and games, 215–217
Functional requirement levels, 22–24

G
Games and fun, 215–217
Glossaries
    basics, 40
    focus of models, 33
    focus questions, 32
    guardians, 153
    requirements model drafts, 153
    scope-level requirements, 34, 35
    structural view, 30
Goal-question-metrics techniques, 268
Grids, visual products, 135
Ground rules (principles), 109–110
    basic rules, 111–113
    culturally aware rules, 114–115
    decision rules, 122–128
    decision rules, examples, 128–129
    decision-making rules (closure),
        119–120
    facilitators, 274–277
    ground rules for ground rules, 112
    group development process, 110–111
    hidden agendas, 117–119
    introducing rules, 116–117
    product- and process-related decisions,
        120–121
    questions for stakeholders, 129–130
    testing rules, 116–117
    value-based, 113–114
Group development process, 110–111
Group dynamics during workshops,
    211–212
Group support systems (GSS), 172
Groupshift and groupthink, group
    dysfunction, 51
Groupware, 172
GSS (group support systems), 172
Guidelines. *See* Business policies

H

Happy sheets, evaluation process, 268
Headlining comments, 113, 210
Hidden agendas, 117–119, 211, 244-245
High-level business rules. *See* Business
    policies
High-level scenarios. *See* Scenarios
High-level workshops
    deliverables, 15–16
    four phases, 65–66
    navigation strategies, horizontal, 226, 240
    navigation strategies, vertical, 235–236,
        236, 240
    navigation strategies, zigzag, 240
Horizontal workshop navigation strategy
    bottom-up approach, 77, 226, 233
    comparing with other strategies, 240
    middle-out approach, 77, 226, 230–232
    selecting types, 226–227
    short dives, 227, 228
    top-down approach, 76, 226, 228–230
    varying with vertical strategies, 236
Huddle, 75-76

I

IAF, facilitators, 272–273
Icebreakers. *See* Opening workshops
Imaging, workshop activities, 193–194
Indirect user participant roles, 90
Initiation documents. *See* Charter
    documents
Input products, requirements workshops
    agenda, 152
    documentation of systems and users,
        154–155
    draft models, 152–153
    iterations, 161
    pre-work, 154–160
    questions for stakeholders, 162
    repositories, 160
    universal models, 153

Invariants. *See* Business rules
Is There a Norm in the Room?
    collaboration pattern, 111, 281–282
Iterative delivery
    requirements models, 142–143
    requirements workshops, 269–271
    software development, 16–17

J

JAD (Joint Application Design),
    requirements workshops origin, 13
    versus meetings, 11–13
"Jelled" teams, 69

K

Kickoffs for workshops, 88–89

L

Latecomer, type of participant, 215
Lateral thinking collaborative technique,
    209
Leading focus questions, 194
Learning styles, workshop success factor,
    61–62
Logic tables. *See* Decision tables
Logistics, workshop physical space, 166–168
Low-fidelity prototypes, iterative software
    development, 17

M

Majority vote decision rule, 123, 124
Marketing managers, project sponsor role,
    87
Matrices
    criteria grids, 207
    doneness testing, 148
    portfolios, 207
    QA (quality assurance), 197
    SWOT matrix collaborative technique,
        209
    visual products, 135

Meetings
  cost of ineffectiveness, 11
  nondelivery of products, 14
  versus requirements workshops, 11–14
Meetingware, 172
Meta focus questions, 194
Metaphors, doneness testing, 149
Method 6-3-5 collaborative technique,
  209
Metrics, evaluation process, 267
Middle-out approach
  horizontal workshop navigation strategy,
    226, 230–232
  horizontal workshop purpose, 77
  storyboards, 201
Mind maps, 135, 136
Mini-tutorials, 185–186
Models, requirements
  actor map basics, 37
  actor tables basics, 37–38
  as-is models, 36
  business policies, basics, 38
  business rules, basics, 38
  communication, primary purpose, 8
  context diagrams, basics, 39
  decision tables, basics, 39
  decision trees, basics, 39
  defined, 7
  domain models, basics, 39–40
  estimating delivery time, 144
  event tables, basics, 40
  focus questions, 30–32
  glossaries, basics, 40
  heuristics for selection, 137
  level of detail, 32–35
  methodology selection, 8–9
  Multi-Model collaboration pattern, 37
  multiple models, 36–37
  process maps, basics, 41
  prototypes, basics, 41
  relationship maps, basics, 41–42

  scenarios, basics, 42
  similarity to BPR (business process
    reengineering), 36–37
  stakeholder classes, basics, 42–43
  statechart diagrams, basics, 43
  use case maps, basics, 44
  use case packages, basics, 44
  use classes, basics, 43
  user interface navigation diagrams,
    basics, 44–45
  views, 28–30
Multi-Model collaboration pattern, 37, 203,
  282–283
  with Divide, Conquer, Correct, Collect
    pattern, 204
Multiple requirements models, 36–37,
  138–139

N
Narrow and deep navigation strategy. *See*
  Vertical workshop navigation
  strategy
Navigation strategies at workshops
  comparing strategies, 240
  horizontal, basics, 225–226
  horizontal, bottom-up approach, 226,
    233
  horizontal, middle-out approach, 226,
    230–232
  horizontal, selecting types, 226–227
  horizontal, short dives, 227, 228
  horizontal, top-down approach, 226,
    228–230
  vertical, basics, 233
  vertical, selecting primary focus, 235
  vertical, selecting scope- or high-level
    models, 235–236
  vertical, selecting starting models,
    233–234
  vertical, varying with horizontal strategy,
    236

Navigation strategies at workshops,
continued
vertical, with multiple workshops,
236–238
zigzag, 238–239
Negotiation decision rule, 123, 124
Nonfunctional requirement levels, 22–24
Norming, group development process,
110–111, 211–212

O
Observers
participant roles, workshops, 85, 103–104
runaway observers, 104
Off-target discussions, 113
addressing, 210
$100 test filtering tool, 207
On-call subject matter experts (SMEs),
participant roles, 85, 105
Open-ended focus questions, 194
Opening workshops, 181–182
Organizational context diagrams. *See*
Relationship maps
Orientation meetings, 155
Output products, requirements models
basics, 134–135
intangibles, 150–151
aligning with business problems, 136–138
decision making and doneness tests,
149, 150
defining detail level, 141–142
defining doneness tests, 145–149
delivering iteratively, 142–143
mixing focus and view models, 140–141
mixing text and diagram models, 139–140
partitioning across workshops, 145, 146
prioritizing delivery, 143–144
selecting multiple models, 138–139
visual deliverables, 135–136
workshop results, 14
Observers, runaway, 104

P
Parallel collaboration mode, 199
Parking lot
addressing issues, 219
basics, 210
Participant roles, workshops
attendance, ensuring, 94
attendance, irregular, 90–91
basics, 84–85
body language, 210
conflicts, 212–213
content participants, 85, 89–91
difficult behavior, 214–215
facilitators, 85, 96–103
fun and games, 215–216
group dynamics, 211–212
group dysfunction, 213–214
observers, 85, 103–104
off-target discussions, 210
on-call subject matter experts (SMEs),
85, 105
parking lot, 210
project sponsors, 85, 86–89
QA (quality assurance) activities, 197
questions for stakeholders, 106
recorders, 85, 95–96
red card technique, 210
surrogate users, 92–94
workshop sponsors, 85, 86
Performance, nonfunctional requirements,
22
Performing, group development process,
110–111, 211–212
Photographing workshop room walls, 85,
95
Place (workshop physical space)
checklists, 176
collaborative technology, 172–174
collaborative technology, warnings, 175
logistics, 166–168
room setup, 168–169

technographers, 171
time and place options, 170–171
videoconferencing, 171
Plan phase, requirements workshops, 65–66
Planning teams, member selection, 75–76
Plenary, 57
Policies. *See* Business policies
Portfolio matrix, 207
Post-work
    data for workshop evaluation, 266
    evaluation surveys, 268
    requirements workshop iterations, 161
Posters, 135
Pre-work
    basics, 154–155
    combining with doneness tests, 150
    data for workshop evaluation, 266
    orientation meetings, 155
    templates, 155–157
    workshop aids, 157–160
    workshop iterations, 161
    workshop success factor, 52–53
Preoccupied one, type of participant, 215
Principles. *See* Ground rules
Prioritization and ranking scales, 207
Priority of delivery, requirements models,
    143–144
Process focus questions, 194
Process maps
    basics, 41
    behavioral view, 30
    focus of models, 33
    focus questions, 32
    models, iterative deliveries, 143
    scope-level requirements, 34, 35
Process variety, workshop success factor,
    56–57
Processes of workshops
    activities, basics, 182–183
    activities, conducting QA, 194–198
    activities, elements of each, 186–188

activities, estimating time, 191, 192
activities, example, 188–191
activities, framing, 185
activities, imaging, 193–194
activities, mini-tutorials, 185–186
activities, sequencing, 183–185
activities, using focus questions,
    191–193, 194
balancing by facilitators, 13
closure, basics, 217–218
closure, dealing with parking lot items,
    219
closure, debriefing, 219–220
closure, show-and-tell, 218
collaboration patterns, combining,
    208–209
collaboration patterns, Divide, Conquer,
    Correct, Collect, 200–201
collaboration patterns, Expand Then
    Contract, 203–205
collaboration patterns, Multi-Model, 203
collaboration patterns, The Sieve,
    205–208
collaboration patterns, Wall of Wonder,
    200–201
collaboration techniques, 209
collaboration techniques, guiding flow,
    210
collaborative modes, 199–200
conflicts, 212–215
fun and games, 215–217
group dynamics, 211–212
opening, 180–182
structure, 180
tools, 220
Product managers
    project sponsor role, 87
    workshop sponsor role, 86
Product output
    basics, 134–135
    intangibles, 150–151

Product output, *continued*
models, aligning with business problems, 136–138
models, decision making and doneness tests, 149, 150
models, defining detail level, 141–142
models, defining doneness tests, 145–149
models, delivering iteratively, 142–143
models, mixing focus and view models, 140–141
models, mixing text and diagram models, 139–140
models, partitioning across workshops, 145, 146
models, prioritizing delivery, 143–144
models, selecting multiple models, 138–139
visual deliverables, 135–136
workshop results, 14
Product- and process-related decisions, 120–121
Products (input), requirements workshops
agenda, 152
documentation of systems and users, 154–155
draft models, 152–153
iterations, 161
pre-work, 154–160
questions for stakeholders, 162
repositories, 160
universal models, 153
Programming language system constraints, 22
Project glossaries. *See* Glossaries
Project scope
scope creep, 72–73
workshop purpose, 72–74
Project sponsors
opening/closing workshops, 88–89
participant roles, 85, 86–89
role if not participants, 88

types, 87
workshop sponsor role, 86
Project visions, linking with workshop purpose, 70–72
Prototypes
basics, 41
behavioral view, 30
detailed-level requirements, 34, 35
focus of models, 33
focus questions, 32
iterative software development, 17
Purpose statements
abandoning assumptions, 68–70
basics, 68
examples, 76–79
incorporating stories, 70, 71
linking purpose with project vision, 70–72
Purpose, workshop framework element
basics, 67–68
defining planning team, 75–76
defining project scope, 72–74
identifying workshop sponsors, 74
writing purpose statement, 68–72
writing purpose statement, examples, 76–79

Q
QA (quality assurance)
basics, 194–195, 197–198
checklists, 147–148, 195
matrices, 197
multiple requirements models, 138
participant-devised, 197
requirements workshop iterations, 161
Self-Reflect collaboration pattern, 197
thumbchecks, 198
walkthroughs, 195
walkthroughs, example, 195–197
workshop processes, 194–198
Quality gate, decision-making process, 120

R

Ranking and prioritization scales, 207
Reciprocal collaboration mode, 199–200
Recorders
    role as participants, 85, 95–96
    role with facilitators, 13–14
Recording tools, 84–85, 95
Red card technique, 210
Refocusing focus questions, 194
Relationship maps
    basics, 41–42
    behavioral view, 30
    focus of models, 33
    focus questions, 32
    scope-level requirements, 34, 35
Releases, iterative software development,
    16
Reports, workshops evaluations, 266
Repositories, workshop product storage,
    160
Requirements
    basics, 4–5
    challenges, 5–6
    documentation methods, 6
    evolution, 22–24
Requirements creep. *See* Scope creep
Requirements levels
    business requirements, 6–7
    software requirements, 6–7
    user requirements, 6–7
Requirements models
    actor map basics, 37
    actor tables basics, 37–38
    as-is models, 36
    business policies, basics, 38
    business rules, basics, 38
    communication, primary purpose, 8
    context diagrams, basics, 39
    decision tables, basics, 39
    decision trees, basics, 39
    defined, 7

domain models, basics, 39–40
estimating delivery time, 144
event tables, basics, 40
focus questions, 30–32
glossaries, basics, 40
heuristics for selection, 137
level of detail, 32–35
methodology selection, 8–9
Multi-Model collaboration pattern, 37
multiple models, 36–37
process maps, basics, 41
prototypes, basics, 41
relationship maps, basics, 41–42
scenarios, basics, 42
similarity to BPR (business process
    reengineering), 36–37
stakeholder classes, basics, 42–43
statechart diagrams, basics, 43
use case maps, basics, 44
use case packages, basics, 44
use classes, basics, 43
user interface navigation diagrams,
    basics, 44–45
views, 28–30
Requirements workshops
    activities, basics, 182–183
    activities, conducting QA, 194–198
    activities, elements of each, 186–188
    activities, estimating time, 191, 192
    activities, example, 188–191
    activities, framing, 185
    activities, imaging, 193–194
    activities, mini-tutorials, 185–186
    activities, sequencing, 183–185
    activities, using focus questions,
        191–193, 194
    and facilitation, 11
    and iterative software development,
        16–17
    basics, 9–10
    best practices, 261–262

Requirements workshops, *continued*
  business users, 274
  business value, 17
  business values, 263–264
  case studies, BestClaims, 255–259
  case studies, HaveFunds, 250–255
  case studies, RegTrak, 245–250
  case studies, SalesTrak, 241–245
  closure, basics, 217–218
  closure, dealing with parking lot items, 219
  closure, debriefing, 219–220
  closure, show-and-tell, 218
  collaboration patterns, combining, 208–209
  collaboration patterns, Divide, Conquer, Correct, Collect, 200–201
  collaboration patterns, Expand Then Contract, 203–205
  collaboration patterns, Multi-Model, 203
  collaboration patterns, The Sieve, 205–208
  collaboration patterns, Wall of Wonder, 200–201
  collaboration techniques, 209
  collaboration techniques, guiding flow, 210
  collaborative modes, 199–200
  common problems, 264–265
  conflicts, 212–215
  disadvantageous uses, 17–18
  distributed teams, 92
  evaluating, reports, 266
  evaluation process, cost-benefit data, 267
  evaluation process, debriefs, 269
  evaluation process, happy sheets, 268
  evaluation process, metrics, 267
  evaluation process, post-workshop surveys, 268
  facilitators, 271–272
  facilitators, ground rules, 274–277
  facilitators, IAF, 272–273
  facilitators, skills/knowlege needed, 273–274
  fun and games, 215–217
  group dynamics, 211–212
  inputs and outputs, 134
  iterations, 269–271
  navigation strategies, comparing, 240
  navigation strategies, horizontal, 225–233
  navigation strategies, vertical, 233–238
  navigation strategies, zigzag, 238–239
  opening, 180–182
  processes, 66
  products, 14
  role in critical success factors, 264
  role in software project success rate, 8
  role of collaboration, 10
  structure, 180
  success factors, collaborative closure, 59–60
  success factors, doneness tests, 57–59
  success factors, flexible structure, 60–61
  success factors, focus questions, 53–54
  success factors, frequent debriefs, 63–64
  success factors, pre-work, 52–53
  success factors, process variety, 56–57
  success factors, right people, 48–50
  success factors, serious play, 54–55
  success factors, shared purpose, 47–48
  success factors, shared space, 50–51
  success factors, trust, 55–56
  success factors, using both sides of brain, 61–62
  success factors, wise groups, 51–52
  tools, 220
  types, 14–16

values to convince management, 262
variant of JAD (Joint Application
Design), 11
versus meetings, 11–14
Retrospectives of workshops, 219–220
Risk plans, 94
Room setup for workshops, 168–169
Runaway observers, 104

S
Scenarios
basics, 42
behavioral view, 30
focus of models, 33
focus questions, 32
high-level requirements, 34, 35
Scope creep
defined, 7
detail level of requirements models, 141
project scope, 72–73
Scope models. *See* Context diagrams
Scope-level workshops
deliverables, 15–16
navigation strategies, horizontal, 226,
240
navigation strategies, horizontal, short
dives, 227, 228
navigation strategies, vertical, 235–236,
240
navigation strategies, zigzag, 240
Screen transition diagrams. *See* User
interface navigation diagrams
Scribes. *See* Recorders
Security, system requirements, 22
Self-Reflect collaboration pattern, 117,
283–284
QA (quality assurance), 197
Sequential collaboration mode, 199–200
Serious play, 216, 217
requirements workshop success factor,
54–55

Shared purpose, workshop success factor,
47–48
Shared space, workshop success factor,
50–51
Shared team space, storyboarding, 201
Short dives, scope-level workshops, 227,
228
Show-and-tell closure processes, 88–89,
218
The Sieve collaboration pattern, 205–208,
284–285
Silent one, type of participant, 215
Six P's
defined, 65
process roles, 66
Six P's, participant roles
basics, 84–85
content participants, 85, 89–91
facilitators, 85, 96–103
observers, 85, 103–104
on-call subject matter experts (SMEs),
85, 105
project sponsors, 85, 86–89
recorders, 85, 95–96
surrogate users, 92–94
workshop sponsors, 85, 86
Six P's, place (workshop physical space)
checklists, 176
collaborative technology, 172–174
collaborative technology, warnings, 175
logistics, 166–168
room setup, 168–169
technographers, 171
time and place options, 170–171
videoconferencing, 171
Six P's, principles (ground rules), 109–110
basic rules, 111–113
culturally aware rules, 114–115
decision rules, 122–128
decision rules, examples, 128–129
decision-making rules (closure), 119–120

Six P's, principles, *continued*
   ground rules for ground rules, 112
   group development process, 110–111
   hidden agendas, 117–119
   introducing rules, 116–117
   product- and process-related decisions, 120–121
   questions for stakeholders, 129–130
   testing rules, 116–117
   value-based, 113–114
Six P's, processes of workshops
   activities, basics, 182–183
   activities, conducting QA, 194–198
   activities, elements of each, 186–188
   activities, estimating time, 191, 192
   activities, example, 188–191
   activities, framing, 185
   activities, imaging, 193–194
   activities, mini-tutorials, 185–186
   activities, sequencing, 183–185
   activities, using focus questions, 191–193, 194
   closure, basics, 217–218
   closure, dealing with parking lot items, 219
   closure, debriefing, 219–220
   closure, show-and-tell, 218
   collaboration patterns, combining, 208–209
   collaboration patterns, Divide, Conquer, Correct, Collect, 200–201
   collaboration patterns, Expand Then Contract, 203–205
   collaboration patterns, Multi-Model, 203
   collaboration patterns, The Sieve, 205–208
   collaboration patterns, Wall of Wonder, 200–201
   collaboration techniques, 209
   collaboration techniques, guiding flow, 210

   collaborative modes, 199–200
   conflicts, 212–215
   fun and games, 215–217
   group dynamics, 211–212
   opening, 180–182
   structure, 180
   tools, 220
Six P's, products (input)
   models, drafts, 152–153
   questions for stakeholders, 162
   workshops, agenda, 152
   workshops, documentation of systems and users, 154–155
   workshops, iterations, 161
   workshops, pre-work, 154–160
   workshops, repositories, 160
Six P's, products (intangible output), 150–151
Six P's, products (output)
   basics, 134–135
   models, aligning with business problems, 136–138
   models, decision making and doneness tests, 149, 150
   models, defining detail level, 141–142
   models, defining doneness tests, 145–149
   models, delivering iteratively, 142–143
   models, mixing focus and view models, 140–141
   models, mixing text and diagram models, 139–140
   models, partitioning across workshops, 145, 146
   models, prioritizing delivery, 143–144
   models, selecting multiple models, 138–139
   models, visual deliverables, 135–136
Six P's, purpose
   basics, 67–68
   defining planning team, 75–76
   defining project scope, 72–74

identifying workshop sponsors, 74
writing statement, 68–72
writing statements, examples, 76–79
Smart filtering, 205–208
SMEs (subject matter experts)
content workshop participants, 89–91
defined, 5
on-call, in participant roles, 85, 105
Snorkeling, scope-level workshops, 227, 228
Software managers, workshop sponsors, 86
Software projects
iterative development, 16–17
reviews, 196
role of requirements workshops in success rate, 8
Software requirements
basics, 27
documentation methods, 6–7
Spokens, 207
Spontaneous agreement decision rule, 124
Stakeholder classes
basics, 42–43
behavioral view, 30
focus of models, 33
focus questions, 32
scope-level requirements, 34
Stakeholder questions
determining purpose, projects, 79–80
from decision makers, 129–130
ground rules, 129–130
participants, 106
products, 162
Stakeholders
business change effects, 26–27
role in requirements workshops, 9
Standards. *See* Business policies
State diagrams and models. *See* Statechart diagrams

Statechart diagrams
basics, 43
detailed-level requirements, 34, 35
dynamic view, 30
focus of models, 33
focus questions, 32
Steering committees, project sponsors, 87
Steps, activities, 186–187, 189
Sticky notes/walls
participant roles, 84–85, 95
room setup for workshops, 168–169
Storming, group development process, 110–111, 211–212
Storyboarding, 200–201, 202
Strategies, workshop navigation
comparing strategies, 240
horizontal, bottom-up approach, 226, 233
horizontal, middle-out approach, 226, 230–232
horizontal, selecting types, 226–227
horizontal, short dives, 227, 228
horizontal, top-down approach, 226, 228–230
vertical, basics, 233
vertical, selecting primary focus, 235
vertical, selecting scope- or high-level models, 235–236
vertical, selecting starting models, 233–234
vertical, varying with horizontal strategy, 236
vertical, with multiple workshops, 236–238
zigzag, 238–239
Structural view
models, 28–30
models, aligning with business problems, 136–138
Subgroups, 188

Subject matter experts (SMEs)
  content workshop participants, 89–91
  defined, 5
  on-call, in participant roles, 85, 105
Suppliers, 5
Surrogate user participant roles, 92–94
Swimlane diagrams. *See* Process maps
SWOT matrix collaborative technique,
  209
Synchronous time, workshops, 170
System constraints, requirement levels,
  22–24
System context use cases. *See* Context
  diagrams
System requirements, requirement levels,
  22–24

T
Techniques, group activities, 187–188
Technographers
  collaborative technology, 171
  defined, 96
  participant roles, 95
Technology of Participation (ToP)
  workshop methods, 200
Templates
  business rules, 156
  pre-work products, 155–156
  workshop activities, 190
Tertiary users. *See* Content advisers
Text and diagram model mixtures,
  139–140
The Sieve collaboration pattern,
  205–208
Thinklets, 172
Thumbchecks, QA (quality assurance),
  198
Time estimations, workshop activities, 191,
  192
Time options for workshops, 170–171
Tools. *See* Workshop aids/tools

ToP (Technology of Participation)
  workshop methods, 200
Top-down approach
  horizontal workshop navigation strategy,
    226, 228–230
  horizontal workshop purpose, 76
  storyboards, 201
Triads, 188
Trust, requirements workshop success
  factor, 55–56

U
UML (Unified Modeling Language),
  statechart diagrams symbols, 43
Undiscussable topics. *See* Hidden agendas
Universal requirements models, 153
Unspokens, 207
Use case activity or dependency diagrams.
  See Use case maps
Use case flow diagram. *See* Use case maps
Use case groups. *See* Use case packages
Use case maps
  basics, 44–45
  behavioral view, 30
  focus of models, 33
  focus questions, 32
  high-level requirements, 34, 35
  requirements models, iterative deliveries,
    143
Use case navigation diagram. *See* Use case
  maps
Use case packages
  basics, 44
  behavioral view, 30
  focus of models, 33
  focus questions, 32
Use case scenarios. *See* Scenarios
Use cases
  basics, 43
  behavioral view, 30
  focus of models, 33

focus questions, 32
harvesting business rules, 140
high-level requirements, 34, 35
User classes. *See* Stakeholder classes
User interface navigation diagrams
behavioral view, 30
detailed-level requirements, 34, 35
focus of models, 33
focus questions, 32
User interface prototype. *See* Prototypes
User requirements
business change effects, 25–27
documentation methods, 6–7
documents, characteristics, 25
functional and nonfunctional, 22
surfacing, 7
user requirements document, 25
users, defined, 25
Users
content workshop participants, 89–91
debate over connotation, 26
defined, 5, 25

V
Value-based ground rules, 114–115
Vertical workshop navigation strategy
basics, 233
comparing with other strategies, 240
multiple workshops, 236–238
purpose, 77–78
selecting primary focus, 235
selecting scope- or high-level models, 235–236
selecting starting models, 233–234
varying with horizontal strategy, 236
Videoconferencing, 171
View models
mixing with focus models, 140–141
Vision documents. *See* Charter documents
Visual deliverables, 135–136
Voice of the customer filtering tool, 207

W
Walkthroughs, QA (quality assurance), 195–197
Wall of Wonder (WoW) collaboration pattern, 187–188, 200–201, 285–286
Warm-ups. *See* Opening workshops
Warnings, 175
Whiteboards, 85, 95
Wide and shallow workshop navigation strategy. *See* Horizontal workshop navigation strategy
Window interface prototype. *See* Prototypes
Wise groups, workshop success factor, 51–52
Workflow maps. *See* Process maps
Workshop aids/tools, 159–160
examples, 158–159
instructions/guidelines, 159
participant role in recording, 84–85, 95
posters, 157–159
shared space factor, 50
supplies, 159–160
visual products, 135, 136
worksheets, 159
workshop physical space
checklists, 176
collaborative technology, 172–174
collaborative technology, warnings, 175
logistics, 166–168
room setup, 168–169
success factor, 50–51
technographers, 171
time and place options, 170–171
videoconferencing, 171
Workshop requirements
activities, basics, 182–183
activities, conducting QA, 194–198
activities, elements of each, 186–188
activities, estimating time, 191, 192
activities, example, 188–191

Workshop requirements, *continued*
  activities, framing, 185
  activities, imaging, 193–194
  activities, mini-tutorials, 185–186
  activities, sequencing, 183–185
  activities, using focus questions,
      191–193, 194
  and facilitation, 11
  and iterative software development,
      16–17
  basics, 9–10
  best practices, 261–262
  business users, 274
  business value, 17
  business values, 263–264
  case studies, BestClaims, 255–259
  case studies, HaveFunds, 250–255
  case studies, RegTrak, 245–250
  case studies, SalesTrak, 241–245
  closure, basics, 217–218
  closure, dealing with parking lot items,
      219
  closure, debriefing, 219–220
  closure, show-and-tell, 218
  collaboration patterns, combining,
      208–209
  collaboration patterns, Divide, Conquer,
      Correct, Collect, 200–201
  collaboration patterns, Expand Then
      Contract, 203–205
  collaboration patterns, Multi-Model, 203
  collaboration patterns, The Sieve,
      205–208
  collaboration patterns, Wall of Wonder,
      200–201
  collaboration techniques, 209
  collaboration techniques, guiding flow,
      210
  collaborative modes, 199–200
  common problems, 264–265
  conflicts, 212–215

  disadvantageous uses, 17–18
  distributed teams, 92
  evaluating, reports, 266
  evaluation process, cost-benefit data,
      267
  evaluation process, debriefs, 269
  evaluation process, happy sheets, 268
  evaluation process, metrics, 267
  evaluation process, post-workshop
      surveys, 268
  facilitators, 271–272
  facilitators, ground rules, 274–277
  facilitators, IAF, 272–273
  facilitators, skills/knowlege needed,
      273–274
  fun and games, 215–217
  group dynamics, 211–212
  inputs and outputs, 134
  iterations, 269–271
  navigation strategies, comparing, 240
  navigation strategies, horizontal,
      225–233
  navigation strategies, vertical, 233–238
  navigation strategies, zigzag, 238–239
  opening, 180–182
  processes, 66
  products, 14
  role in critical success factors, 264
  role in software project success rate, 8
  role of collaboration, 10
  structure, 180
  success factors, collaborative closure,
      59–60
  success factors, doneness tests, 57–59
  success factors, flexible structure, 60–61
  success factors, focus questions, 53–54
  success factors, frequent debriefs, 63–64
  success factors, pre-work, 52–53
  success factors, process variety, 56–57
  success factors, right people, 48–50
  success factors, serious play, 54–55

success factors, shared purpose, 47–48
success factors, shared space, 50–51
success factors, trust, 55–56
success factors, using both sides of
    brain, 61–62
success factors, wise groups, 51–52
tools, 220
types, 14–16
values to convince management, 262
variant of JAD (Joint Application
    Design), 11
versus meetings, 11–14
Workshop retrospectives, 219–220

Workshop sponsors
    identifying, 74
    opening/closing workshops, 88–89
    participant roles, 85, 86
    role if not participants, 88
WoW (Wall of Wonder) collaboration
    pattern, 187–188, 200–201, 285–286

Z
Zigzag workshop navigation strategy,
    238–239
    comparing with other strategies, 240
    purpose, 78

informIT.com
THE TRUSTED TECHNOLOGY LEARNING SOURCE

PEARSON

InformIT is a brand of Pearson and the online presence for the world's leading technology publishers. It's your source for reliable and qualified content and knowledge, providing access to the top brands, authors, and contributors from the tech community.

Addison-Wesley · **Cisco Press** · EXAM/**CRAM** · **IBM** Press. · QUE · PRENTICE HALL · **SAMS** | Safari Books Online

LearnIT at InformIT

Looking for a book, eBook, or training video on a new technology? Seeking timely and relevant information and tutorials? Looking for expert opinions, advice, and tips? **InformIT has the solution.**

- Learn about new releases and special promotions by subscribing to a wide variety of newsletters.
  Visit **informit.com/newsletters**.

- Access FREE podcasts from experts at **informit.com/podcasts**.

- Read the latest author articles and sample chapters at **informit.com/articles**.

- Access thousands of books and videos in the Safari Books Online digital library at **safari.informit.com**.

- Get tips from expert blogs at **informit.com/blogs**.

Visit **informit.com/learn** to discover all the ways you can access the hottest technology content.

Are You Part of the IT Crowd?

Connect with Pearson authors and editors via RSS feeds, Facebook, Twitter, YouTube, and more! Visit **informit.com/socialconnect**.